Simply Shakespeare

Original Shakespearean Text
With a Modern Line-for-Line Translation

DISCARD

HAMLET

BARRON'S

© Copyright 2002 by Barron's Educational Series, Inc.

All rights reserved.
No part of this book may be reproduced in any form, by photostat, microfilm, xerography, or any other means, or incorporated into any information retrieval system, electronic or mechanical, without the written permission of the copyright owner.

All inquiries should be addressed to:
Barron's Educational Series, Inc.
250 Wireless Boulevard
Hauppauge, New York 11788
http://www.barronseduc.com

International Standard Book No. 0-7641-2084-0

Library of Congress Catalog Card No. 2001043295

Library of Congress Cataloging-in-Publication Data

Shakespeare, William, 1564–1616.
    Hamlet / edited and rendered into modern English by Jenny Mueller.
       p. cm. — (Simply Shakespeare)
    Includes bibliographical references.
    Summary: Presents the original text of Shakespeare's play side by side with a modern version, with discussion questions, role-playing scenarios, and other study activities.
    ISBN 0-7641-2084-0
       1. Hamlet—Juvenile drama. 2. Princes—Juvenile drama. 3. Denmark—Juvenile drama. 4. Fathers—Death—Juvenile drama. 5. Murder victims' families—Juvenile drama. 6. Children's plays, English. [1. Shakespeare, William, 1564–1616. Hamlet. 2. Plays. 3. English literature—History and criticism.] I. Mueller, Jenny, 1962– II. Title.

PR2807 .A25 2002
822.3'3—dc21

                                                      2001043295

PRINTED IN THE UNITED STATES OF AMERICA
9 8 7 6 5

Simply Shakespeare

Titles in the Series

Contents

Introduction

William Shakespeare, 1564–1616

Who was William Shakespeare? This simple question has challenged scholars for years. The man behind vivid, unforgettable characters like Hamlet, Romeo and Juliet, and King Lear is a shadow compared to his creations. Luckily, official records of Shakespeare's time have preserved some facts about his life.

Shakespeare was born in April 1564 in Stratford-upon-Avon, England. His father, John Shakespeare, was a prominent local merchant. Shakespeare probably attended grammar school in Stratford, learning basic Latin and Greek and studying works by ancient Roman writers. In 1582, when Shakespeare was 18, he married Anne Hathaway. Eventually, the couple had three children—but, like many families in their day, they were forced to endure a tragic loss when Hamnet, their only son, died at age 11.

No records document Shakespeare's life from 1585 to 1592, when he was between the ages of 21 and 28. In his writings, Shakespeare seems to know so much about so many things that it's tempting to make guesses about how he supported his young family during this period. Over the years, it's been speculated that he worked as a schoolteacher, a butcher, or an actor—and even that he did a little poaching as a young man. Thanks to some London theater gossip left behind by a professional rival, we know that Shakespeare was living in London as a playwright and actor by 1592. Meanwhile, Anne and the children stayed in Stratford.

This must have been a thrilling time for Shakespeare. In 1592, England was becoming a powerful nation under its great and clever queen, Elizabeth I. English explorers and colonists crossed seas to search strange new worlds. London was a bustling, exciting center of commerce, full of travelers from abroad. And though many Europeans still looked down on English culture, they admitted that London's stages boasted some of the best plays and actors to be found. Travelers from all over admired the dramas of Christopher Marlowe, Thomas Kyd, and the new name on the scene, William Shakespeare.

Nevertheless, the life of the theater had its hazards. London's actors, playwrights, and theatrical entrepreneurs chose a risky and somewhat shady line of work. Religious leaders condemned the theater for encouraging immorality and idleness among the London populace. London's city leaders, fearful of crowds, closed the theaters in times of unrest or plague. Luckily, the London troupes had some powerful "fans"—members of the nobility who acted as patrons, protecting the troupes from their enemies. Queen Elizabeth herself loved plays. Special performances were regularly given for her at court.

By 1594, two theatrical companies had emerged as the most popular. Archrivals, The Lord Admiral's Men and The Lord Chamberlain's Men performed at the Rose and the Theatre, respectively. However, The Lord Chamberlain's Men had an ace: Shakespeare was both a founding member and the company's main playwright. The company's fine lead actor was Richard Burbage, the first man to play such roles as Hamlet, Othello, and Macbeth. With a one-two punch like that, it's not surprising that The Lord Chamberlain's Men soon emerged as London's top troupe. By 1597, Shakespeare had written such works as *Romeo and Juliet, The Merchant of Venice,* and *A Midsummer Night's Dream.* His finances grew with his reputation, and he was able to buy land and Stratford's second-largest house, where Anne and the children moved while he remained in London.

Then as now, owning property went a long way. Like many acting companies to this day, The Lord Chamberlain's Men got involved in a bitter dispute with their landlord. However, they owned the actual timbers of the Theatre building—which turned out to be useful assets. Eventually the exasperated troupe hired a builder to secretly take apart the Theatre, then transported its timbers across London to the south bank of the River Thames. There, they used the Theatre's remains to construct their new home—The Globe.

At The Globe, many of Shakespeare's greatest plays first came to life. From 1599 until his death in 1616, the open-air Globe served as Shakespeare's main stage. Audiences saw the first performances of *Hamlet, Macbeth, Twelfth Night,* and *King Lear* there. (In winter, Shakespeare's company performed at London's Blackfriars, the indoor theater that housed the first performance of *The Tempest.*) In 1603, after the death of Queen Elizabeth, Shakespeare's troupe added a new triumph to its résumé. Changing its name to The King's Men, it became the official theatrical company of England's new monarch, James I. The company performed frequently at court and state functions for its powerful new patron.

Around 1611–1612, Shakespeare returned permanently to Stratford. Unfortunately, we know little about his domestic life there. Where Shakespeare is concerned, there's no "tell-all" biography to reveal his intimate life. Was he happily wed to Anne, or did he live for so long in London to escape a bad marriage? Do the sonnets Shakespeare published in 1609 tell us a real-life story of his relationships with a young man, a "Dark Lady," and a rival for the lady's love? What were Shakespeare's political beliefs? From his writings, it's clear that Shakespeare understood life's best and worst emotions very deeply. But we'll never know how much of his own life made its way into his art. He died at the age of 53 on April 23, 1616, leaving behind the almost 40 plays and scores of poems that have spoken for him to generations of readers and listeners. Shakespeare is buried in Holy Trinity Church in Stratford, where he lies under a stone that warns the living—in verse—never to disturb his bones.

Shakespeare's Theater

Going to a play in Shakespeare's time was a completely different experience than going to a play today. How theaters were built, who attended, what happened during the performance, and who produced the plays were all quite unlike most theater performances today.

Theaters in Shakespeare's time were mainly outside the walls of the city of London—and away from the authorities *in* London. In those times, many religious authorities (especially radical Protestants) condemned plays and playgoing. They preached that plays, being stage illusions, were acts of deception and therefore sinful. The city authorities in London agreed that the theaters encouraged immorality. Despite this, theaters did exist in and around the city of London. They were, however, housed in neighborhoods known as Liberties. Liberties were areas that previously had religious functions and therefore were under the control of the crown, not the city of London. Luckily for playgoers, the monarchs Elizabeth and James were more tolerant of the amusements offered by the stage than the London authorities.

Who enjoyed what the stage had to offer? Almost all of London society went to the theater. Merchants and their wives, prostitutes, lawyers, laborers, and visitors from other countries would attend. Once you were at the theater, your social station dictated what you could pay and where you sat. If you could only afford a pence (about a penny), you would stand in the yard immediately surrounding the stage.

(These members of Shakespeare's audience were called "groundlings.") As many as a thousand other spectators might join you there. In the yard everyone would be exposed to the weather and to peddlers selling fruit and nuts. Your experience would probably be more active and less quiet than attending a play today. Movement was not uncommon. If you wanted a better or different view, you might rove about the yard. If you paid another pence, you could move into a lower gallery.

The galleries above and surrounding the stage on all sides could accommodate up to 2,000 more people. However, because the galleries were vertical and surrounded the stage, no matter where you sat, you would never be more than 35 feet away from the stage. The galleries immediately behind the stage were reserved for members of the nobility and royalty. From behind the stage a noble could not only see everything, but—more importantly—could be seen by others in the audience! Queen Elizabeth and King James were less likely to attend a theater performance, although they protected theater companies. Instead, companies performed plays for them at court.

The Globe's stage was similar to the other outdoor theaters in Shakespeare's time. These stages offered little decoration or frills. Consequently, the actors and the text carried the burden of delivering the drama. Without the help of scenery or lighting, the audience had to imagine what was not represented on the stage (the storms, shipwrecks, and so forth). The Globe's stage was rectangular—with dimensions of about 27 by 44 feet. At the back of the stage was a curtained wall containing three entrances onto the stage. These entrances led directly from the tiring (as in "attiring") house, where the actors would dress. The middle entrance was covered by a hanging tapestry and was probably used for special entrances—such as a ceremonial procession or the delivery of a prologue.

Unlike the yard, the stage was covered by a canopied roof that was suspended by two columns. This canopy was known as the *heavens*. Its underside was covered with paintings of the sun, moon, stars, and sky and was visible to all theatergoers. *Hell* was the area below the stage with a trapdoor as the entrance. Immediately behind and one flight above the stage were the dressing rooms, and above them lay the storage area for props and costumes.

Indoor theaters were similar to outdoor theaters in many respects. They featured a bare stage with the heavens, a trapdoor leading to hell, and doors leading to the tiring house. Builders created indoor theaters from preexisting space in already constructed buildings. These theaters were smaller, and because they were in town they were also more expensive. Standing in the yard of an outdoor theater cost a pence. The cheapest seat in an *indoor* theater was sixpence. The most fashionable and wealthy members of London society attended indoor theaters as much to see as to be seen. If you were a gallant (a fashionable theatergoer), you could pay 24 pence and actually sit on a stool at the edge of the stage—where everyone could see you.

The actors' costumes were also on display. Whether plays were performed indoors or outdoors, costumes were richly decorated. They were one of the main assets of a theater company and one of the draws of theater. However, costumes didn't necessarily match the period of the play's setting. How spectacular the costumes looked was more important than how realistic they were or if they matched the period setting.

These costumes were worn on stage only by men or boys who were a part of licensed theater companies. The actors in the companies were exclusively male and frequently doubled up on parts. Boys played female roles before their voices changed. Some actors were also shareholders—the most important members of a theater company. The shareholders owned the company's assets (the play texts, costumes, and props) and made a profit from the admissions gathered. Besides the shareholders and those actors who did not hold shares, other company members were apprentices and hired men and musicians.

The actors in Shakespeare's day worked hard. They were paid according to the house's take. New plays were staged rapidly, possibly with as little as three weeks from the time a company first received the play text until opening night. All the while, the companies appeared to have juggled a large number of new and older plays in performance. In lead roles, the most popular actors might have delivered as many as 4,000 lines in six different plays during a London working week! Working at this pace, it seems likely that teamwork was key to a company's success.

The Sound of Shakespeare

Shakespeare's heroes and heroines all share one quality: They're all great talkers. They combine Shakespeare's powerful imagery and vocabulary with a sound that thunders, trills, rocks, and sings.

When Shakespearean actors say their lines, they don't just speak lines of dialogue. Often, they're also speaking lines of dramatic poetry that are written in a sound pattern called *iambic pentameter*. When these lines don't rhyme and are not grouped in stanzas, they're called *blank verse*. Though many passages in Shakespeare plays are written in prose, the most important and serious moments are almost always in iambic pentameter. As Shakespeare matured, the sound of his lines began to change. Late plays like *The Tempest* are primarily in a wonderfully flowing blank verse. Earlier works, such as *Romeo and Juliet*, feature much more rhymed iambic pentameter, often with punctuation at the end of each line to make the rhymes even stronger.

Terms like "iambic pentameter" sound scarily technical—like part of a chemistry experiment that will blow up the building if you measure it wrong. But the Greeks, who invented iambic pentameter, used it as a dance beat. Later writers no longer used it as something one could literally shimmy to, but it was still a way to organize the rhythmic noise and swing of speech. An *iamb* contains one unaccented (or unstressed) syllable and one accented (stressed) syllable, in that order. It borrows from the natural swing of our heartbeats to go *ker-THUMP, ker-THUMP*. Five of these ker-thumping units in a row make a line of iambic *penta*meter.

Dance or rock music needs a good, regular thumping of drums (or drum machine) and bass to get our feet tapping and bodies dancing, but things can get awfully monotonous if that's all there is to the sound. Poetry works the same way. With its ten syllables and five ker-thumps, a line like "he WENT to TOWN toDAY to BUY a CAR" is perfect iambic pentameter. It's just as regular as a metronome. But it isn't poetry. "In SOOTH/ I KNOW/ not WHY/ I AM/ so SAD" is poetry (*The Merchant of Venice*, Act 1, Scene 1). Writers like Shakespeare change the iambic pentameter pattern of their blank verse all the time to keep things sounding interesting. The melody of vowels and other sound effects makes the lines even more musical and varied. As it reaches the audience's ears, this mix of basic, patterned beat and sound variations carries powerful messages of meaning and emotion. The beating, regular rhythms of blank verse also help actors remember their lines.

Why did Shakespeare use this form? Blank verse dominated through a combination of novelty, tradition, and ease. The Greeks and Romans passed on a tradition of combining poetry and drama. English playwrights experimented with this tradition by using all sorts of verse and prose for their plays. By the 1590s, blank verse had caught on with some of the best new writers in London. In the hands of writers like the popular Christopher Marlowe and the up-and-coming Will Shakespeare, it was more than just the latest craze in on-stage sound.

Blank verse also fit well with the English language itself. Compared to languages like French and Italian, English is hard to rhyme. It's also heavily accentual—another way of saying that English really bumps and thumps.

The words and sounds coming from the stage were new and thrilling to Shakespeare's audience. England was falling in love with its own language. English speakers were still making up grammar, spelling, and pronunciation as they went along—giving the language more of a "hands-on" feel than it has today. The grammar books and dictionaries that finally fixed the "rules" of English did not appear until after Shakespeare's death. The language grew and grew, soaking up words from other languages, combining and making new words. Politically, the country also grew in power and pride.

Shakespeare's language reflects this sense of freedom, experimentation, and power. When he put his words in the beat of blank verse and the mouths of London's best actors, it must have sounded a little like the birth of rock and roll—mixing old styles and new sounds to make a new, triumphant swagger.

Publishing Shakespeare

Books of Shakespeare's plays come in all shapes and sizes. They range from slim paperbacks like this one to heavy, muscle-building anthologies of his collected works. Libraries devote shelves of space to works by and about "the Bard." Despite all that paper and ink, no printed text of a Shakespeare play can claim to be an exact, word-by-word copy of what Shakespeare wrote.

Today, most writers work on computers and can save their work electronically. Students everywhere know the horror of losing the only copy of something they've written and make sure they always have a backup version! In Shakespeare's time, a playwright delivered a hand-written copy of his work to the acting company that asked him to write a play. This may have been his only copy—which was now the property of the company, not the writer. In general, plays were viewed as mere "entertainments"—not literary art. They were written quickly and were often disposed of when the acting companies had no more use for them.

The draft Shakespeare delivered was a work in progress. He and the company probably added, deleted, and changed some material—stage directions, entrances and exits, even lines and character names—during rehearsals. Companies may have had a clean copy written out by a scribe (a professional hand-writer) or by the writer himself. Most likely they kept this house copy for future performances. No copies of Shakespeare's plays in his own handwriting have survived.

Acting companies might perform a hit play for years before it was printed, usually in small books called *quartos*. However, the first published versions of Shakespeare's plays vary considerably. Some of these texts are thought to be of an inferior, incomplete quality. Because of this, scholars have speculated that they are not based on authoritative, written copies, but were re-created from actors' memories or from the shorthand notes of a scribe working for a publisher.

Shakespearean scholars often call these apparently faulty versions of his plays "bad quartos." Why might such texts have appeared? Scholars have guessed that they are "pirated versions." They believe that acting companies tried to keep their plays out of print to prevent rival troupes from stealing popular material. However, booksellers sometimes printed unauthorized versions of Shakespeare's plays that were used by competing companies. The pirated versions may have been done with help from actors who had played minor roles in the play, memorized it, and then sold their unreliable, memorized versions. (In recent years, this theory has been challenged by some scholars who argue that the "bad" quartos may be based on Shakespeare's own first drafts or that they reliably reflect early performance texts of the plays.)

"Good" quartos were printed with the permission of the company that owned the play and were based on written copies. However, even these authorized versions were far from perfect. The printers had to work either by deciphering the playwright's handwriting or by using a flawed version printed earlier. They also had to memorize lines as they manually set type on the press. And they decided how a line should be punctuated and spelled—not always with foolproof judgment!

The first full collection of Shakespeare's plays came out in 1623, seven years after his death. Called the "First Folio," this collection included 36 plays compiled by John Heminge and Henry Condell, actor-friends of Shakespeare from The King's Men troupe.

To develop the First Folio texts, Heminge, Condell, and their co-editors probably worked with a mix of handwritten and both good and bad printed versions of their friend's plays. Their 1623 version had many errors, and though later editions of that text corrected some mistakes, they also added new ones. The First Folio also contained no indications of where acts and scenes began and ended. The scene and act divisions that appear standard in most modern editions of Shakespeare actually rely on the shrewd guesses of generations of editors and researchers.

Most modern editors of Shakespeare depend on a combination of trustworthy early publications to come up with the most accurate text possible. They often use the versions in the First Folio, its later editions, and other "good," authorized publications of single plays. In some cases, they also consult "bad" versions or rely on pure guesswork to decide the most likely reading of some words or lines. Because of such uncertainties, modern editions of Shakespeare often vary, depending on editors' research and choices. This version of William Shakespeare's *Hamlet* is taken from the Folio Edition of 1623.

Hamlet

Introduction to the Play

Hamlet is Shakespeare's most famous tragedy. In a way, it is also a mystery. Throughout the play, the title character is obsessed with trapping a culprit and bringing him to justice. Sorting fact from fiction and appearance from reality is a major theme of the play. But the most mysterious thing about *Hamlet* is the character of Hamlet himself. What makes him tick? Why does he take so long to enact his revenge? Audiences, actors, directors, and scholars have been fascinated for centuries by this troubled prince.

When audiences try to "solve" the play's mysteries, they often look inside their own hearts and minds. *Hamlet* offers a deep and sometimes frightening look at human nature. Its characters seem to be both good and evil. Our feelings about them change from scene to scene, because Shakespeare does not provide easy answers for sorting out who is innocent and who is guilty. In the middle of it all stands Hamlet himself, struggling to take action in a world full of plots, doubts, and dirty secrets.

It's easy to understand why so many actors (and some actresses) have longed to play Prince Hamlet. He's brilliant, brave, charismatic, and even funny. He's fatally attractive and romantically doomed. He thinks in complex, ironic ways that seem thoroughly up-to-date, even to twenty-first-century audiences. Many scholars feel that Hamlet is the first "modern" character in literature.

Hamlet is also fond of asking difficult questions, like his famous "To be, or not to be." But Shakespeare's plays never sacrifice drama for philosophical depth. *Hamlet* is not a dull lecture on the meaning of life. It's a tragedy, a mystery, a revenge story, a ghost story, and a political thriller—with some good jokes thrown in.

The world of *Hamlet* is full of sinister threats. Shakespeare's powerful images of disease, poison, and nature gone wrong create a perilous and paranoid environment. In this world, corruption spreads just below the surface, threatening to consume all. Meanwhile, the characters try to hide their real thoughts and actions by playing roles. *Hamlet* is the greatest example of how Shakespeare used his own profession as a favorite metaphor. In *Hamlet,* "playing" is an image for how humans try to hide or to reveal the truth.

With *Hamlet,* Shakespeare began to write some of his greatest plays. *Macbeth, Othello, King Lear, Twelfth Night, Antony and Cleopatra,* and *The Tempest* all follow after it. It was also one of his first works to be performed by Shakespeare's company at their new home, The Globe, probably in 1600 or 1601. Scholars believe that The Globe's painted sign featured an image of Hercules carrying the Earth on his shoulders. In *Hamlet,* Shakespeare may be paying tribute to his new stage with his references to "Hercules and his load" and "this distracted globe."

Hamlet's Sources

Shakespeare's plays tell great stories. However, Shakespeare rarely invented his plots on his own. For *Hamlet,* he took almost his entire plot from preexisting materials.

Shakespeare scholars have traced *Hamlet*'s origins as far back as some Danish legends collected by a twelfth-century historian called Saxo Grammaticus. Published in the early sixteenth century, these tales included the story of a young noble named Amleth. Compared to Shakespeare's *Hamlet,* Amleth's story is long on gore and short on psychology. More like an epic or saga than a tragedy, Saxo's plot includes early models not only for Hamlet, but also for Claudius, Gertrude, Polonius, Ophelia, Rosencrantz, and Guildenstern. The story was translated into French around 1576 and Shakespeare probably knew the French version or a translation.

In addition, there was already an English-language play named *Hamlet* that was performed before Shakespeare wrote his version. Scholars think this play existed because it is referred to in some publications and a diary that were written before 1599–1601, when Shakespeare seems to have created his version. Unfortunately, this earlier English version of the Hamlet story has been lost for a long time. No one knows who wrote it, but the most likely suspect is Thomas Kyd (1558–1594). Kyd's play *The Spanish Tragedy*—which was highly influential—is similar to Shakespeare's Danish revenge drama. In fact, almost every event that occurs in the story we think of today as "Shakespeare's *Hamlet*" also occurred in some earlier version of the tale.

Some readers might wonder, what's so great about Shakespeare if he didn't invent his own stories? Shakespeare could perform miracles with a dusty old tale. In *Hamlet,* he took a story of murder, deception, and revenge and retold it in a way that added boundless psychological, moral, and metaphysical depth—*without* sacrificing any of the story's entertainment value! Pushing the English language and stage to new heights of poetry and drama, he took a minor character from an obscure legend and turned him into one of the most fascinating, best-loved heroes in the history of literature.

Readers who are troubled by Shakespeare's borrowing habits might think about their favorite movies or songs. How many movies have wholly "original" plots? What separates *The Godfather* or *Citizen Kane* from countless other rise-and-fall stories? Why do many people remember *Psycho* as a scary classic, while very few recall the original book version? In the same way, much of today's music—from dance-club tunes to modern classical composers performing in symphony halls—uses "samples" and borrowed themes to create something brand new out of old elements. Shakespeare's originality does not lie in *what* plot elements he used, but in *how* he used these materials.

The Text of *Hamlet*

Hamlet's plot is full of mysteries about what's real and what isn't. Scholars face similar questions when they turn to the text of the play.

Hamlet was probably written and first performed at The Globe between 1599 and 1601. A version of the Shakespeare play first appeared in print in 1603. However, many scholars believe that this edition (called *Q1*) is a pirated version based on passages memorized by actors who played minor and bit parts. In 1604 a new version of *Hamlet* was published, claiming to be "the true and perfect Coppie" of Shakespeare's work. Far longer than Q1, this edition (called *Q2*) seems to have been based on an authentic copy of Shakespeare's own manuscript.

But Q2 also presents some problems. The printers seem to have borrowed from Q1 when they couldn't read Shakespeare's handwriting, and the text contains many printing errors. It also omits a few passages (such as Hamlet's calling Denmark "a prison" in Act 2) that were Shakespeare's work. Despite this, most modern editions of *Hamlet* start from Q2 as the closest text to what Shakespeare would have considered the best version.

In 1623, *Hamlet* was published as part of the First Folio (see "Printing Shakespeare"). The First Folio corrects many minor errors in Q2, but it also cuts some material. These cuts may reflect changes Shakespeare himself made to its performance. (Even today, modern-day productions often make small cuts from the text to make *Hamlet* a comfortable evening at the theater.)

Because of these complications, no modern edition can claim to be an absolutely perfect mirror of Shakespeare's intentions for his play. Like so many aspects of its title character and plot, the "real" *Hamlet* text is still a fascinating mystery.

Hamlet

Original text and modern version

Characters

Hamlet Prince of Denmark

Claudius (King) King of Denmark, and Hamlet's uncle

Gertrude (Queen) Hamlet's mother, Queen of Denmark, widow of
the former King and now remarried to Claudius

The ghost of Hamlet's father, the late King

Polonius a councillor to the King

Laertes Polonius's son

Ophelia Polonius's daughter

Horatio Hamlet's friend

Rosencrantz } members of the court, previously fellow
Guildenstern } students of Hamlet

Fortinbras Prince of Norway

Voltemand } members of the Danish court and
Cornelius } ambassadors to Norway

Marcellus
Barnardo } members of the King's guard
Francisco

Osric a fashionable courtier

Reynaldo Polonius's servant

A gravedigger

The gravedigger's coworker

Players members of a touring company of actors

Ambassadors from England

A captain in Fortinbras's army

A gentleman of the Danish court

A priest

Sailors

Lords, Ladies, Soldiers, Messengers, and **Attendants**

Scene: Elsinore, the court of the King of Denmark

All the World's a Stage Introduction

"Who's there?" Two military guards nervously greet each other at midnight and *Hamlet* begins. The mood of the opening scene is anxious, dark, and mysterious. So is much of the play. While the guards (called *sentries*) keep watch on the walls of a Danish castle, their discussion suggests that all is not well. Denmark is not at war, but the country is active with military preparations. The royal family is in a state of confusion: The king is dead and power has shifted to his brother, Claudius. In Scene 2, Claudius tells the audience about conditions in Denmark—but fails to mention that his marriage to Gertrude, his widowed sister-in-law, brings scandal to the throne. In Shakespeare's time, such a marriage was considered incestuous.

Hamlet is set in Elsinore, English for the Danish city Helsingør, not far from Copenhagen. The characters come from Danish legend.

What's in a Name? Characters

Act 1 introduces all the play's major characters. Chief among these is Hamlet, Prince of Denmark. Hamlet's dead father, the late king, appears as the night-walking Ghost. Hamlet's mother, Queen Gertrude, is now remarried to the current king, Claudius, who is also Hamlet's uncle. (As king, Claudius sometimes calls himself "we" when he means "I." This was a standard way for royalty to speak in Shakespeare's day.)

Hamlet is many things: angry, brave, clever, and—at times—fragile. He shares private thoughts with the audience in brief remarks to himself (called *asides*) and longer speeches alone (called *soliloquies*). His appearance also tells you who he is. Imagine how he dresses, where he stands, and how he moves.

Dialogue clues will help you imagine how the characters behave on stage. Looking for these clues is often the only way to understand characters–since Shakespeare provides few stage directions in his plays. Characters comment privately about one another; in other words, they gossip! In Scene 2, Claudius and Gertrude talk about how Hamlet's clothing stands out at court.

Have you ever noticed that someone's tired expression is connected to some inner conflict or turmoil? Or perhaps someone is good looking and neat in appearance but cleverly hiding some inner troubles? Hamlet's emotions about recent events have something to do with his appearance. The royal couple is also keeping *up* appearances, despite troubles in the kingdom.

COME WHAT MAY Things to Watch For

In Elsinore's environment, signs of order and disorder appear. Behind the harmonious mask of a new king and marriage, chaos and confusion reign. What holds the kingdom together? Or are things falling apart? Who shows a great face and displays good manners? Who is behaving poorly or confused? Look at the court with a very critical eye.

Which "truths" are worth keeping, and which ones conceal lies? Watch for characters' comments on order and disorder—truth and lies. Shakespeare backs up these ideas with images of sickness and health, joining and being "out of joint." Are things in balance, or is something a bit "off" in *Hamlet*'s world?

All Our Yesterdays **Historical and Social Context**

Ghosts often appeared in plays in Shakespeare's London. But although ghosts made popular fictional characters, many people also feared them in real life. Belief in the supernatural was widespread and freely mixed Christian faith with folk superstition. People believed that ghosts, goblins, and other restless spirits came from hell to tempt the living. Their words and appearance were powerful, but very untrustworthy.

The Play's the Thing **Staging**

At public theaters like Shakespeare's Globe, actors generally entered and exited the stage through doors at the back of the stage. At times, however, a player might dramatically enter or leave through a trapdoor in the middle of the stage. Combined with the other doors, this device allows the Ghost in *Hamlet* to move mysteriously around and under the stage.

Playgoers did have to use their imaginations. The first scene takes place after midnight, in cold and gloomy darkness. But the Globe was an outdoor theater, so Shakespeare's actors performed it in summer daylight.

My Words Fly Up **Language**

Act 1's language raises questions about words we might think we know—words like *natural*. What is natural behavior (that between a mother and son, between a father-uncle and a son-nephew)? What is unnatural or rather phony behavior (loyalty to the new king)? Watch for frequent double meanings. When Hamlet says that he is "too much in the sun," for example, his pun on *sun* and *son* says much about his difficult position. Is he truly a son? Hamlet's remark that he is "A little more than kin, and less than kind" is bursting with clues about his state of mind. He is more than a nephew to Claudius, but Hamlet hardly feels "kind" affection toward the new king. Nor does he feel the loyalty that is expected when meeting with a king.

Act I

Scene I

Elsinore. A platform before the castle. Enter **Barnardo** *and* **Francisco,** *two Sentinels.*

Barnardo Who's there?

Francisco Nay, answer me. Stand and unfold yourself.

Barnardo Long live the King!

Francisco Barnardo?

5 **Barnardo** He.

Francisco You come most carefully upon your hour.

Barnardo 'Tis now struck twelve. Get thee to bed, Francisco.

Francisco For this relief much thanks. 'Tis bitter cold,
And I am sick at heart.

10 **Barnardo** Have you had quiet guard?

Francisco Not a mouse stirring.

Barnardo Well, good night.
If you do meet Horatio and Marcellus,
The rivals of my watch, bid them make haste.

15 **Francisco** I think I hear them.

[*Enter* **Horatio** *and* **Marcellus**]

Stand ho! Who's there?

Elsinore. A guard platform on the castle walls. Two sentries, **Barnardo** *and* **Francisco,** *enter the stage.*

Barnardo Who's there?

Francisco No, you answer *me.* Stand still and say who you are.

Barnardo Long live the King!

Francisco Barnardo?

Barnardo Yes.

Francisco You're here right on time.

Barnardo It struck twelve just now. Go to bed, Francisco.

Francisco Many thanks for relieving me. It's bitter cold, and I feel sick at heart.

Barnardo Has it been quiet?

Francisco Not so much as a mouse stirring.

Barnardo Well, good night. If you run into Horatio and Marcellus, my partners on duty, tell them to hurry.

Francisco I think I hear them.

[**Horatio** *and* **Marcellus** *enter*]

Stop! Who's there?

Horatio Friends to this ground.

Marcellus   And liegemen to the Dane.

Francisco Give you good night.

20 **Marcellus** Oh, farewell honest soldier. Who hath relieved
     you?

Francisco Barnardo hath my place. Give you good
     night.
                                              [*Exit*]

Marcellus Holla, Barnardo!

25 **Barnardo** Say, what, is Horatio there?

Horatio A piece of him.

Barnardo Welcome, Horatio. Welcome, good Marcellus.

Horatio What, has this thing appeared again tonight?

Barnardo I have seen nothing.

30 **Marcellus** Horatio says 'tis but our fantasy,
     And will not let belief take hold of him,
     Touching this dreaded sight twice seen of us.
     Therefore I have entreated him along
     With us to watch the minutes of this night,
35   That if again this apparition come,
     He may approve our eyes and speak to it.

Horatio Tush, tush, 'twill not appear.

Barnardo   Sit down awhile,
     And let us once again assail your ears,
40   That are so fortified against our story,
     What we two nights have seen.

Horatio   Well, sit we down.
     And let us hear Barnardo speak of this.

Horatio Friends.

Marcellus And loyal subjects to the King of Denmark.

Francisco Good night to you.

Marcellus Oh, good night, worthy soldier. Who relieved you?

Francisco Barnardo took my place. Good night to you.

[**Francisco** *exits*]

Marcellus Hello, Barnardo!

Barnardo Yes—what, is Horatio there?

Horatio A piece of him.

Barnardo Welcome, Horatio. Welcome, good Marcellus.

Horatio Well, has this thing appeared again tonight?

Barnardo I haven't seen anything.

Marcellus Horatio says it's just our imagination, and won't let himself believe in this horrible sight we've already seen twice. So I asked him to take the watch with us tonight, so that if this apparition comes again he can confirm that we're not seeing things, and he can speak to it.

Horatio Oh, really! It won't appear.

Barnardo Sit down a while, and we'll try telling you again about what we've seen the last two nights, even though your ears don't want to listen.

Horatio All right, let's sit down and hear what Barnardo has to say.

Barnardo   Last night of all,
45   When yond same star that's westward from the pole,
Had made his course t'illume that part of heaven
Where now it burns, Marcellus and myself,
The bell then beating one –

[*Enter* **Ghost**]

Marcellus   Peace, break thee off. Look where it comes again.

50   **Barnardo**   In the same figure like the King that's dead.

Marcellus   Thou art a scholar. Speak to it, Horatio.

Barnardo   Looks it not like the King? Mark it, Horatio.

Horatio   Most like. It harrows me with fear and wonder.

Barnardo   It would be spoke to.

55   **Marcellus**   Question it, Horatio.

Horatio   What art thou that usurp'st this time of night,
Together with that fair and warlike form
To which the majesty of buried Denmark
Did sometimes march? By heaven, I charge thee speak.

60   **Marcellus**   It is offended.

Barnardo   See, it stalks away.

Horatio   Stay, speak, speak, I charge thee speak!

[*Exit* **Ghost**]

Marcellus   'Tis gone and will not answer.

Barnardo   How now, Horatio! You tremble and look pale.
65   Is not this something more than fantasy?
What think you on't?

Horatio   Before my God, I might not this believe
Without the sensible and true avouch
Of mine own eyes.

Barnardo Last night, when that same star that's west of the North Star had moved to where it's shining now, Marcellus and I—just when the bell struck one—

[*The **Ghost** enters*]

Marcellus Shh! Look! Here it comes again.

Barnardo Looking like the dead King, just like last time.

Marcellus Horatio, you speak better than I. Speak to it!

Barnardo Doesn't it look like the King? Look, Horatio!

Horatio Very much like him. It racks me with fear and wonder.

Barnardo It wants to be spoken to.

Marcellus Ask it something, Horatio.

Horatio Who are you and why are you intruding here at this time of night, wearing the armor in which the late King used to march? In heaven's name, I command you to speak.

Marcellus It's offended.

Barnardo Look, it's stalking away.

Horatio Stay, speak, speak; I command you to speak!

[*The **Ghost** exits*]

Marcellus It's gone. It won't answer.

Barnardo Well, Horatio? You're trembling and you look pale. Isn't this more than just our imaginations? What do you think?

Horatio As God is my witness, I wouldn't have believed this if I hadn't seen it with my own eyes.

70 **Marcellus**   Is it not like the King?

Horatio As thou art to thyself:
    Such was the very armour he had on
    When he th'ambitious Norway combated.
    So frowned he once, when in an angry parle
75   He smote the sledded Polacks on the ice.
    'Tis strange.

Marcellus Thus twice before, and jump at this dead hour,
    With martial stalk hath he gone by our watch.

Horatio In what particular thought to work I know not,
80   But in the gross and scope of my opinion,
    This bodes some strange eruption to our state.

Marcellus Good now, sit down, and tell me, he that knows,
    Why this same strict and most observant watch
    So nightly toils the subject of the land,
85   And why such daily cast of brazen cannon
    And foreign mart for implements of war,
    Why such impress of shipwrights, whose sore task
    Does not divide the Sunday from the week:
    What might be toward that this sweaty haste
90   Doth make the night joint-labourer with the day?
    Who is't that can inform me?

Horatio   That can I.
    At least the whisper goes so. Our last King,
    Whose image even but now appeared to us,
95   Was as you know by Fortinbras of Norway,
    Thereto pricked on by a most emulate pride,
    Dared to the combat; in which our valiant Hamlet
    (For so this side of our known world esteemed him)
    Did slay this Fortinbras, who by a sealed compact
100   Well ratified by law and heraldry
    Did forfeit, with his life, all those his lands
    Which he stood seized of to the conqueror;
    Against the which a moiety competent

Marcellus Doesn't it look like the King?

Horatio As you look like yourself. He had on that same armor when he fought the old King of Norway. He frowned that same frown when he killed the Poles in battle while they tried to cross the ice on their sledges. It's strange.

Marcellus Twice before, and just at this same hour in the dead of night, he's gone past us, walking in that warlike way.

Horatio I don't exactly know why, but it's my opinion that this means some awful upheaval is about to occur in Denmark.

Marcellus All right then; sit down, and tell me—anyone that can—why our countrymen are being made to keep watch so carefully and strictly every night? Why are they making new brass cannons every day and trading for arms in foreign markets? Why are the shipmakers being forced to work hard all week, even Sunday? What are we getting ready for with all this sweaty haste, twenty-four hours a day? Can anyone tell me?

Horatio I can. Or at least, this is what people are whispering. Our last King, whose image just now appeared to us, was arrogantly challenged to single combat by King Fortinbras of Norway. He was proud enough to think he was our King's match. Our valiant King Hamlet—for so all our part of the world regarded him—killed this Fortinbras in combat. According to a formal agreement based on the laws of combat, this meant that all the land Fortinbras possessed was forfeited to our King. (By the same token, if Fortinbras had won, Hamlet would have lost the same amount of territory.

105 Was gaged by our King, which had returned
To the inheritance of Fortinbras,
Had he been vanquisher; as, by the same cov'nant
And carriage of the article designed,
His fell to Hamlet. Now, sir, young Fortinbras,
110 Of unimproved mettle, hot and full,
Hath in the skirts of Norway here and there
Sharked up a list of lawless resolutes
For food and diet to some enterprise
That hath a stomach in't; which is no other,
115 As it doth well appear unto our state,
But to recover of us by strong hand
And terms compulsatory those foresaid lands
So by his father lost. And this, I take it,
Is the main motive of our preparations,
The source of this our watch, and the chief head
120 Of this post-haste and rummage in the land.

Barnardo I think it be no other but e'en so.
Well may it sort that this portentous figure
Comes armed through our watch so like the King
That was and is the question of these wars.

125 **Horatio** A mote it is to trouble the mind's eye.
In the most high and palmy state of Rome,
A little ere the mightiest Julius fell,
The graves stood tenantless and the sheeted dead
Did squeak and gibber in the Roman streets;
130 As stars with trains of fire, and dews of blood,
Disasters in the sun; and the moist star,
Upon whose influence Neptune's empire stands,
Was sick almost to doomsday with eclipse.
And even the like precurse of feared events,
135 As harbingers preceding still the fates
And prologue to the omen coming on,
Have heaven and earth together demonstrated
Unto our climatures and countrymen

He had agreed to give that up if he lost, since he had staked it according to the same contractual terms.) Well, sir, Fortinbras's son, the young Prince Fortinbras, is hot to prove his untested worth. He's gone through the Norwegian provinces hastily recruiting a group of mercenaries, who'll fight for any purpose that keeps them employed and that satisfies their appetite for daring. It's obvious to Denmark that young Fortinbras plans to use his military strength against us and force us to give back that very same land, which his father had lost. And this, as I understand it, is the main motive for our preparations, the reason why we're on this guard duty, and the source of this furious hasty activity throughout the land.

Barnardo   I think that's exactly right. It fits well with the way that this ominous figure comes to us here on our watch, armed and looking so much like the King who was, and still is, the reason for these wars.

Horatio   It troubles the mind, the way one's vision can be troubled by a floating speck. During the height of Rome's power and peace, just before the mighty Julius Caesar was assassinated, the graves opened and were empty while the dead went shrieking their gibberish through the Roman streets, still wearing their burial shrouds. Comets with fiery tails, streaming like bloody dews, came as ominous signs from the sun. And the moon, which rules over the tides, was almost completely darkened by an eclipse. It was almost as dark as it will be at the end of the world. And similar omens giving advance warning of terrible events have appeared in our regions and to our countrymen, both in the skies and on the earth.

[*Enter* **Ghost**]

But soft, behold. Lo, where it comes again.
140 I'll cross it though it blast me.   [**Ghost** *spreads its arms*]
                                        Stay, illusion:
If thou hast any sound or use of voice,
Speak to me.
If there be any good thing to be done
145 That may to thee do ease, and grace to me,
Speak to me;
If thou art privy to thy country's fate,
Which, happily, foreknowing may avoid,
Oh speak!
150 Or if thou hast uphoarded in thy life
Extorted treasure in the womb of earth,
For which, they say, you spirits oft walk in death,
Speak of it. Stay and speak!   [*The cock crows*]
                                        Stop it, Marcellus.

155 **Marcellus**   Shall I strike at it with my partisan?

Horatio   Do if it will not stand.

Barnardo   'Tis here.

Horatio   'Tis here.

[*Exit* **Ghost**]

Marcellus   'Tis gone.
160 We do it wrong, being so majestical,
To offer it the show of violence,
For it is as the air, invulnerable,
And our vain blows malicious mockery.

Barnardo   It was about to speak when the cock crew.

165 **Horatio**   And then it started like a guilty thing
Upon a fearful summons. I have heard

[*The* **Ghost** *enters*]

But hush! Look! Look, here it comes again. I'll confront it, even though it might blast me. [*The* **Ghost** *spreads its arms*]

Stop, phantom! If you can talk, speak to me. [**Horatio** *pauses; the* **Ghost** *is silent*] If there is any good thing that can be done to give you peace, and to bring me grace, speak to me! [*Silence*] If you know something about your country's future that perhaps might be avoided, oh speak! [*Silence*] Or if you buried a hoard of stolen treasure when you were still alive—which is the reason why (so they say) your spirits still walk the earth after death—speak of it! Stay here and speak! [*The rooster crows*] Stop it, Marcellus!

Marcellus Should I strike at it with my spear?

Horatio Yes, if it won't stay there.

Barnardo It's here.

Horatio It's here.

[*The* **Ghost** *exits*]

Marcellus It's gone. It's wrong for us to threaten such a majestic figure. It's like the air; it can't be hurt. We only mock it with our pointless blows.

Barnardo It was about to speak when the rooster crowed.

Horatio And then it gave a start, like some guilty being who's been summoned to face something terrible. I've heard

The cock, that is the trumpet to the morn,
Doth with his lofty and shrill-sounding throat
Awake the god of day, and at his warning,
170   Whether in sea or fire, in earth or air,
Th'extravagant and erring spirit hies
To his confine; and of the truth herein
This present object made probation.

Marcellus   It faded on the crowing of the cock.
175   Some say that ever 'gainst that season comes
Wherein our Savior's birth is celebrated,
The bird of dawning singeth all night long;
And then, they say, no spirit dare stir abroad,
The nights are wholesome; then no planets strike,
180   No fairy takes, nor witch hath power to charm,
So hallowed and so gracious is that time.

Horatio   So have I heard and do in part believe it.
But look, the morn in russet mantle clad
Walks o'er the dew of yon high eastward hill.
185   Break we our watch up, and by my advice
Let us impart what we have seen tonight
Unto young Hamlet; for upon my life
This spirit, dumb to us, will speak to him.
Do you consent we shall acquaint him with it
190   As needful in our loves, fitting our duty?

Marcellus   Let's do't, I pray, and I this morning know
Where we shall find him most conveniently.

[*Exeunt*]

that the rooster wakes up the god of day with his high, shrill call that announces morning like a trumpeter. At this warning call, the spirit that's been wandering far and wide hurries back to where it belongs, whether that home is in the sea, fire, earth, or air. What we've just seen proves that this story is true.

Marcellus It faded when the rooster crowed. Some people say that before Christmas the rooster always crows all night long. And then, they say, no spirit dares to wander. The nights are free of danger, the influence of the planets doesn't cause us any harm, the fairies don't cast charms, and witches can't cast spells, because that time of year is so holy and so blessed.

Horatio So I have heard, and I partly believe it. But look, the dawn is coming up over the tip of the hill to the east. It's spreading out like somebody's grayish-brown cloak. Let's separate. My advice is that we should tell young Hamlet what we've seen tonight. I'd bet my life that this spirit will speak to him even though it won't talk to us. Do you agree that we should tell him what we saw, as friendship and duty require?

Marcellus Yes, please, let's do that. I know where we can find him easily this morning.

[*They exit*]

Act I

Scene II

Flourish. Enter **Claudius** *the* **King of Denmark, Gertrude** *the* **Queen,** *Council, including* **Voltemand, Cornelius, Polonius** *and his son* **Laertes, Hamlet,** *with others.*

King Though yet of Hamlet our dear brother's death
     The memory be green; and that it us befitted
     To bear our hearts in grief, and our whole kingdom
     To be contracted in one brow of woe;
5   Yet so far hath discretion fought with nature
     That we with wisest sorrow think on him,
     Together with remembrance of ourselves.
     Therefore our sometime sister, now our Queen,
     Th'imperial jointress of this warlike state,
10   Have we, as 'twere with a defeated joy,
     With an auspicious and a dropping eye,
     With mirth in funeral and with dirge in marriage,
     In equal scale weighing delight and dole,
     Taken to wife. Nor have we herein barred
15   Your better wisdoms, which have freely gone
     With this affair along. For all, our thanks.
     Now follows that you know: young Fortinbras,
     Holding a weak supposal of our worth,
     Or thinking by our late dear brother's death
20   Our state to be disjoint and out of frame,
     Colleagued with this dream of his advantage,
     He hath not failed to pester us with message

Sound of trumpets, announcing the entry of **Claudius, King of Denmark.** *He is accompanied by* **Gertrude, Queen of Denmark**, *and the Council. The Council includes* **Voltemand; Cornelius; Polonius** *and his son,* **Laertes; Hamlet;** *and others.*

King [*using the royal "we" to mean "I"*] Although the memory of the death of Hamlet, our dear brother-in-law, is still recent—and although we fittingly grieved for him, and the whole kingdom all mourned as one—nevertheless, common sense dictates that we should mourn for him wisely. We think of ourselves as well. Therefore we have married our former sister-in-law, who is now our Queen. She joins us in ruling this warlike country, and in feeling this warlike state of mixed emotions. We married with, so to speak, a feeling of defeated joy: with one eye sad and one eye hopeful, with cheerful feelings at the funeral and sorrowful emotion at the wedding. Our delight and our misery were balanced equally. In this, we have not ignored your wise advice, since you have approved of our actions from the start. For all of this you have our thanks. Now, to speak of what you already know. Young Fortinbras has a low estimate of our worth, and perhaps he thinks that our late brother's death has thrown our country off-balance. Acting in league with his own ambitious dreams, he has not failed to pester us with messages. These messages demand that we

Importing the surrender of those lands
Lost by his father, with all bonds of law,
25 To our most valiant brother. So much for him.
Now for ourself, and for this time of meeting,
Thus much the business is: we have here writ
To Norway, uncle of young Fortinbras –
Who, impotent and bedrid, scarcely hears
30 Of this his nephew's purpose – to suppress
His further gait herein, in that the levies,
The lists, and full proportions are all made
Out of his subject; and we here dispatch
You, good Cornelius, and you, Voltemand,
35 For bearers of this greeting to old Norway,
Giving to you no further personal power
To business with the King more than the scope
Of these dilated articles allow.
Farewell, and let your haste commend your duty.

40 **Corn.,Volt.** In that, and all things, will we show our duty.

King We doubt it nothing. Heartily farewell.

[*Exeunt* **Voltemand** *and* **Cornelius**]

And now, Laertes, what's the news with you?
You told us of some suit; what is't, Laertes?
You cannot speak of reason to the Dane
45 And lose your voice. What wouldst thou beg, Laertes,
That shall not be my offer, not thy asking?
The head is not more native to the heart,
The hand more instrumental to the mouth,
Than is the throne of Denmark to thy father.
50 What wouldst thou have, Laertes?

Laertes   My dread lord,
Your leave and favour to return to France,
From whence though willingly I came to Denmark

surrender all those lands that his father lost, entirely legally, to our valiant brother. So much for Fortinbras. Now, as for us, and as for why we've called this meeting, this is how things stand. [*He shows the Council a letter*] We have written in this letter to the King of Norway, young Fortinbras's uncle, who is helpless and bedridden and has barely heard of his nephew's intentions. We have asked him to stop Fortinbras from going further in this enterprise, since the troops and supplies are all taken from Norway's subjects. We send you, good Cornelius, and you, Voltemand, as bearers of this greeting to the old King of Norway—giving you no more personal powers to do business with the King than is detailed at length in the articles here. Farewell, and let your swift actions show your sense of duty.

Corn., Volt.   In that, and in all things, we will express our loyalty.

King   We don't doubt it. Our hearty farewell.

[**Voltemand** *and* **Cornelius** *exit*]

And now, Laertes, what's the news with you? You told us you had a request: What is it, Laertes? You cannot ask anything reasonable of the King of Denmark that won't be well heard. What could you ask for, Laertes, that I wouldn't offer before you requested it? The head is not in closer accord with the heart, and the hand is not more helpful to the mouth, than the throne of Denmark is to your father. What would you like, Laertes?

Laertes   My august lord, your permission to return to France. I came from there willingly, to show my sense of loyalty at your coronation. But now I must confess that after performing

To show my duty in your coronation,
55   Yet now I must confess, that duty done,
My thoughts and wishes bend again towards France
And bow them to your gracious leave and pardon.

King Have you your father's leave? What says Polonius?

Polonius He hath, my lord, wrung from me my slow leave
60   By laboursome petition, and at last
Upon his will I sealed my hard consent.
I do beseech you give him leave to go.

King Take thy fair hour, Laertes, time be thine,
And thy best graces spend it at thy will.
65   But now, my cousin Hamlet, and my son –

Hamlet [*aside*] A little more than kin, and less than kind.

King How is it that the clouds still hang on you?

Hamlet Not so, my lord, I am too much i'th'sun.

Queen Good Hamlet, cast thy nighted colour off,
70   And let thine eye look like a friend on Denmark.
Do not for ever with thy vailed lids
Seek for thy noble father in the dust.
Thou know'st 'tis common: all that lives must die,
Passing through nature to eternity.

75 **Hamlet** Ay, madam, it is common.

Queen   If it be,
Why seems it so particular with thee?

Hamlet Seems, madam? Nay, it is. I know not seems.
'Tis not alone my inky cloak, good mother,
80   Nor customary suits of solemn black,
Nor windy suspiration of forced breath,
No, nor the fruitful river in the eye,
Nor the dejected haviour of the visage,
Together with all forms, moods, shapes of grief,

this duty my thoughts and desires turn again toward France, submitting to your gracious permission and tolerance.

King Do you have your father's permission? Polonius?

Polonius My lord, he has wrung out of me my reluctant permission, by repeatedly begging, until finally his request won my consent. I request that you give him permission to go.

King Enjoy your youth, Laertes, and may your best qualities guide you in spending this time. [*He turns to address* **Hamlet**] But now, my nephew Hamlet, and my son—

Hamlet [*aside*] More than just a relative, but less than a friend.

King Why are the clouds still hanging over you?

Hamlet Not so, my lord, I'm getting too much sun.

Queen My dear Hamlet, throw off your black clothes and black mood, and look at the King in a friendlier manner. Don't keep looking down at the ground forever, as if you were searching for your noble father in the dust. You know that it's common for all that lives to die, and to pass through the natural world to eternity.

Hamlet Yes, madam. It is common.

Queen If it's common, why does it seem so special to *you*?

Hamlet *Seems,* madam? No, it *is.* I don't know what's meant by "seems." It's not just my gloomy covering, my good Mother, or my traditional mourning clothes, or my windy sighs that can truly show my inner feelings. No, nor is it the river cried from my eye, nor the depressed look on my face, along with all the other moods, forms, and shapes that grief

85 That can denote me truly. These indeed seem,
For they are actions that a man might play;
But I have that within which passes show,
These but the trappings and the suits of woe.

King 'Tis sweet and commendable in your nature, Hamlet,
90 To give these mourning duties to your father,
But you must know your father lost a father,
That father lost, lost his; – and the survivor bound
In filial obligation for some term
To do obsequious sorrow. But to persever
95 In obstinate condolement is a course
Of impious stubbornness 'tis unmanly grief,
It shows a will most incorrect to heaven,
A heart unfortified, a mind impatient,
An understanding simple and unschooled;
100 For what we know must be, and is as common
As any the most vulgar thing to sense –
Why should we in our peevish opposition
Take it to heart? Fie, 'tis a fault to heaven,
A fault against the dead, a fault to nature,
105 To reason most absurd; whose common theme
Is death of fathers, and who still hath cried
From the first corse till he that died today,
'This must be so.' We pray you throw to earth
This unprevailing woe, and think of us
110 As of a father; for let the world take note
You are the most immediate to our throne,
And with no less nobility of love
Than that which dearest father bears his son
Do I impart towards you. For your intent
115 In going back to school in Wittenberg,
It is most retrograde to our desire,
And we beseech you bend you to remain
Here in the cheer and comfort of our eye,
Our chiefest courtier, cousin, and our son.

can assume. All these things do just *seem,* because they're all actions someone can pretend. But what I have inside me goes beyond show. These other things are just outward signs and costumes of woe.

King It's sweet and praiseworthy in your nature, Hamlet, to dutifully mourn your father this way. But you must know that your father lost a father; while that lost father also lost his own; and the survivor was bound by his duties as a son to observe the rites of mourning. But to persevere mourning, obstinately, is a disrespectfully stubborn course. It's unmanly grief; it displays a will that won't submit to heaven, a weak-willed heart, an impatient mind, and a simple and untrained understanding. Why, in our perverse stubbornness, should we take to heart what we know must occur, what's just as plain as any simple fact? For shame; it's an offense against heaven, an offense against the dead, an offense against nature, an absurdity to reasonable thought. The death of fathers is the world's way. "This must be so!" it has declared, from the first corpse to the one that died today. We hope you'll throw off this pointless sorrow, and think of us like a father. For let the world take note: you are next in line for the throne. And my love for you is no less strong than the love that the most affectionate father feels for his son. Your intention to go back to school in Wittenberg strongly contradicts our wishes. We implore you to stay here, in the cheer and comfort of our presence, as our court's most important member, our kin, and our son.

120 **Queen** Let not thy mother lose her prayers, Hamlet:
   I pray thee stay with us, go not to Wittenberg.

Hamlet I shall in all my best obey you, madam.

King Why, 'tis a loving and a fair reply.
   Be as ourself in Denmark. Madam, come.
125 This gentle and unforced accord of Hamlet
   Sits smiling to my heart; in grace whereof
   No jocund health that Denmark drinks today
   But the great cannon to the clouds shall tell,
   And the King's rouse the heaven shall bruit again,
130 Re-speaking earthly thunder. Come away.

[*Flourish. Exeunt all but* **Hamlet**]

Hamlet O that this too too solid flesh would melt,
   Thaw and resolve itself into a dew,
   Or that the Everlasting had not fixed
   His canon 'gainst self-slaughter. O God! God!
135 How weary, stale, flat, and unprofitable
   Seem to me all the uses of this world!
   Fie on't, ah fie! 'Tis an unweeded garden
   That grows to seed; things rank and gross in nature
   Possess it merely. That it should come to this!
140 But two months dead – nay, not so much, not two –
   So excellent a king, that was to this
   Hyperion to a satyr; so loving to my mother
   That he might not beteem the winds of heaven
   Visit her face too roughly. Heaven and earth!
145 Must I remember? Why, she would hang on him
   As if increase of appetite had grown
   By what it fed on; and yet within a month –
   Let me not think on't! Frailty, thy name is woman!
   A little month, or ere those shoes were old
150 With which she followed my poor father's body,
   Like Niobe, all tears – why she, even she –

Queen   Hamlet, don't let your mother's prayers go unanswered. Please stay with us; don't go to Wittenberg.

Hamlet   I'll do my best to obey you, madam.

King   Why, that's a loving and a civil reply. Act the way we do in Denmark. Madam, come. Hamlet's gentle and willing consent brings happiness to my heart. In thanks for this, for every toast I drink today the great cannon will fire toward the clouds, so the King's rounds of drink will resound in the heavens, re-echoing the thunder made below. Let us go.

[*Sound of trumpets. All exit except* **Hamlet**]

Hamlet   Oh, if only my too too solid flesh would melt, thaw, and end up as dew, or if only the Everlasting Father had not forbidden suicide! Oh God! God! How tiresome, stale, flat, and pointless everything in this world seems to me! A curse on it all! It's an untended garden that's gone to seed, completely overgrown with disgusting common weeds. That it should come to this! Just two months dead—no, not even *that* much, not even two! Such an excellent king! He was like a sun god, compared to *this* king who's half-man, half-beast. He was so loving to my mother that he wouldn't let the wind blow too roughly on her face. Heaven and earth! Must I remember? Why, she would hang onto him, as if the more she had of him the more she wanted. And yet, within a month . . . I don't want to think about it! *Woman* is just another word for weakness! One little month, even before the shoes were old in which she'd followed my poor father's corpse, weeping endlessly like Niobe in the Greek myth— why she, even she . . . oh, God! A beast that can't even think

O God! A beast that wants discourse of reason
Would have mourned longer – married with my uncle,
My father's brother – but no more like my father
155   Than I to Hercules. Within a month,
Ere yet the salt of most unrighteous tears
Had left the flushing in her galled eyes,
She married. O most wicked speed! To post
With such dexterity to incestuous sheets!
160   It is not, nor it cannot come to good.
But break, my heart, for I must hold my tongue. |

[*Enter* **Horatio, Marcellus,** *and* **Barnardo**]

Horatio Hail to your lordship.

Hamlet   I am glad to see you well.
Horatio, or I do forget myself.

165 **Horatio** The same, my lord, and your poor servant ever.

Hamlet Sir, my good friend, I'll change that name with you.
And what make you from Wittenberg, Horatio? –
Marcellus?

Marcellus My good lord.

170 **Hamlet** I am very glad to see you. [*To* **Barnardo**] Good
even, sir.
But what in faith make you from Wittenberg?

Horatio A truant disposition, good my lord.

Hamlet I would not have your enemy say so,
175   Nor shall you do my ear that violence
To make it truster of your own report
Against yourself. I know you are no truant.
But what is your affair in Elsinore?
We'll teach you to drink deep ere you depart.

180 **Horatio** My lord, I came to see your father's funeral.

with reason would have mourned longer! She married my uncle, my father's brother. But he's no more like my father than I'm like Hercules. Within a month, before the salt of those hypocritical tears had been flushed out of her reddened eyes, she married. Oh, such wicked speed! To hurry so expertly into an incestuous bed! It's not good; it can't come to any good. But you must break, my heart, since I must hold my tongue.

[**Horatio, Marcellus,** *and* **Barnardo** *enter*]

Horatio Greetings, your lordship.

Hamlet I am glad to see you well. It's Horatio, or have I got it wrong?

Horatio Yes, my lord, and always your humble servant.

Hamlet Sir, my good friend, I'll exchange that name of "friend" with you. Why aren't you in Wittenberg, Horatio? [*Turning to* **Marcellus**] Marcellus?

Marcellus My dear lord.

Hamlet I am very glad to see you. [*To* **Barnardo**] Good evening to you, sir. [*To* **Horatio**] But truly, what brings you here from Wittenberg?

Horatio A tendency to play the truant, my good lord!

Hamlet I wouldn't let your enemy say that, and I won't let you do such an injustice to my ears that I'll let them believe your words. I know you are no truant. But what is your business in Elsinore? We'll teach you how to drink heavily before you leave.

Horatio My lord, I came to see your father's funeral.

Hamlet I prithee do not mock me, fellow-student.
I think it was to see my mother's wedding.

Horatio Indeed, my lord, it followed hard upon.

Hamlet Thrift, thrift, Horatio. The funeral baked meats
185   Did coldly furnish forth the marriage tables.
Would I had met my dearest foe in heaven
Or ever I had seen that day, Horatio!
My father – methinks I see my father –

Horatio Where, my lord?

190 **Hamlet**   In my mind's eye, Horatio.

Horatio I saw him once; he was a goodly king.

Hamlet He was a man, take him for all in all:
I shall not look upon his like again.

Horatio My lord, I think I saw him yesternight.

195 **Hamlet** Saw? Who?

Horatio   My lord, the King your father.

Hamlet The King my father?

Horatio Season your admiration for a while
With an attent ear till I may deliver
200   Upon the witness of these gentlemen
This marvel to you.

Hamlet   For God's love, let me hear!

Horatio Two nights together had these gentlemen,
Marcellus and Barnardo, on their watch
205   In the dead waste and middle of the night
Been thus encountered: a figure like your father
Armed at point exactly, cap-a-pe,
Appears before them, and with solemn march
Goes slow and stately by them; thrice he walked
210   By their oppressed and fear-surprised eyes

Hamlet Please don't make a fool of me, fellow student. I think it was to see my mother's wedding.

Horatio Indeed, my lord, it followed very soon afterwards.

Hamlet Thrift, thrift, Horatio. The meat pies baked for the funeral were served cold at the wedding feast. I would rather have met my worst enemy in heaven than ever have seen that day, Horatio! My father—I think I can see my father—

Horatio Where, my lord?

Hamlet In my mind's eye, Horatio.

Horatio I saw him once; he was a fine king.

Hamlet He was a man; take him for a perfect example—I'll never see anyone like him again.

Horatio My lord, I think I saw him last night.

Hamlet Saw? Who?

Horatio My lord, your father, the King.

Hamlet My father the King?

Horatio Hold off your sense of wonder for a while, and listen closely while I tell you about this marvel, with these gentlemen as my witnesses.

Hamlet For the love of God, let me hear!

Horatio For two nights in a row these gentlemen, Marcellus and Barnardo, have had the following encounter while they served guard duty in the dead of night. A figure looking like your father, armed exactly like him in every detail from head to foot, has appeared in front of them and marched solemnly, slowly, and in a stately manner past them. Three times he walked in front of their overwhelmed and fear-struck eyes,

Within his truncheon's length, whilst they, distilled
Almost to jelly with the act of fear,
Stand dumb and speak not to him. This to me
In dreadful secrecy impart they did,
215 And I with them the third night kept the watch,
Where, as they had delivered, both in time,
Form of the thing, each word made true and good,
The apparition comes. I knew your father;
These hands are not more like.

220 **Hamlet**   But where was this?

Marcellus My lord, upon the platform where we watch.

Hamlet Did you not speak to it?

Horatio   My lord, I did,
But answer made it none. Yet once methought
225 It lifted up its head and did address
Itself to motion like as it would speak.
But even then the morning cock crew loud,
And at the sound it shrunk in haste away
And vanished from our sight.

230 **Hamlet**   'Tis very strange.

Horatio As I do live, my honoured lord, 'tis true;
And we did think it writ down in our duty
To let you know of it.

Hamlet Indeed, sirs; but this troubles me.
235 Hold you the watch tonight?

All   We do, my lord.

Hamlet Armed, say you?

All   Armed, my lord.

Hamlet From top to toe?

240 **All**   My lord, from head to foot.

passing within the length of his military staff. Each time they stood dumbly and didn't speak to him, almost turning to jelly with their sense of fear. They told me this in solemn secrecy, and I kept watch with them on the third night. There, just as they reported—as to both the timing and the form of the thing, every word proved true—the apparition came. I knew your father—these two hands couldn't look more alike. [*He shows his hands*]

Hamlet But where was this?

Marcellus My lord, upon the platform where we keep watch.

Hamlet Didn't you speak to it?

Horatio My lord, I did, but it gave no answer. Yet once, I thought, it lifted up its head and made a motion as if it wanted to speak. But just then the morning rooster loudly crowed, and at the sound it shrank hastily away and vanished from our sight.

Hamlet It's very strange.

Horatio As sure as I live, my honored lord, it's true. We thought duty required us to let you know about it.

Hamlet Indeed, sirs. But this troubles me. Are you on guard duty tonight?

All We are, my lord.

Hamlet "Armed," you said?

All Armed, my lord.

Hamlet From top to toe?

All My lord, from head to foot.

Hamlet Then saw you not his face?

Horatio Oh yes, my lord, he wore his beaver up.

Hamlet What looked he, frowningly?

Horatio A countenance more in sorrow than in anger.

245 **Hamlet** Pale, or red?

Horatio Nay, very pale.

Hamlet   And fixed his eyes upon you?

Horatio Most constantly.

Hamlet   I would I had been there.

250 **Horatio** It would have much amazed you.

Hamlet   Very like.
    Stayed it long?

Horatio While one with moderate haste might tell a hundred.

Mar., Bar. Longer, longer.

255 **Horatio** Not when I saw't.

Hamlet His beard was grizzled, no?

Horatio It was as I have seen it in his life,
    A sable silvered.

Hamlet   I will watch tonight.
260   Perchance 'twill walk again.

Horatio   I warrant it will.

Hamlet If it assume my noble father's person,
    I'll speak to it though hell itself should gape
    And bid me hold my peace. I pray you all,
265   If you have hitherto concealed this sight,
    Let it be tenable in your silence still;

Hamlet Then you didn't see his face?

Horatio Oh yes, my lord, he wore his helmet visor up.

Hamlet How did he look, was he scowling?

Horatio His face looked more sorrowful than angry.

Hamlet Pale, or red?

Horatio Oh, very pale.

Hamlet And he looked at you fixedly?

Horatio Constantly.

Hamlet I wish I had been there.

Horatio You would have been utterly astonished.

Hamlet Very probably. Did it stay long?

Horatio For as long as it might take to count a hundred fairly quickly.

Mar., Bar. [*together*] Longer, longer.

Horatio Not when I saw it.

Hamlet His beard was graying, no?

Horatio It was like I saw it when he was alive, black streaked with silver.

Hamlet I'll watch tonight. Perhaps it will walk again.

Horatio I'm sure it will.

Hamlet If it takes on the image of my noble father, I'll speak to it, even if the mouth of hell itself opens to make me hold my tongue. I ask all of you, if you have kept this sight secret up till now, keep it in silence still. And whatever else may happen

And whatsomever else shall hap tonight,
Give it an understanding but no tongue.
I will requite your loves. So fare you well.
270   Upon the platform 'twixt eleven and twelve,
I'll visit you.

All   Our duty to your honour.

Hamlet Your loves, as mine to you. Farewell.

[*Exeunt* **Horatio, Marcellus,** *and* **Barnardo**]

My father's spirit – in arms! All is not well.
275   I doubt some foul play. Would the night were come.
Till then sit still, my soul. Foul deeds will rise,
Though all the earth o'erwhelm them, to men's eyes.

[*Exit*]

tonight, pay good attention to it but don't speak of it. I will repay your loyalty. So, farewell. I'll join you on the platform between eleven and twelve.

All   We offer our duty to your honor.

Hamlet   And your love, as I offer my love to you. Farewell.

[**Horatio, Marcellus,** *and* **Barnardo** *exit*]

My father's spirit—in arms! All is not well. I suspect some foul play. If only night would come. Till then, my soul, sit still! Foul deeds will come to light, no matter how deeply they're covered by earth.

[**Hamlet** *exits*]

Act I

Scene III

Enter **Laertes** *and* **Ophelia.**

Laertes My necessaries are embarked. Farewell.
And sister, as the winds give benefit
And convoy is assistant, do not sleep,
But let me hear from you.

5 **Ophelia**   Do you doubt that?

Laertes For Hamlet, and the trifling of his favours,
Hold it a fashion and a toy in blood,
A violet in the youth of primy nature,
Forward, not permanent, sweet, not lasting,
10   The perfume and suppliance of a minute,
No more.

Ophelia   No more but so?

Laertes   Think it no more.
For nature crescent does not grow alone
15   In thews and bulk, but as this temple waxes,
The inward service of the mind and soul
Grows wide withal. Perhaps he loves you now,
And now no soil nor cautel doth besmirch
The virtue of his will; but you must fear,
20   His greatness weighed, his will is not his own.
For he himself is subject to his birth:
He may not, as unvalued persons do,
Carve for himself, for on his choice depends

Laertes *and* **Ophelia** *enter.*

Laertes My luggage is stowed on board. Farewell. And sister, so long as there's wind and a ship that can sail, don't sleep before you've written to me.

Ophelia Can you doubt I would do so?

Laertes As for Hamlet and the signs of his affection, consider that just a phase and a passing attraction, like a violet in very early spring. It's quick to bloom but not permanent, sweet but not lasting, the perfume and passing fancy of a minute, but no more.

Ophelia No more than that?

Laertes Think of it as nothing more. For growth is not just the development of muscles and sinews. As the body's structure grows, so do the inner powers of the mind and soul. Perhaps he loves you now, and perhaps now no sin or lie dirties his good intentions. But you must remember, considering his noble rank, that his will is not his own. He is subject to the responsibilities of his birth. Unlike ordinary people, he can't do what he'd like, because this whole country's safety and

The safety and health of this whole state;
25 And therefore must his choice be circumscribed
Unto the voice and yielding of that body
Whereof he is the head. Then if he says he loves you,
It fits your wisdom so far to believe it
As he in his particular act and place
30 May give his saying deed; which is no further
Than the main voice of Denmark goes withal.
Then weigh what loss your honour may sustain
If with too credent ear you list his songs,
Or lose your heart, or your chaste treasure open
35 To his unmastered importunity.
Fear it, Ophelia, fear it, my dear sister,
And keep you in the rear of your affection
Out of the shot and danger of desire.
The chariest maid is prodigal enough
40 If she unmask her beauty to the moon.
Virtue itself scapes not calumnious strokes;
The canker galls the infants of the spring
Too oft before their buttons be disclosed,
And in the morn and liquid dew of youth
45 Contagious blastments are most imminent.
Be wary then: best safety lies in fear.
Youth to itself rebels, though none else near.

Ophelia I shall the effect of this good lesson keep
As watchman to my heart. But good my brother,
50 Do not as some ungracious pastors do,
Show me the steep and thorny way to heaven,
Whiles like a puffed and reckless libertine
Himself the primrose path of dalliance treads,
And recks not his own rede.

55 **Laertes**   Oh fear me not.

[*Enter* **Polonius**]

well-being depend upon what he chooses. His choice must
be limited by the approval and consent of Denmark, for
Denmark is the body of which he is the head. So if he says he
loves you, you'd be wise to believe it only so far as a man in
his position can act on his words—and that's no further than
popular consent in Denmark will allow. So consider the
damage to your honor if you listen to his songs too trustfully,
or lose your heart, or open the treasure of your chastity to his
uncontrolled pleadings. Fear it, Ophelia; fear it, my dear
sister. Don't let your affections carry you away and leave you
exposed to lust. Even the most modest young woman
behaves wantonly if she lets her beauty show. Virtue offers
no escape from scandal. Too often, roses are ruined in the
spring by canker worms, before their buds can open.
Likewise, the fresh early beauties of youth are especially
prone to the spread of blights. So beware; the safest option
is to fear. The young will always rebel, against themselves if
nothing else is near.

Ophelia I'll take the meaning of this worthy lesson to heart.
But, dear brother, don't be like some hypocritical preacher
who preaches the hard and painful way to heaven when he
himself behaves like a bloated, reckless libertine, taking the
easy way of pleasure and failing to follow his own advice.

Laertes Oh, don't worry on my account.

[**Polonius** *enters*]

I stay too long. But here my father comes.
A double blessing is a double grace:
Occasion smiles upon a second leave.

Polonius Yet here, Laertes? Aboard, aboard for shame.
60   The wind sits in the shoulder of your sail,
And you are stayed for. There, my blessing with thee.
And these few precepts in thy memory
Look thou character. Give thy thoughts no tongue,
Nor any unproportioned thought his act.
65   Be thou familiar, but by no means vulgar;
The friends thou hast, and their adoption tried,
Grapple them unto thy soul with hoops of steel,
But do not dull thy palm with entertainment
Of each new-hatched, unfledged comrade. Beware
70   Of entrance to a quarrel, but being in,
Bear't that th'opposed may beware of thee.
Give every man thy ear, but few thy voice;
Take each man's censure, but reserve thy judgment.
Costly thy habit as thy purse can buy,
75   But not expressed in fancy; rich, not gaudy;
For the apparel oft proclaims the man,
And they in France of the best rank and station
Are of a most select and generous chief in that.
Neither a borrower nor a lender be,
80   For loan oft loses both itself and friend,
And borrowing dulls the edge of husbandry.
This above all: to thine own self be true,
And it must follow as the night the day
Thou canst not then be false to any man.
85   Farewell: my blessing season this in thee!

Laertes Most humbly do I take my leave, my lord.

Polonius The time invests you; go, your servants tend.

Laertes Farewell, Ophelia, and remember well
What I have said to you.

I'm late. But here comes my father. Two farewell blessings are twice as fortunate: here's a lucky chance for a second good-bye.

Polonius Still here, Laertes? Get aboard, get aboard the ship; shame on you! The wind gathers in the sail; they're waiting for you. There, here's my blessing. And record these few principles in your memory. Don't say what you're thinking; don't act without thinking things through. Be sociable, but don't be friendly with everyone. Clasp to your soul with bonds of steel those friends who've been tried and tested as true. But don't give your hand in fellowship to every newfound, untested comrade. Beware of getting into quarrels, but once in, make sure your opponent fears you. Listen to everyone, but say little yourself. Listen to each man's opinion, but keep your own judgment private. Your clothes should be as costly as your wallet will allow, but not outlandish—expensive quality, not flashiness. For you can tell a man by his clothes, and the top people in France have the most discriminating, best tastes in this regard. Be neither a borrower nor a lender, since a loan often loses both the money and the friend, and borrowing weakens the habit of thrift. This above all: Be true to yourself, and it must follow— just as night follows day—that you cannot deceive any man. Farewell. May my blessing promote all these principles in you!

Laertes I leave you most humbly, my lord.

Polonius Time is running short. Go, your servants are waiting.

Laertes Farewell, Ophelia, and remember well what I said to you.

Ophelia   'Tis in my memory locked,
90   And you yourself shall keep the key of it.

Laertes Farewell.

[*Exit* **Laertes**]

Polonius What is't, Ophelia, he hath said to you?

Ophelia So please you, something touching the Lord
95   Hamlet.

Polonius Marry, well bethought!
         'Tis told me he hath very oft of late
         Given private time to you, and you yourself
         Have of your audience been most free and bounteous.
100   If it be so – as so 'tis put on me,
         And that in way of caution – I must tell you
         You do not understand yourself so clearly
         As it behoves my daughter and your honour.
         What is between you? Give me up the truth.

105 **Ophelia** He hath, my lord, of late made many tenders
         Of his affection to me.

Polonius Affection? Pooh! You speak like a green girl,
         Unsifted in such perilous circumstance.
         Do you believe his tenders, as you call them?

110 **Ophelia** I do not know, my lord, what I should think.

Polonius Marry, I will teach you. Think yourself a baby
         That you have ta'en these tenders for true pay
         Which are not sterling. Tender yourself more dearly
         Or – not to crack the wind of the poor phrase,
115   Running it thus – you'll tender me a fool.

Ophelia My lord, he hath importuned me with love
         In honourable fashion.

Polonius Ay, fashion you may call it. Go to, go to.

Ophelia It's locked in my memory, and you yourself shall keep the key.

Laertes Farewell.

[**Laertes** *exits*]

Polonius What did he say to you, Ophelia?

Ophelia If you please, sir, something about the Lord Hamlet.

Polonius Indeed, very prudent! I'm told that lately he's often met with you in private, and that you yourself have freely and generously given him your attention. If this is so—as it has been related to me, by way of warning—I must tell you that you don't understand yourself as clearly as is proper for my daughter and for your honor. What's between you? Tell me the truth.

Ophelia He has, my lord, tendered many offers of affection to me lately.

Polonius Affection? Ridiculous! You speak like a young girl who's inexperienced in such perilous circumstances. Do you believe his "tenders," as you call them?

Ophelia I don't know what I should think, my lord.

Polonius Indeed, then I'll teach you. Consider yourself a baby, since you have taken these "tenders" for legal tender, when they're really counterfeit. "Tender" yourself at a higher value, or—not to overwork this poor way of speaking by belaboring it this way—you'll tender me a fool, making a fool of me by foolishly getting pregnant.

Ophelia My lord, he has pleaded his love for me in an honorable fashion.

Polonius Yes, you might well call it "fashion." Tut tut, tut tut.

Ophelia And hath given countenance to his speech, my lord,
120   With almost all the holy vows of heaven.

Polonius Ay, springes to catch woodcocks! I do know,
When the blood burns, how prodigal the soul
Lends the tongue vows. These blazes, daughter,
Giving more light than heat, extinct in both,
125   Even in their promise as it is a-making,
You must not take for fire. From this time
Be something scanter of your maiden presence,
Set your entreatments at a higher rate
Than a command to parley. For Lord Hamlet,
130   Believe so much in him that he is young,
And with a larger tether may he walk
Than may be given you. In few, Ophelia,
Do not believe his vows; for they are brokers
Not of that dye which their investments show,
135   But mere implorators of unholy suits,
Breathing like sanctified and pious bawds
The better to beguile. This is for all.
I would not, in plain terms, from this time forth
Have you so slander any moment leisure
140   As to give words or talk with the Lord Hamlet.
Look to't, I charge you. Come your ways.

Ophelia I shall obey, my lord.

[*Exeunt*]

Ophelia And he has added weight to his words, my lord, with almost all the holy vows of heaven.

Polonius Yes, traps to catch woodcocks, those foolish birds. I know what lavish vows are made when souls feel the heat of passion. Daughter, you must not take these blazes for fire. They give more light than heat, and they extinguish at the very moment they promise to spark. From now on, be more withholding of your maidenly presence. Don't surrender and grant a meeting, just because he asks you. As for Lord Hamlet, believe no more of him than this: that he is young, with more license to act than you have. In short, Ophelia, don't believe his vows. They're brokers who don't show their true colors, but falsely represent sinful desires. They plead their case in a saintly, pious way in order to deceive. This is my last word: In plain terms, from now on I don't want you to disgrace a moment of your free time by talking to the Lord Hamlet. Take heed; I order you. Come along.

Ophelia I shall obey, my lord.

[**Polonius** *and* **Ophelia** *exit*]

Act I

Scene IV

The platform. Enter **Hamlet, Horatio,** *and* **Marcellus.**

Hamlet The air bites shrewdly, it is very cold.

Horatio It is a nipping and an eager air.

Hamlet What hour now?

Horatio   I think it lacks of twelve.

5   **Marcellus** No, it is struck.

Horatio   Indeed? I heard it not.
It then draws near the season
Wherein the spirit held his wont to walk.

[*A flourish of trumpets, and two pieces of ordnance go off*]

What does this mean, my lord?

10 **Hamlet** The King doth wake tonight and takes his rouse,
Keeps wassail, and the swagg'ring upspring reels;
And, as he drains his draughts of Rhenish down,
The kettle-drum and trumpet thus bray out
The triumph of his pledge.

15 **Horatio**   Is it a custom?

Hamlet Ay marry is't,
But to my mind, though I am native here
And to the manner born, it is a custom

The guard platform on top of the castle walls. **Hamlet,**
Horatio, *and* **Marcellus** *enter.*

Hamlet   The air bites sharply. It's very cold.

Horatio   It's a nipping, keen air.

Hamlet   What time is it?

Horatio   I think it's just before twelve.

Marcellus   No, it's struck midnight.

Horatio   Indeed? I didn't hear it. Then it's close to the time
when the spirit tends to walk.

[*A trumpet fanfare is heard, and a cannon is fired twice*]

What does this mean, my lord?

Hamlet   The King's up late tonight carousing, revelling, and
joining in swaggering wild dances. And while he drains his
deep cups of Rhine wine, the kettledrum and trumpet blare
out his accomplishment in finishing his toasts.

Horatio   Is it a custom?

Hamlet   Yes, indeed it is. But although I'm a native here and
born into this way of life, I think it's more honorable to break
than to observe this custom. This drunken revelry throughout

More honoured in the breach than the observance.
20 This heavy-headed revel east and west
Makes us traduced and taxed of other nations –
They clepe us drunkards, and with swinish phrase
Soil our addition; and indeed it takes
From our achievements, though performed at height,
25 The pith and marrow of our attribute.
So, oft it chances in particular men
That for some vicious mole of nature in them,
As in their birth, wherein they are not guilty
(Since nature cannot choose his origin),
30 By the o'ergrowth of some complexion,
Oft breaking down the pales and forts of reason,
Or by some habit, that too much o'erleavens
The form of plausive manners – that these men,
Carrying, I say, the stamp of one defect,
35 Being Nature's livery or Fortune's star,
His virtues else, be they as pure as grace,
As infinite as man may undergo,
Shall in the general censure take corruption
From that particular fault. The dram of evil
40 Doth all the noble substance of a doubt
To his own scandal.

[*Enter* **Ghost**]

Horatio   Look, my lord, it comes.

Hamlet Angels and ministers of grace defend us!
Be thou a spirit of health or goblin damned,
45 Bring with thee airs from heaven or blasts from hell,
Be thy intents wicked or charitable,
Thou com'st in such a questionable shape
That I will speak to thee. I'll call thee Hamlet,
King, father, royal Dane. O, answer me!
50 Let me not burst in ignorance, but tell
Why thy canonized bones, hearsed in death,

the land, east and west, makes us objects of criticism and shame in other nations. They call us drunkards, and they ridicule our noble titles by comparing us to swine. And, indeed, this drunkenness does detract from even our highest achievements by diminishing our reputation. Something similar is often true of particular men. They might have some small blemish on their character—such as something that they were born with and that isn't their fault, since no one can choose his ancestors. Because of this blemish (or because of some quality of disposition that overtakes and breaks down their reason, or because of some compulsive habit that corrupts their conventional behavior) popular opinion will consider these men to be corrupted by that one particular fault. And this is true of such men (who, as I say, bear the mark of one fault, whether they were born with it or acquired it through misfortune) no matter what other virtues they may have. The tiniest bit of evil overshadows all the good, so that the whole man is disgraced.

[*The* **Ghost** *enters*]

Horatio   Look, my lord. Here it comes!

Hamlet   Angels and saints defend us! Whether you are a good spirit or a goblin damned to hell, whether you bring with you heavenly airs or blasts from hell, whether your intentions are wicked or friendly, you come in a shape that invites so many questions that I will speak to you. I'll call you Hamlet, King, father, royal Dane. Oh, answer me! Don't let me burst in my ignorance. Tell me why your bones—which were buried with the proper religious rites and coffined in death—have burst from their burial shroud. Why has the tomb in which we saw

Have burst their cerements; why the sepulchre
Wherein we saw thee quietly inurned
Hath op'd his ponderous and marble jaws
55 To cast thee up again. What may this mean,
That thou, dead corse, again in complete steel
Revisits thus the glimpses of the moon,
Making night hideous and we fools of nature
So horridly to shake our disposition
60 With thoughts beyond the reaches of our souls?
Say why is this? Wherefore? What should we do?

[**Ghost** *beckons*]

Horatio It beckons you to go away with it,
As if it some impartment did desire
To you alone.

65 **Marcellus** Look with what courteous action
It waves you to a more removed ground.
But do not go with it.

Horatio   No, by no means.

Hamlet It will not speak. Then I will follow it.

70 **Horatio** Do not, my lord.

Hamlet   Why, what should be the fear?
I do not set my life at a pin's fee,
And for my soul, what can it do to that,
Being a thing immortal as itself?
75 It waves me forth again. I'll follow it.

Horatio What if it tempt you toward the flood, my lord,
Or to the dreadful summit of the cliff
That beetles o'er his base into the sea,
And there assume some other horrible form
80 Which might deprive your sovereignty of reason
And draw you into madness? Think of it:

you quietly buried opened its heavy marble doors like jaws, to cast you back up again? What can it mean that you, dead corpse, come back again in full armor under the pale moonlight—making the nights horrifying and turning us mere men into fools, shocked to the depths of our souls with thoughts beyond the powers of our imaginations? Tell us why! For what purpose? What should we do?

[*The* **Ghost** *beckons*]

Horatio   It beckons you to go away with it, as if it wants to say something to you alone.

Marcellus   Look at the courteous way it waves you toward a more remote place. But don't go with it.

Horatio   No, by no means.

Hamlet   It won't speak. So I'll follow it.

Horatio   Don't, my lord.

Hamlet   Why, what's there to fear? I don't value my life as highly as it costs to buy a pin. And as for my soul, what can it do to that, since the soul is also immortal? It waves me forward again. I'll follow it.

Horatio   What if it tempts you toward the ocean, my lord, or to the dangerous summit of the cliff that drops off sharply to the sea, and there takes on some other terrifying shape that might cause you to lose control of your reason, and lead you into madness? Think of it. By itself, that place puts

The very place puts toys of desperation,
Without more motive, into every brain
That looks so many fathoms to the sea
85 And hears it roar beneath.

Hamlet   It waves me still.
Go on, I'll follow thee.

Marcellus You shall not go, my lord.

Hamlet   Hold off your hands.

90 **Horatio** Be ruled; you shall not go.

Hamlet   My fate cries out
And makes each petty artery in this body
As hardy as the Nemean lion's nerve.
Still am I called. Unhand me, gentlemen.
95 By heaven, I'll make a ghost of him that lets me.
I say away! Go on, I'll follow thee.

[*Exeunt* **Ghost** *and* **Hamlet**]

Horatio He waxes desperate with imagination.

Marcellus Let's follow. 'Tis not fit thus to obey him.

Horatio Have after. To what issue will this come?

100 **Marcellus** Something is rotten in the state of Denmark.

Horatio Heaven will direct it.

Marcellus   Nay, let's follow him.

[*Exeunt*]

desperate thoughts in the mind when it looks so far down at the sea, and hears it roar below.

Hamlet It's still waving me forward. [*To the* **Ghost**] Go on, I'll follow you.

Marcellus You shall not go, my lord.

Hamlet Let go of me!

Horatio Let us restrain you; you shall not go.

Hamlet My fate cries out and fills my body's weakest sinews with the courage of the lion killed by Hercules! It still calls me. Let me go, gentlemen. By heaven, I'll make a ghost of anyone who hinders me. Get away, I say! [*To the* **Ghost**] Go on, I'll follow you.

[**Hamlet** *and the* **Ghost** *exit*]

Horatio His fantasies are making him desperate.

Marcellus Let's follow. It's not right to obey his orders.

Horatio Follow him. How will this turn out?

Marcellus Something rotten is up in the state of Denmark.

Horatio Heaven will determine it.

Marcellus No, let's follow him.

[*They exit*]

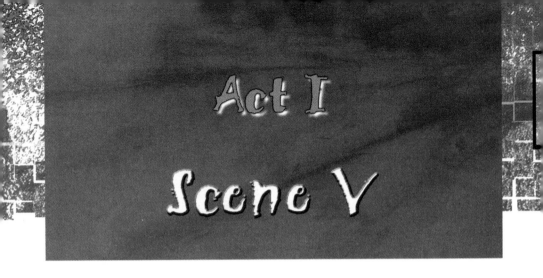

Act I

Scene V

Enter **Ghost** *and* **Hamlet.**

Hamlet Whither wilt thou lead me? Speak, I'll go no further.

Ghost Mark me.

Hamlet   I will.

Ghost   My hour is almost come
5   When I to sulph'rous and tormenting flames
       Must render up myself.

Hamlet   Alas, poor ghost.

Ghost Pity me not, but lend thy serious hearing
       To what I shall unfold.

10 **Hamlet**   Speak, I am bound to hear.

Ghost So art thou to revenge when thou shalt hear.

Hamlet What?

Ghost I am thy father's spirit,
       Doomed for a certain term to walk the night,
15   And for the day confined to fast in fires,
       Till the foul crimes done in my days of nature
       Are burnt and purged away. But that I am forbid
       To tell the secrets of my prison-house,
       I could a tale unfold whose lightest word
20   Would harrow up thy soul, freeze thy young blood,
       Make thy two eyes like stars start from their spheres,

The **Ghost** *and* **Hamlet** *enter.*

Hamlet Where are you leading me? Speak; I'll go no further.

Ghost Listen well.

Hamlet I will.

Ghost The hour is almost here when I must give myself up to hellish, tormenting flames.

Hamlet Alas, poor ghost!

Ghost Don't pity me, but listen carefully to what I shall reveal.

Hamlet Speak; I'm bound to listen.

Ghost And so are you bound to revenge, when you hear.

Hamlet What?

Ghost I am your father's ghost, doomed to walk the night for a certain time, and forced to do penance in fires during the day, until the foul sins committed while I was alive are burnt and purged away. If I weren't forbidden to tell the secrets of my prison, I could tell you a tale whose most trivial word could strike terror throughout your soul, freeze your young blood, make your two eyes pop out of their sockets,

Thy knotted and combined locks to part,
And each particular hair to stand on end
Like quills upon the fretful porpentine.
25 But this eternal blazon must not be
To ears of flesh and blood. List, list, o, list!
If thou didst ever thy dear father love –

Hamlet O, God!

Ghost Revenge his foul and most unnatural murder.

30 **Hamlet** Murder!

Ghost Murder most foul, as in the best it is,
But this most foul, strange and unnatural.

Hamlet Haste me to know't, that I with wings as swift
As meditation or the thoughts of love
35 May sweep to my revenge.

Ghost   I find thee apt;
And duller shouldst thou be than the fat weed
That roots itself in ease on Lethe wharf,
Wouldst thou not stir in this. Now, Hamlet, hear.
40 'Tis given out that, sleeping in my orchard,
A serpent stung me; so the whole ear of Denmark
Is by a forged process of my death
Rankly abused; but know, thou noble youth,
The serpent that did sting thy father's life
45 Now wears his crown.

Hamlet O my prophetic soul! My uncle!

Ghost Ay, that incestuous, that adulterate beast,
With witchcraft of his wit, with traitorous gifts –
O wicked wit, and gifts that have the power
50 So to seduce! – won to his shameful lust
The will of my most seeming-virtuous Queen.
O Hamlet, what a falling off was there,
From me, whose love was of that dignity

uncurl your hair, and make each individual hair stand on end, like quills on a frightened porcupine. But this report of eternity must not be spoken to ears of flesh and blood. Listen, listen, oh, listen! If you ever loved your father—

Hamlet Oh, God!

Ghost Revenge his foul and most unnatural murder.

Hamlet Murder!

Ghost Murder most foul, as it must always be. But this one especially evil, strange, and unnatural.

Hamlet Tell me quickly, so I may swoop to my revenge with wings as swift as meditation or as the thoughts of love.

Ghost An apt response. You'd be more sluggish than the lazy weed that comfortably roots on the banks of the river of forgetfulness, if this didn't stir you to react. Now, Hamlet, listen. It's been reported that a snake bit me while I slept in my garden. And so all of Denmark has been vilely deceived by a false tale of my death. But know this, noble youth. The snake whose bite took your father's life now wears his crown.

Hamlet Oh, I sensed this! My uncle!

Ghost Yes, that incestuous, that adulterous beast, working witchcraft with his wits, with a gift for treachery—oh wicked wits and gifts that have such seductive power!—he conquered the will of my seemingly virtuous Queen to satisfy his shameful lust. Oh Hamlet, what a fall from grace that was!

That it went hand in hand even with the vow
55   I made to her in marriage; and to decline
Upon a wretch whose natural gifts were poor
To those of mine!
But virtue, as it never will be moved,
Though lewdness court it in a shape of heaven,
60   So lust, though to a radiant angel linked,
Will sate itself in a celestial bed
And prey on garbage.
But soft! Methinks I scent the morning air:
Brief let me be. Sleeping within my orchard,
65   My custom always of the afternoon,
Upon my secure hour thy uncle stole
With juice of cursed hebenon in a vial,
And in the porches of my ears did pour
The leperous distilment; whose effect
70   Holds such an enmity with blood of man
That swift as quicksilver it courses through
The natural gates and alleys of the body,
And with a sudden vigour it doth posset
And curd, like eager droppings into milk,
75   The thin and wholesome blood. So did it mine,
And a most instant tetter barked about,
Most lazar-like, with vile and loathsome crust
All my smooth body.
Thus was I, sleeping, by a brother's hand
80   Of life, of crown, of queen at once dispatched,
Cut off even in the blossoms of my sin,
Unhouseled, disappointed, unaneled,
No reck'ning made, but sent to my account
With all my imperfections on my head.
85   O horrible! O horrible! Most horrible!
If thou has nature in thee, bear it not,
Let not the royal bed of Denmark be
A couch for luxury and damned incest.
But howsoever thou pursuest this act,

From me, whose love was so noble it perfectly matched the words of my wedding vow—and to stoop to the level of a despicable man whose qualities were poor compared to mine! Virtue cannot be corrupted even when lewdness woos it in heavenly form. And lust is the same, even when it's linked to a radiant angel: it will satisfy its sinfulness in a celestial bed and feed on garbage. But hush! I think I smell the scent of morning air. Let me be brief. While I was sleeping in my garden, my usual habit in the afternoon, your uncle stole upon me in my unguarded hour, with a poison extract in a vial. He poured this leprous extract into the openings of my ears. Its effect in the blood is so virulent that it flows through the body's passageways as swiftly as mercury. With a sudden strength it thickens and curdles the thin and healthy blood, like acid dropped into milk. It did this to mine, and I was instantly covered with bark-like scabs, much like a leper, with a vile and loathsome crust all over my smooth body. And in this way, while I was sleeping, I was deprived by my brother all at once of my life, of my crown, of my Queen—I was cut off while all my sins flourished, without benefit of sacraments, without rites, without extreme unction, without asking forgiveness for my sins, sent to make my final account with all my sins on my head. Oh, horrible! Oh, horrible! Most horrible! If you have natural feelings in you, don't allow this; don't let the royal bed of Denmark be a couch for lust and damnable incest. But however you act to

90 Taint not thy mind nor let thy soul contrive
Against thy mother aught. Leave her to heaven,
And to those thorns that in her bosom lodge
To prick and sting her. Fare thee well at once:
The glow-worm shows the matin to be near
95 And 'gins to pale his uneffectual fire.
Adieu, adieu, adieu. Remember me.

[*Exit*]

Hamlet O all you host of heaven! O earth! What else?
And shall I couple hell? O fie! Hold, hold, my heart,
And you, my sinews, grow not instant old,
100 But bear me stiffly up. Remember thee?
Ay, thou poor ghost, whiles memory holds a seat
In this distracted globe. Remember thee?
Yea, from the table of my memory
I'll wipe away all trivial fond records,
105 All saws of books, all forms, all pressures past
That youth and observation copied there,
And thy commandment all alone shall live
Within the book and volume of my brain,
Unmixed with baser matter. Yes, by heaven!
110 O most pernicious woman!
O villain, villain, smiling damned villain!
My tables. Meet it is I set it down
That one may smile, and smile, and be a villain –
At least I am sure it may be so in Denmark. [*Writes*]
115 So, uncle, there you are. Now to my word.
It is 'Adieu, adieu, remember me.'
I have sworn't.

[*Enter* **Horatio** *and* **Marcellus**]

Horatio My lord, my lord.

Marcellus Lord Hamlet.

prevent this, don't poison your mind or let your soul scheme against your mother. Leave her to heaven and to the thorns of conscience in her heart that prick and sting her. And now farewell: the firefly's ineffective blaze begins to fade, showing the morning is near. Good-bye, good-bye, good-bye. Remember me.

[*The* **Ghost** *exits*]

Hamlet Oh, all you angels of heaven! Oh earth! And what else? Should I also invoke hell? Oh, shame! Hold fast, hold fast, my heart. And you, my sinews, don't suddenly grow old, but hold me up stiffly. Remember you? Yes, you poor ghost, while memory still sits in my head, this distracted globe. Remember you? Yes, I'll clear the pages of my memory, I'll wipe away all trivial, foolish items, all the maxims in books, all images, all past impressions noted with youth and powers of observation. Your commandment, all alone, shall live in the book and volume of my brain, unmixed with less serious matters. Yes, by heaven! Oh, wicked woman! Oh, villain, villain, smiling damned villain! My notes. I should write this down: that one may smile, and smile, and be a villain— at least, I'm sure this may be the case in Denmark. [*He writes in a notebook*] So, uncle, there you are. Now to my command. It is, "Good-bye, good-bye, remember me." I have sworn to obey.

[**Horatio** *and* **Marcellus** *enter*]

Horatio My lord, my lord!

Marcellus Lord Hamlet!

120 **Horatio** Heavens secure him.

Hamlet [*aside*] So be it.

Marcellus Hillo, ho, ho, my lord.

Hamlet Hillo, ho, ho, boy. Come, bird come.

Marcellus How is't, my noble lord?

125 **Horatio** What news, my lord?

Hamlet O, wonderful!

Horatio Good my lord, tell it.

Hamlet No, you will reveal it.

Horatio Not I, my lord, by heaven.

130 **Marcellus** Nor I, my lord.

Hamlet How say you then, would heart of man once think
    it –
    But you'll be secret?

Hor., Mar. Ay, by heaven.

135 **Hamlet** There's never a villain dwelling in all Denmark
    But he's an arrant knave.

Horatio There needs no ghost, my lord, come from the grave
    To tell us this.

Hamlet   Why, right, you are i'th'right.
140   And so without more circumstance at all,
    I hold it fit that we shake hands and part,
    You as your business and desires shall point you –
    For every man hath business and desire,
    Such as it is; and for my own poor part,
145   I will go pray.

Horatio These are but wild and whirling words, my lord.

Horatio   May heaven keep him safe.

Hamlet   [*aside*] So be it.

Marcellus   [*using a hunting cry*] Hillo, ho, ho, my lord!

Hamlet   Hillo, ho, ho, boy! Come, bird, come.

Marcellus   How are you, my noble lord?

Horatio   What's your news, my lord?

Hamlet   Oh, wonderful!

Horatio   My good lord, tell it.

Hamlet   No, you'll reveal it.

Horatio   By heaven, I won't, my lord.

Marcellus   Neither will I, my lord.

Hamlet   What do you say to this, then—could anyone believe it—but you'll keep this secret?

Hor., Mar.   Yes, by heaven.

Hamlet   There's no villain living in all of Denmark who's not a complete rascal.

Horatio   There's no need for a ghost to come from the grave to tell us this, my lord.

Hamlet   Why, right, right you are. And so, without any more ceremony, I think we should shake hands and part. You shall go as your business and as your wills direct you—for every man has business and will, such as it is. And for my own part, I'll go pray.

Horatio   These are just wild and whirling words, my lord.

Hamlet I am sorry they offend you, heartily –
Yes faith, heartily.

Horatio   There's no offence, my lord.

150 **Hamlet** Yes by Saint Patrick but there is, Horatio,
And much offence too. Touching this vision here,
It is an honest ghost, that let me tell you.
For your desire to know what is between us,
O'ermaster't as you may. And now, good friends,
155 As you are friends, scholars, and soldiers,
Give me one poor request.

Horatio   What is't, my lord? We will.

Hamlet Never make known what you have seen tonight.

Hor., Mar. My lord, we will not.

160 **Hamlet** Nay, but swear't.

Horatio In faith, my lord, not I.

Marcellus Nor I, my lord, in faith.

Hamlet Upon my sword.

Marcellus We have sworn, my lord, already.

165 **Hamlet** Indeed, upon my sword, indeed.

Ghost [*beneath*] Swear.

Hamlet Ah ha, boy, say'st thou so? Art thou there,
truepenny?
Come on, you hear this fellow in the cellarage.
170 Consent to swear.

Horatio   Propose the oath, my lord.

Hamlet Never to speak of this that you have seen.
Swear by my sword.

Ghost Swear. [*They swear*]

Hamlet   I am heartily sorry if they offend you. Yes, truly, heartily sorry.

Horatio   There's no offense, my lord.

Hamlet   Yes, by Saint Patrick, but there *is,* Horatio—and much offense, too. Concerning this vision here, it's an actual ghost, let me tell you that. As for your desire to know what passed between us, control that as well as you can. And now, good friends, as you are friends, scholars, and soldiers, grant me one minor request.

Horatio   What is it, my lord? We will.

Hamlet   Never make known what you have seen tonight.

Hor., Mar.   My lord, we won't.

Hamlet   No, but swear to it.

Horatio   Truly, my lord, I won't.

Marcellus   Nor will I, my lord, truly.

Hamlet   Swear upon my sword.

Marcellus   We have already sworn, my lord.

Hamlet   Indeed, upon my sword, indeed.

Ghost   [*from under the stage*]   Swear.

Hamlet   Aha, boy, is that what you say? Are you there, old trustworthy one? Come, you hear this fellow in the cellar. Agree to swear.

Horatio   Speak the oath, my lord.

Hamlet   Never to speak of what you have seen. Swear by my sword.

Ghost   Swear.

[**Horatio** *and* **Marcellus** *swear the oath*]

175 **Hamlet** Hic et ubique? Then we'll shift our ground.
Come hither, gentlemen,
And lay your hands again upon my sword.
Swear by my sword
Never to speak of this that you have heard.

180 **Ghost** Swear by his sword. [*They swear*]

Hamlet Well said, old mole. Canst work i'th'earth so fast?
A worthy pioneer! Once more remove, good friends.

Horatio O, day and night, but this is wondrous strange.

Hamlet And therefore as a stranger give it welcome.
185 There are more things in heaven and earth, Horatio,
Than are dreamt of in your philosophy.
But come,
Here, as before, never, so help you mercy,
How strange or odd so e'er I bear myself –
190 As I perchance hereafter shall think meet
To put an antic disposition on –
That you, at such time seeing me, never shall,
With arms encumbered thus, or this head-shake,
Or by pronouncing of some doubtful phrase,
195 As 'Well, we know,' or 'We could and if we would,'
Or 'If we list to speak,' or 'There be and if there might,'
Or such ambiguous giving out, to note
That you know aught of me – this do swear,
So grace and mercy at your most need help you.

200 **Ghost** Swear. [*They swear*]

Hamlet Rest, rest, perturbed spirit! So, gentlemen,
With all my love I do commend me to you;
And what so poor a man as Hamlet is
May do t'express his love and friending to you,
205 God willing, shall not lack. Let us go in together.
And still your fingers on your lips, I pray.

Hamlet   Here and everywhere? Then we'll change our position. Come here, gentlemen, and lay your hands on my sword again. Swear by my sword that you will never speak of what you have heard.

Ghost   [*from a different position below stage*]   Swear by his sword.   [**Horatio** *and* **Marcellus** *swear the oath*]

Hamlet   Well said, old mole. Can you burrow through the earth so fast? Worthy explorer! Let's move away again, good friends.

Horatio   Oh, day and night, but this is astoundingly strange.

Hamlet   And therefore give it the welcome due to strangers. There are more things in heaven and earth, Horatio, than your so-called philosophy imagines. But come. . . . Here, as before, swear never, so help you God (no matter how strangely or peculiarly I behave, since it's possible that after this I may think it's best to act like a madman), that when you see me at such times you will never give away that you know anything more about me. Don't give me away by crossing your arms like this, or by shaking your head in this manner, or by making some mysterious comment like "Well, we know," or "We could, if we wanted to," or "If we wanted to speak," or "Some people might say more about this," or by other ambiguous hints. Swear this, by God's mercy at your time of need.

Ghost   Swear.   [**Horatio** *and* **Marcellus** *swear again*]

Hamlet   Rest, rest, distressed spirit! So, gentlemen, I give you my best with all my love. And whatever such a poor man as Hamlet might do to express his love and friendship to you, God willing, I'll do. Let us go in together. And please, keep mum.

The time is out of joint. O, cursed spite,
That ever I was born to set it right!
Nay, come, let's go together.

[*Exeunt*]

The time is off kilter. Oh, what cursed bad luck, that I was ever born to make things right again! [**Marcellus** *and* **Horatio** *wait for* **Hamlet** *to go first*] No, come, let's go together.

[*They exit*]

Comprehension Check What You Know

1. Describe the state of affairs between Denmark and Norway.

2. Who is Laertes and what does he note about Hamlet's behavior?

3. In Scene 2, how does Hamlet describe himself to his mother?

4. What do you know about Hamlet's interaction with Ophelia?

5. How would you describe Polonius? What parental behavior does he display toward his son and daughter?

6. How does Hamlet feel about his mother and his uncle's marriage?

7. Which characters are guessing about the behaviors of others in the first act? How are the characters testing one another?

8. What does Hamlet learn from the Ghost and what does Hamlet plan to do?

Activities & Role-Playing Classes or Informal Groups

You may choose to complete one of the following activities as time permits:

The Sons of Denmark Make a two-column chart comparing and contrasting Hamlet and Laertes. Use these questions to help get you started. What do they have in common? (young) How do they differ? (Hamlet has no father from whom to seek advice. Laertes has a father who gives advice.)

©Hulton/Archive

Friends in Times of Trouble List the characteristics that make a good friend. Then identify lines that show the friendship between Hamlet and Horatio.

In a Black Mood As a group, role-play the beginning of Scene 2 (lines 1–161). Take the roles of Laertes, Hamlet, the Queen, and the King. Use the following list of descriptions to prepare for speaking the lines of your part:

- Laertes: young, has lived away from home, servant to the King
- Hamlet: young, admired and loved his father, in mourning, sarcastic at times
- Queen: mother of Hamlet, just married, worried about her son
- King: powerful, just married, new stepfather to Hamlet

Discussion **Classes or Informal Groups**

1. Discuss how Elizabethans interpreted the marriage of Claudius and Gertrude. Discuss the exchange in Scene 2 between Hamlet, the King (Claudius), and Gertrude, Hamlet's mother. Is the conversation easy and comfortable or confusing and tense? How do you know? What trouble are the characters having with their "roles" within the royal family?

2. As a group, begin a profile of Hamlet's character. Identify lines about him—either his own words or other characters' descriptions of him. Then develop a list of characteristics that describe him. If Hamlet was your friend today, what advice would you give him regarding his feelings about his father, mother, and uncle?

Suggestions for Writing **Improve Your Skills**

1. In one paragraph, explain the importance of the setting in this play. To begin, answer the following questions: Act 1 begins at what time of day? What event has caused a change of power in the kingdom? How does this event affect Hamlet? What physical characteristics of the kingdom reflect the setting or mood? Support your explanation with details.

2. Choose a key speech in this act. Identify the main idea of the speech. Then write a paragraph that paraphrases the statements or lines that were difficult or puzzling to you. Refer to the material that precedes the act for more information or key ideas that explain a specific character or event.

3. Use first-person point of view and imagine that you are Hamlet. Write a brief autobiographical sketch of him. Using clues from the text, have Hamlet explain the marriage of his mother and his uncle. Also describe his encounter with the Ghost and how he feels about events in Denmark.

4. Write a sentence or two to explain the relationship between two of the characters, a description of a character's motivation or goals, and imagery in Act 1.

All the World's a Stage Introduction

Who's in the know? Act 1 reveals that guilty secrets lie behind the royal smiles at Elsinore. But who has helped us to discover this? Even if we believe in ghosts, should we believe *Hamlet*'s ghost?

Hamlet thinks he might trust this frightening figure and its story of treasonous murder. Claiming to be the spirit of Hamlet's father, the Ghost demands that his son take revenge. At the close of Act 1, Hamlet seems to think up a plan. He warns Horatio and Marcellus that they may soon see him behaving as if he has gone insane. And he asks them not to tell his secrets.

What's in a Name? Characters

Act 2 introduces Rosencrantz and Guildenstern, two of Hamlet's old friends. These visitors to Elsinore are soon caught up in some unfolding, cat-and-mouse (life-and-death) games.

In these games *Hamlet*'s audience has a great advantage. Shakespeare allows playgoers to see behind the masks the characters present to each other. We can judge how well they play this dangerous game. Is Polonius as smart as he thinks he is? How well does Hamlet understand the game?

COME WHAT MAY Things to Watch For

Many readers have wondered why Shakespeare included the conversation between Polonius and Reynaldo that opens Act 2, Scene 1. They put audiences on the alert for one of Elsinore's most common and least attractive activities: spying. In Act 2, watch for how playacting, secret observation, and tale-telling start to take over the Danish court.

All Our Yesterdays Historical and Social Context

"Frailty, thy name is woman!" Feminists might well wish Shakespeare had never written this famous phrase from Act 1. Although Hamlet says it, he expresses ideas about feminine nature that ran deep throughout European society. Women were considered both morally and physically "frail." They were also less able to think with reason than men. Religious authorities pointed to the Bible. Eve was seen as the typical woman who gave in weakly to temptation, then tempted her more virtuous husband to his doom. The ideal woman was the Virgin Mary, who was completely obedient to God. Women were taught to be similarly obedient to their spouses, clergy, and fathers.

Hamlet says harsh and sometimes degrading things about women, but no one knows what Shakespeare privately thought about the opposite sex. He did create some wonderfully thoughtful and virtuous heroines, such as Viola in *Twelfth Night*. *Hamlet*'s women are trickier cases. How do Gertrude's or Ophelia's real or perceived "frailty" affect events? Intentionally or not, these female characters are movers and shakers—real players in the action of the play.

The Play's the Thing Staging

Women were not allowed to perform on the theatrical stage in Elizabethan times. Boys dressed in women's costumes played the roles of Ophelia and Gertrude. Such casting did not prevent audiences from enjoying the plays—in fact, some theatrical companies consisted entirely of boys. They began as choirboys, performing in the houses of the powerful. Later, these boys' companies rented a private indoor theater in London and began performing plays written for them. They were a big hit with a hip, rich audience. Their popularity was a serious threat to the actors in Shakespeare's plays. This real-life battle for audiences is discussed early in *Hamlet*'s Act 2.

Early in the play, the King and Queen were offended by Hamlet's black clothes in court. In Act 2, Scene 1, Ophelia gives us more information about how Hamlet is now dressed. How might Hamlet's costume continue to stand out in the ceremonies of Elsinore's royal court? As you read Act 2, Scene 2, imagine how the action might look on stage. The scene opens with trumpets announcing the King and Queen's arrival. How might the other characters behave around this royal couple? Would they bow or kneel? Do the royals leave in the same ceremonial style with which they entered?

My Words Fly Up Language

If you're not careful, some words and lines could pass by and you might not catch their full meaning. "What is the matter, my lord?" When Polonius asks this in Act 2, Scene 2, he's not quite asking Hamlet what's wrong. *Matter* here means *content,* as in the content of a letter. It could also refer to a cause of something, such as an argument. Hamlet uses this meaning when he asks who the matter is "between." Hamlet also is clever with words when he says he knows the difference between "a hawk and a handsaw." Both were types of tools. But Hamlet is also using another sense of "hawk." He means that he knows a predator when he sees one.

Shakespeare borrowed the characters Hecuba, Priam, and Pyrrhus in Scene 2 from a story about the ancient Trojan War. Priam and Hecuba were the king and queen of Troy, which was defeated and sacked by Greek troops that included Pyrrhus. Pyrrhus was the son of the fierce warrior Achilles. Other mythical figures mentioned in the story include the Cyclops—one-eyed giants who worked as blacksmiths in the underworld.

Act II

Scene I

Enter **Polonius** *and* **Reynaldo.**

Polonius Give him this money and these notes, Reynaldo.

Reynaldo I will, my lord.

Polonius You shall do marvellous wisely, good Reynaldo,
Before you visit him, to make inquire
5   Of his behaviour.

Reynaldo   My lord, I did intend it.

Polonius Marry, well said, very well said. Look you, sir,
Inquire me first what Danskers are in Paris,
And how, and who, what means, and where they keep,
10   What company, at what expense; and finding
By this encompassment and drift of question
That they do know my son, come you more nearer
Than your particular demands will touch it.
Take you as 'twere some distant knowledge of him,
15   As thus, 'I know his father, and his friends,
And in part him.' Do you mark this, Reynaldo?

Reynaldo Ay, very well, my lord.

Polonius 'And in part him. But,' you may say, 'not well;
But if't be he I mean, he's very wild,
20   Addicted so and so' – and there put on him
What forgeries you please – marry, none so rank
As may dishonour him – take heed of that –

Polonius *and his servant* **Reynaldo** *enter.*

Polonius Give him this money and these notes, Reynaldo.

Reynaldo I will, my lord.

Polonius You'd be wonderfully wise, Reynaldo, to make inquiries about his behavior before you see him.

Reynaldo My lord, I intended to do that.

Polonius Indeed; well said, well said. Look now, sir, first find out which Danes are in Paris, and how they wound up there, and who they are, and by what means they support themselves, and where they live, who they keep company with, and how much they spend. When you find out through these roundabout and indirect questions that they know my son, you'll get nearer to the truth than if you asked for it directly. Act as if you knew him distantly, like this: "I know his father, and his friends, and I know him somewhat." Are you getting this, Reynaldo?

Reynaldo Yes, very well, my lord.

Polonius "And I know him somewhat. But," you might say, "not well. But if he's the one I think he is, he's very wild, addicted to such-and-such. . . ." And there make up whatever false charges you please—though certainly nothing so evil that it might dishonor him. Be careful of that.

But, sir, such wanton, wild, and usual slips
As are companions noted and most known
25   To youth and liberty.

Reynaldo As gaming, my lord?

Polonius   Ay, or drinking, fencing, swearing,
      Quarrelling, drabbing – you may go so far.

30 **Reynaldo** My lord, that would dishonour him.

Polonius 'Faith no, as you may season it in the charge.
      You must not put another scandal on him,
      That he is open to incontinency;
      That's not my meaning. But breathe his faults so quaintly
35   That they may seem the taints of liberty,
      The flash and outbreak of a fiery mind,
      A savageness in unreclaimed blood,
      Of general assault.

Reynaldo But my good lord –

40 **Polonius**   Wherefore should you do this?

Reynaldo Ay my lord, I would know that.

Polonius Marry, sir, here's my drift,
      And I believe it is a fetch of warrant.
45   You laying these slight sullies on my son,
      As 'twere a thing a little soiled i'th'working,
      Mark you,
      Your party in converse, him you would sound,
      Having ever seen in the prenominate crimes
50   The youth you breathe of guilty, be assured
      He closes with you in this consequence
      'Good sir,' or so, or 'friend,' or 'gentleman,'
      According to the phrase or the addition
      Of man and country.

But sir, the kind of frisky, wild, and typical mistakes that are known to go with youth and freedom.

Reynaldo Like gambling, my lord?

Polonius Yes, or drinking, fencing, swearing, quarrelling, or visiting prostitutes. You can go that far.

Reynaldo My lord, that would dishonor him.

Polonius Oh, no, since you can water it down while you're making the charge. You must not make a scandal out of him by accusing him of being reckless. That's not what I mean. But mention his faults in such an artful way that they seem like the defects that accompany freedom, like the fiery flash and outbreak of an energetic mind, a wildness in the untamed blood. Young men are often subject to these things.

Reynaldo But my good lord—

Polonius Why should you do this?

Reynaldo Yes, my lord, I'd like to know that.

Polonius Well, sir, here's my drift—and I think it's a clever plan. By your assigning these slight blemishes to my son—as if they were all just the kind of faults that just come from living, mind you—you'll sound out the person you're talking with. If he's ever seen the young man you're discussing behaving in ways that show he's guilty of the previously mentioned defects, you can be sure he'll agree with your comments, responding like this: "Good sir" or something like that, or "friend," or "gentleman," according to the style in which he and his countrymen talk.

55 **Reynaldo**   Very good, my lord.

Polonius   And then, sir, does a this – a does – what was I
    about to say? By the mass, I was about to say something.
    Where did I leave?

Reynaldo   At 'closes in the consequence.'

60 **Polonius**   At 'closes in the consequence,' ay, marry.
    He closes thus: 'I know the gentleman,
    I saw him yesterday,' or 'th'other day,'
    Or then, or then, with such or such, 'and as you say,
    There was a gaming,' 'there o'ertook in's rouse,'
65   'There falling out at tennis,' or perchance
    'I saw him enter such a house of sale' –
    Videlicet a brothel, or so forth.
    See you now,
    Your bait of falsehood takes this carp of truth;
70   And thus do we of wisdom and of reach,
    With windlasses and with assays of bias,
    By indirections find directions out.
    So by my former lecture and advice
    Shall you my son. You have me, have you not?

75 **Reynaldo**   My lord, I have.

Polonius   God be wi' you, fare you well.

Reynaldo   Good my lord.

Polonius   Observe his inclination in yourself.

Reynaldo   I shall, my lord.

80 **Polonius**   And let him ply his music.

Reynaldo   Well, my lord.

                                      [*Exit*]

[*Enter* **Ophelia**]

Reynaldo Very good, my lord.

Polonius And then, sir, he does this . . . he does . . . what was I going to say? By heaven, I was about to say something. Where did I break off?

Reynaldo At "responds to you like this."

Polonius At "responds to you like this," yes, indeed. He responds this way: "I know that gentleman, I saw him yesterday," or "the other day" (or at this time or that time, with so-and-so), "and, like you say, he was there gambling"; "there he was, overcome by drink"; "there he was, fighting over a tennis match"; or perhaps, "I saw him enter such a business establishment"—in other words, a brothel—or so forth. You see? Your little lie serves as bait to catch the big fish, the larger truth. And this is the way we men of wisdom and understanding, through roundabout and angling methods, use indirect means to get the direct story. In this way you'll find out about my son by heeding the lesson and advice I just gave you. You understand me, do you not?

Reynaldo My lord, I do.

Polonius Good-bye. Fare you well.

Reynaldo My good lord.

Polonius And keep an eye on him.

Reynaldo I will, my lord.

Polonius And see that he still practices his music.

Reynaldo Certainly, my lord.

[**Reynaldo** *exits*]

[**Ophelia** *enters*]

Polonius   Farewell. How now, Ophelia, what's the matter?

Ophelia   Oh, my lord, my lord, I have been so affrighted.

Polonius   With what, i'th'name of God?

85 **Ophelia**   My lord, as I was sewing in my chamber,
Lord Hamlet, with his doublet all unbraced,
No hat upon his head, his stockings fouled,
Ungartered and down-gyved to his ankle,
Pale as his shirt, his knees knocking each other,
90 And with a look so piteous in purport
As if he had been loosed out of hell
To speak of horrors, he comes before me.

Polonius   Mad for thy love?

Ophelia   My lord, I do not know,
95 But truly I do fear it.

Polonius   What said he?

Ophelia   He took me by the wrist and held me hard.
Then goes he to the length of all his arm,
And with his other hand thus o'er his brow
100 He falls to such perusal of my face
As he would draw it. Long stayed he so.
At last, a little shaking of mine arm,
And thrice his head thus waving up and down,
He raised a sigh so piteous and profound
105 As it did seem to shatter all his bulk
And end his being. That done, he lets me go,
And with his head over his shoulder turned
He seemed to find his way without his eyes,
For out o'doors he went without their helps,
110 And to the last bended their light on me.

Polonius   Come, go with me, I will go seek the King.
This is the very ecstasy of love,
Whose violent property fordoes itself
And leads the will to desperate undertakings

Polonius Farewell. Well now, Ophelia; what's the matter?

Ophelia Oh, my lord, my lord, I've been so frightened.

Polonius Of what, in the name of God?

Ophelia My lord, while I was sewing in my room, Lord Hamlet came before me with his vest all undone, no hat on his head, his stockings dirty and hanging down around his ankles like chains, pale as his shirt, with his knees knocking together, and with such a pathetic look it was as if he had been hurled out of hell to relate its horrors.

Polonius Gone mad for your love?

Ophelia My lord, I don't know, but I do indeed fear it.

Polonius What did he say?

Ophelia He took me by the wrist and held me hard. Then he stretched out his arm, and with the other hand on his forehead, like this, he began studying my face so hard it was as if he wanted to draw it. He stayed that way a long time. Finally, giving my arm a little shake, and nodding his head up and down three times, like this, he let out a sigh so sad and deep it seemed to shatter his whole body and end his life. After doing that, he let me go. Twisting his head over his shoulder, he seemed to find his way without looking, since he went out the door without using his eyes and fixed their light on me to the end.

Polonius Come with me. I'll go find the King. This is love at the height of madness. Its violence is self-destructive. It leads to desperate acts, as much as any passion under the sun that

115   As oft as any passion under heaven
    That does afflict our natures. I am sorry –
    What, have you given him any hard words of late?

Ophelia No, my good lord, but as you did command,
    I did repel his letters and denied
120   His access to me.

Polonius   That hath made him mad.
    I am sorry that with better heed and judgment
    I had not quoted him. I feared he did but trifle
    And meant to wrack thee. But beshrew my jealousy!
125   By heaven, it is as proper to our age
    To cast beyond ourselves in our opinions
    As it is common for the younger sort
    To lack discretion. Come, go we to the King.
    This must be known, which, being kept close, might move
130   More grief to hide than hate to utter love.
    Come.

          [Exeunt]

afflicts our human natures. I'm sorry— [*He interrupts himself*] Now wait, have you spoken harsh words to him lately?

Ophelia   No, my good lord. But, as you commanded, I sent back his letters and refused to let him see me.

Polonius   That has driven him insane. I'm sorry I didn't read him with more care and judgment. I was afraid he was only trifling with you and that he wanted to ruin you. Curse my suspicious ways! By heaven, it's as typical of my generation to be overly suspicious as it is for younger people to be foolish. Come, let's go to the King. We must tell of this. Keeping it secret might cause more grief than it will cause anger by being revealed. Come.

[**Polonius** *and* **Ophelia** *exit*]

Act II

Scene II

Flourish. Enter **King** *and* **Queen, Rosencrantz** *and*
Guildenstern, *with Attendants.*

King Welcome, dear Rosencrantz and Guildenstern!
Moreover that we much did long to see you,
The need we have to use you did provoke
Our hasty sending. Something have you heard
5   Of Hamlet's transformation – so I call it,
Since nor th'exterior nor the inward man
Resembles that it was. What it should be,
More than his father's death, that thus hath put him
So much from th'understanding of himself
10   I cannot dream of. I entreat you both
That, being of so young days brought up with him,
And since so neighboured to his youth and haviour,
That you vouchsafe your rest here in our court
Some little time, so by your companies
15   To draw him on to pleasures and to gather,
So much as from occasion you may glean,
Whether aught to us unknown afflicts him thus
That, opened, lies within our remedy.

Queen Good gentlemen, he hath much talked of you,
20   And sure I am, two men there is not living
To whom he more adheres. If it will please you
To show us so much gentry and good will

106

Sound of trumpets. The **King** *and* **Queen** *enter, accompanied by* **Rosencrantz** *and* **Guildenstern** *and Attendants.*

King [*sometimes using the royal "we" to mean "I"*] Welcome, dear Rosencrantz and Guildenstern! Besides the fact that we longed to see you, we sent for you hastily because we needed your services. You've heard a bit about Hamlet's "transformation." I call it that, since he's not the man he used to be, either outside or inside. Besides his father's death, I can't imagine what has unhinged him this way. Since you grew up with him and have been so closely linked with his life and behavior as a young man, I ask you both to agree to stay here in our court for a while. That way your company will cause him to take pleasure in things again. And that way you can find out, as much as possible, whether he's suffering from anything that we don't know about and that we could set right once it's revealed.

Queen Good gentlemen, he's talked about you frequently, and I'm sure that there are no two men alive to whom he feels so close. If you would be so kind as to show us such courtesy and goodwill that you would spend your time with us a

As to expend your time with us awhile
For the supply and profit of our hope,
25 Your visitation shall receive such thanks
As fits a king's remembrance.

Rosencrantz   Both your Majesties
Might, by the sovereign power you have of us,
Put your dread pleasures more into command
30 Than to entreaty.

Guildenstern   But we both obey,
And here give up ourselves in the full bent
To lay our service freely at your feet
To be commanded.

35 **King** Thanks, Rosencrantz and gentle Guildenstern.

Queen Thanks, Guildenstern and gentle Rosencrantz.
And I beseech you instantly to visit
My too much changed son. Go, some of you,
And bring these gentlemen where Hamlet is.

40 **Guildenstern** Heavens make our presence and our practices
Pleasant and helpful to him.

Queen   Ay, amen.

[*Exeunt* **Rosencrantz** *and* **Guildenstern**]

[*Enter* **Polonius**]

Polonius The ambassadors from Norway, my good lord,
Are joyfully returned.

45 **King** Thou still hast been the father of good news.

Polonius Have I, my lord? I assure my good liege
I hold my duty as I hold my soul,
Both to my God and to my gracious King;
And I do think – or else this brain of mine

while, thereby promoting our hopes, you'll be thanked for your visit with royal compensation.

Rosencrantz With your sovereign powers, both your Majesties could command us to fulfill your honored wishes, rather than asking.

Guildenstern But we will both obey, and we put ourselves at your service to the utmost of our abilities, ready to be commanded.

King Thanks, Rosencrantz and kind Guildenstern.

Queen Thanks, Guildenstern and kind Rosencrantz. And I ask you to immediately visit my son, who has changed too much. [*To the Attendants*] Some of you go and bring these gentlemen to where Hamlet is.

Guildenstern May heaven make our presence and activities pleasing and helpful to him.

Queen Indeed; amen.

[**Rosencrantz** *and* **Guildenstern** *exit*]

[**Polonius** *enters*]

Polonius Happily, the ambassadors have returned from Norway, my good lord.

King You have always been the father of good news.

Polonius Have I, my lord? I assure you, my good lord, that I maintain my duty as I maintain my soul, both dedicated to God and to my gracious King. And I think—unless this brain

50   Hunts not the trail of policy so sure
       As it hath used to do – that I have found
       The very cause of Hamlet's lunacy.

King   O, speak of that: that I do long to hear.

Polonius   Give first admittance to th'ambassadors.
55   My news shall be the fruit to that great feast.

King   Thyself do grace to them and bring them in.

                              [*Exit* **Polonius**]

       He tells me, my dear Gertrude, he hath found
       The head and source of all your son's distemper.

Queen   I doubt it is no other than the main,
60   His father's death and our o'er-hasty marriage.

King   Well, we shall sift him.

    [*Enter* **Polonius, Voltemand,** *and* **Cornelius**]

                        Welcome, my good friends.
       Say, Voltemand, what from our brother Norway?

Voltemand   Most fair return of greetings and desires.
65   Upon our first, he sent out to suppress
       His nephew's levies, which to him appeared
       To be a preparation 'gainst the Polack;
       But better looked into, he truly found
       It was against your highness. Whereat grieved,
70   That so his sickness, age, and impotence
       Was falsely borne in hand, sends out arrests
       On Fortinbras; which he, in brief, obeys,
       Receives rebuke from Norway, and, in fine,
       Makes vow before his uncle never more
75   To give th'assay of arms against your Majesty.
       Whereon old Norway, overcome with joy,

of mine isn't as shrewd as it used to be—that I have found out the real cause of Hamlet's lunacy.

King Oh, tell me more about that; I'm longing to hear.

Polonius Admit the ambassadors first. My news will be like the dessert after their great feast.

King Do the honors yourself and bring them in.

[**Polonius** *exits*]

He tells me, my dear Gertrude, that he's found the source of your son's disorder.

Queen I suspect it's the obvious one: his father's death and our too-hasty marriage.

King Well, we'll question him closely.

[**Polonius, Voltemand,** *and* **Cornelius** *enter*]

Welcome, my good friends. Voltemand, what's the message from our brother the King of Norway?

Voltemand A most pleasing return of your greetings and requests. As soon as we spoke of this matter, he sent out orders to disband the troops mustered by his nephew. He had believed the troops were a preparation for battle against the King of Poland. But once he looked into it more, he found it was actually a preparation against your Highness. Whereupon, grieved that his sickness, age, and lack of power had been taken advantage of, he sent out orders for Fortinbras to stop. To be brief, Fortinbras obeyed; he was rebuked by the King; and, in conclusion, he vowed to his uncle that he would never again challenge your Majesty militarily. Whereupon the old King, overcome with joy, gave

Gives him three thousand crowns in annual fee
And his commission to employ those soldiers
So levied, as before, against the Polack,
80   With an entreaty, herein further shown, [*Giving a paper*]
That it might please you to give quiet pass
Through your dominions for this enterprise,
On such regards of safety and allowance
As therein are set down.

85 **King**   It likes us well;
And at our more considered time we'll read,
Answer, and think upon this business.
Meantime, we thank you for your well-took labour.
Go to your rest; at night we'll feast together.
90   Most welcome home.

[*Exeunt* **Voltemand** *and* **Cornelius**]

Polonius   This business is well ended.
My liege and madam, to expostulate
What majesty should be, what duty is,
Why day is day, night night, and time is time,
95   Were nothing but to waste night, day, and time.
Therefore, since brevity is the soul of wit,
And tediousness the limbs and outward flourishes,
I will be brief. Your noble son is mad.
Mad call I it, for to define true madness,
100   What is't but to be nothing else but mad?
But let that go.

Queen   More matter with less art.

Polonius Madam, I swear I use no art at all.
That he is mad 'tis true; 'tis true 'tis pity;
105   And pity 'tis 'tis true. A foolish figure!
But farewell it, for I will use no art.
Mad let us grant him then. And now remains
That we find out the cause of this effect,

him an annual sum of three thousand crowns and a
commission to use the soldiers he'd mustered against
Poland. He also gave a request, which is further detailed here
[*he gives the* **King** *a document*], that your Majesty might
consent to allow this expedition safe passage through your
domain, with such safeguards and terms as are outlined
therein.

King This pleases us well, and when we have more time for
thought we'll read, answer, and consider this business.
Meanwhile, we thank you for your well-received work. Go
and rest; tonight we'll feast together. You are most welcome
home.

[**Voltemand** *and* **Cornelius** *exit*]

Polonius This matter has ended well. My King and Queen: To
deliberate what kingliness should be, what duty is, why day
is day and night is night and time is time, would simply
waste night, day, and time. Therefore, since being brief is
at the core of good judgment, and dullness dwells in
elaboration and unnecessary flourishes, I will be brief. Your
noble son is mad. I call it mad, since isn't it madness itself to
define true madness? But let that be.

Queen More content, less artfulness.

Polonius Madam, I swear I'm not being artful at all. That he is
mad, it's true. It's true that it's a pity, and it's a pity that it's
true. A silly figure of speech! But let it go, so I won't be artful.
Let's grant that he is mad, then. And now it remains that we
should find out what caused this effect—or rather what

Or rather say the cause of this defect,
110 For this effect defective comes by cause:
Thus it remains; and the remainder thus:
Perpend,
I have a daughter – have whilst she is mine –
Who in her duty and obedience, mark,
115 Hath given me this. Now gather and surmise.
[*Reads*] *To the celestial and my soul's idol, the most beautified*
Ophelia – That's an ill phrase, a vile phrase, 'beautified' is a
vile phrase. But you shall hear thus: *in her excellent white*
bosom, these, etc.

120 **Queen** Came this from Hamlet to her?

Polonius Good madam, stay awhile, I will be faithful.

> *Doubt that the stars are fire,*
> *Doubt that the sun doth move,*
> *Doubt truth to be a liar,*
125 > *But never doubt I love.*
Oh dear Ophelia, I am ill at these numbers. I have not art to
reckon my groans. But that I love thee best, oh, most best,
believe it. Adieu. Thine evermore, most dear lady, whilst this
machine is to him, Hamlet.

130 This in obedience hath my daughter shown me,
And, more above, hath his solicitings,
As they fell out by time, by means, and place,
All given to mine ear.

King But how hath she received his love?

135 **Polonius** What do you think of me?

King As of a man faithful and honourable.

Polonius I would fain prove so. But what might you think,
When I had seen this hot love on the wing –
As I perceived it, I must tell you that,
140 Before my daughter told me – what might you

caused this *defect*—for there must be a cause that effects this defect. Thus it remains, and the remainder is therefore: Consider this. [*He pauses*] I have a daughter—have her while she is still with me—who in her sense of duty and obedience, please note, has given me this. Now listen and judge. [*He reads a letter*]

To the idol of the heavens and my soul, the most beautified Ophelia—That's a badly chosen word, a vile word; *beautified* is a vile word. But you'll hear more: . . . *to the heart in her admirable white breast these words are sent, etc.*

Queen   Did this come to her from Hamlet?

Polonius   Good madam, wait a while, I'll read it all.

> *Doubt that the stars are fire,*
> *Doubt that the sun does move,*
> *Think that truth is a liar,*
> *But never doubt I love.*
> *Oh, dear Ophelia, I am bad at writing verse. I lack the skill to express my pains in rhythm and rhyme. But that I love you more than anyone, oh, more than anyone, believe me. Good-bye. Yours forever, dearest lady, as long as my body, lives, Hamlet.*

My daughter has obediently shown me this. Furthermore, she has told me of all his attempts to woo her: when and where and how they occurred.

King   But how has she responded to his love?

Polonius   How do you think of me?

King   As a faithful, honorable man.

Polonius   I would gladly be so. But what would you have thought, as I saw this passionate love taking wing—and I observed it, I must tell you that, before my daughter told me

Or my dear Majesty your queen here think
If I had played the desk or table-book,
Or given my heart a winking mute and dumb,
Or looked upon this love with idle sight –
145   What might you think? No, I went round to work,
And my young mistress thus I did bespeak:
'Lord Hamlet is a prince out of thy star.
This must not be.' And then I prescripts gave her,
That she should lock herself from his resort,
150   Admit no messengers, receive no tokens;
Which done, she took the fruits of my advice,
And he, repelled – a short tale to make –
Fell into sadness, then into a fast,
Thence to a watch, thence into a weakness,
155   Thence to a lightness, and, by this declension,
Into the madness wherein now he raves
And all we mourn for.

King   Do you think 'tis this?

Queen It may be; very like.

160 **Polonius** Hath there been such a time – I would fain know
that –
That I have positively said ''Tis so,'
When it proved otherwise?

King   Not that I know.

165 **Polonius** [*points to his head and shoulder*] Take this from
this if this be otherwise:
If circumstances lead me, I will find
Where truth is hid, though it were hid indeed
Within the centre.

170 **King**   How may we try it further?

Polonius You know sometimes he walks four hours together
Here in the lobby.

about it—what would you or my dear majesty, your Queen here, have thought if I'd carried messages? Or if I'd kept my heart's eyes, ears, and mouth closed, or if I'd witnessed this love without comprehending it? What would you think? No, I went right to work. I said to my young miss, "Lord Hamlet is a prince, out of your sphere. This must not be." And then I gave her orders that she should lock herself away from his attempts to visit, admit no messengers, and accept no tokens of his love. That being done, she took my advice to heart. And he, being rejected (to make a long story short) fell into a depression, then couldn't eat, then couldn't sleep, then became weak, then became light-headed, and, following this pattern of decline, he fell into the madness he's raving in now, which causes us all to mourn.

King [*to* **Gertrude**] Do you think this is it?

Queen It may be; very likely.

Polonius Has there ever been a time—I would like to know— when I have positively said, "This is so," and it turned out otherwise?

King Not that I know of.

Polonius [*pointing to his head and shoulders*] Take *this* from *this* if I'm wrong. Given the right circumstances, I'll find out where the truth is hidden, even if it's hidden at the center of the earth.

King How can we test this theory further?

Polonius You know that he sometimes walks for four whole hours here in this hall.

Queen So he does indeed.

Polonius At such a time I'll loose my daughter to him.
175   Be you and I behind an arras then.
Mark the encounter: if he love her not,
And be not from his reason fall'n thereon,
Let me be no assistant for a state,
But keep a farm and carters.

180 **King** We will try it.

[*Enter* **Hamlet,** *reading a book*]

Queen But look where sadly the poor wretch comes reading.

Polonius Away, I do beseech you both, away.
I'll board him presently. Oh, give me leave.

[*Exeunt* **King** *and* **Queen** *and Attendants*]

How does my good Lord Hamlet?

185 **Hamlet** Well, God-a-mercy.

Polonius Do you know me, my lord?

Hamlet Excellent well. You are a fishmonger.

Polonius Not I, my lord.

Hamlet Then I would you were so honest a man.

190 **Polonius** Honest, my lord?

Hamlet Ay sir. To be honest, as this world goes, is to be one
man picked out of ten thousand.

Polonius That's very true, my lord.

Hamlet For if the sun breed maggots in a dead dog, being a
195   good kissing carrion – Have you a daughter?

Polonius I have, my lord.

Queen   So he does, indeed.

Polonius   At such a time, I'll set my daughter before him. Let's you and I hide behind a hanging tapestry. Watch the encounter: If he doesn't love her, and if he hasn't lost his reason because of that, let me no longer be a state councillor, but run a farm and employ wagon drivers instead.

King   We'll give it a try.

[**Hamlet** *enters, reading a book*]

Queen   But look how sadly the poor, miserable man comes, reading.

Polonius   Go, please, both of you go. I'll confront him at once. Oh, let me do so.

[*The* **King, Queen,** *and Attendants exit*]

How is my good Lord Hamlet?

Hamlet   God's mercy on you; I'm well.

Polonius   Do you recognize me, my lord?

Hamlet   Very well. You're a fish dealer.

Polonius   Not I, my lord.

Hamlet   Then I wish you were that honest a man.

Polonius   Honest, my lord?

Hamlet   Yes, sir. To be honest, as this world goes, is to be one man in ten thousand.

Polonius   That's very true, my lord.

Hamlet   For, if the sun breeds maggots in a dead dog—it being good enough for the sun to kiss . . . Do you have a daughter?

Polonius   I have, my lord.

Hamlet Let her not walk i'th'sun. Conception is a blessing, but as your daughter may conceive – friend, look to't.

200 **Polonius** [*aside*] How say you by that? Still harping on my daughter. Yet he knew me not at first; he said I was a fishmonger. He is far gone. And truly in my youth I suffered much extremity for love, very near this. I'll speak to him again. What do you read, my lord?

Hamlet Words, words, words.

205 **Polonius** What is the matter, my lord?

Hamlet Between who?

Polonius I mean the matter that you read, my lord.

Hamlet Slanders, sir. For the satirical rogue says here that old men have grey beards, that their faces are wrinkled, their
210 eyes purging thick amber and plumtree gum, and that they have a plentiful lack of wit, together with most weak hams – all which, sir, though I most powerfully and potently believe, yet I hold it not honesty to have it thus set down. For you yourself, sir, shall grow old as I am – if like a crab
215 you could go backward.

Polonius [*aside*] Though this be madness, yet there is method in't. Will you walk out of the air, my lord?

Hamlet Into my grave?

Polonius Indeed, that's out of the air. [*Aside*] How pregnant
220 sometimes his replies are – a happiness that often madness hits on, which reason and sanity could not so prosperously be delivered of. I will leave him and suddenly contrive the means of meeting between him and my daughter. My lord, I will take my leave of you.

225 **Hamlet** You cannot, sir, take from me anything that I will not more willingly part withal – except my life, except my life, except my life.

Hamlet Don't let her walk in the sun. Conception (when it means "understanding") is a blessing, but since your daughter may conceive in another way—friend, be careful.

Polonius [*aside*] What do you think of that! Continually harping on about my daughter. Yet at first he didn't know me; he said I was a fish dealer. He's far gone. And to be sure, in my youth I suffered terribly over love, much like this. I'll speak to him again. What are you reading, my lord?

Hamlet Words, words, words.

Polonius What is the matter, my lord?

Hamlet What's the matter? Between who?

Polonius I mean the subject you're reading about, my lord.

Hamlet Slander, sir. For the satirical rascal says here [*indicating his book*] that old men have gray beards, that their faces are wrinkled, that their eyes discharge a gummy resin, and that they suffer a plentiful lack of wits, along with very weak haunches. All of which, sir, I powerfully and potently believe, but I don't think it's proper to have written it down like that. For you, yourself, sir, will grow as old as I am—if, like a crab, you could go backward.

Polonius [*aside*] Though this is madness, it still makes its own kind of sense. [*To* **Hamlet**] Will you walk in out of the air, my lord?

Hamlet Into my grave?

Polonius Indeed, that's out of the air. [*Aside*] How full of meaning his replies are sometimes. It's a knack that madness often arrives at, which reason and sanity couldn't deliver as fruitfully. I'll leave him, and immediately think up a way for he and my daughter to meet. [*To* **Hamlet**] My lord, I'll take my leave of you.

Hamlet Sir, there's nothing you can take from me that I wouldn't rather part with. Except my life, except my life, except my life.

Polonius Fare you well, my lord.

Hamlet These tedious old fools!

[*Enter* **Rosencrantz** *and* **Guildenstern**]

230 **Polonius** You go to seek the Lord Hamlet. There he is.

Rosencrantz God save you, sir.

[*Exit* **Polonius**]

Guildenstern My honoured lord.

Rosencrantz My most dear lord.

Hamlet My excellent good friends. How dost thou,
235 Guildenstern? Ah, Rosencrantz. Good lads, how do you
both?

Rosencrantz As the indifferent children of the earth.

Guildenstern Happy in that we are not over-happy: on
Fortune's cap we are not the very button.

240 **Hamlet** Nor the soles of her shoes?

Rosencrantz Neither, my lord.

Hamlet Then you live about her waist, or in the middle of
her favours?

Guildenstern Faith, her privates we.

245 **Hamlet** In the secret parts of Fortune? Oh most true, she
is a strumpet. What news?

Rosencrantz None, my lord, but the world's grown honest.

Hamlet Then is doomsday near. But your news is not true.
Let me question more in particular. What have you, my
250 good friends, deserved at the hands of Fortune that she sends
you to prison hither?

Polonius Farewell, my lord.

Hamlet These tedious old fools!

[**Rosencrantz** and **Guildenstern** enter]

Polonius You've come to find the Lord Hamlet. There he is.

Rosencrantz God save you, sir.

[**Polonius** exits]

Guildenstern My honored lord.

Rosencrantz My dearest lord.

Hamlet My excellent good friends. How are you, Guildenstern? Ah, Rosencrantz. Good fellows, how are you both?

Rosencrantz As well as the average children of the earth.

Guildenstern Happy in that we're not overly happy. We're not the brightest button on Lady Fortune's cap!

Hamlet Nor the sole of her shoe?

Rosencrantz Neither, my lord.

Hamlet Then you live around her waist, or in the middle of her favors?

Guildenstern In faith, we're her privates.

Hamlet In the private parts of Fortune? Oh, most true, she is a strumpet. What's new?

Rosencrantz Nothing, my lord, except that the world's grown honest.

Hamlet Then Doomsday must be near. But your news isn't true. Let me ask something more specific. What, my good friends, have you done to deserve being punished by Fortune so that she sends you to prison here?

Guildenstern Prison, my lord?

Hamlet Denmark's a prison.

Rosencrantz Then is the world one.

255 **Hamlet** A goodly one, in which there are many confines, wards, and dungeons, Denmark being one o'th'worst.

Rosencrantz We think not so, my lord.

Hamlet Why then 'tis none to you; for there is nothing either good or bad but thinking makes it so. To me it is a prison.

260 **Rosencrantz** Why, then your ambition makes it one: 'tis too narrow for your mind.

Hamlet O, God, I could be bounded in a nutshell and count myself a king of infinite space – were it not that I have bad dreams.

265 **Guildenstern** Which dreams indeed are ambition; for the very substance for the ambitious is merely the shadow of a dream.

Hamlet A dream itself is but a shadow.

Rosencrantz Truly, and I hold ambition of so airy and light a quality that it is but a shadow's shadow.

270 **Hamlet** Then are our beggars bodies, and our monarchs and outstretched heroes the beggars' shadows. Shall we to th' court? For by my fay, I cannot reason.

Both We'll wait upon you.

Hamlet No such matter. I will not sort you with the rest of
275 my servants; for, to speak to you like an honest man, I am most dreadfully attended. But in the beaten way of friendship, what make you at Elsinore?

Rosencrantz To visit you, my lord, no other occasion.

Hamlet Beggar that I am, I am even poor in thanks, but I
280 thank you. And sure, dear friends, my thanks are too dear

Guildenstern Prison, my lord?

Hamlet Denmark's a prison.

Rosencrantz Then the world is one too.

Hamlet A good-sized one, in which there are many blocks, cells, and dungeons, Denmark being one of the worst.

Rosencrantz We don't think so, my lord.

Hamlet Well, then, it isn't one to you. Nothing's either good or bad unless you think it's that way. To me, it's a prison.

Rosencrantz Well, then your ambition turns it into one. It's too narrow for your mind.

Hamlet Oh God, I could be enclosed in a nutshell and consider myself a king of infinite space—if it weren't for the fact that I have bad dreams.

Guildenstern Those dreams are also ambition. The substantial thing an ambitious man desires is just a shadow of a dream.

Hamlet A dream itself is only a shadow.

Rosencrantz That's true, and I consider ambition to be so light and insubstantial that it's merely a shadow's shadow.

Hamlet Then our beggars are like bodies, and our monarchs and far-reaching heroes are like the beggars' shadows. Shall we take this to court? By my faith, I can't figure it out.

Ros., Guild. We'll attend you.

Hamlet You'll do no such thing. I won't put you in the class of the rest of my servants—since, frankly speaking, I'm very poorly attended to. But to return to the familiar ways of friendship: What brings you to Elsinore?

Rosencrantz We came to visit you, my lord—no other reason.

Hamlet Beggar that I am, I'm even lacking in thanks. But I thank you. And to be sure, dear friends, my thanks aren't a halfpenny. Were you not sent for? Is it your own inclining? Is it a free visitation? Come, come, deal justly with me. Come, come. Nay, speak.

Guildenstern   What should we say, my lord?

285   **Hamlet**   Why, anything. But to the purpose. You were sent for, and there is a kind of confession in your looks, which your modesties have not craft enough to colour. I know the good King and Queen have sent for you.

Rosencrantz   To what end, my lord?

290   **Hamlet**   That, you must teach me. But let me conjure you, by the rights of our fellowship, by the consonancy of our youth, by the obligation of our ever-preserved love, and by what more dear a better proposer can charge you withal, be even and direct with me whether you were sent for or no.

295   **Rosencrantz**   [*aside to* **Guildenstern**]   What say you?

Hamlet   Nay, then I have an eye of you. If you love me, hold not off.

Guildenstern   My lord, we were sent for.

Hamlet   I will tell you why; so shall my anticipation prevent
300   your discovery, and your secrecy to the King and Queen
moult no feather. I have of late, but wherefore I know not,
lost all my mirth, forgone all custom of exercise; and indeed
it goes so heavily with my disposition that this goodly frame
the earth seems to me a sterile promontory, this most
305   excellent canopy the air, look you, this brave o'erhanging
firmament, this majestical roof fretted with golden fire, why,
it appeareth nothing to me but a foul and pestilent
congregation of vapours. What a piece of work is a man, how
noble in reason, how infinite in faculties, in form and
310   moving how express and admirable, in action how like an
angel, in apprehension how like a god: the beauty of the
world, the paragon of animals – and yet, to me, what is this

worth half a penny. Weren't you sent for, then? Did you come because you wanted to? Is your visit completely voluntary? Come, come, deal with me honestly. Come, come. No, please speak.

Guildenstern What should we say, my lord?

Hamlet Why, anything. So long as it's straightforward. You were sent for. Your expressions give you away, and you've got too much sense of shame to craftily disguise that. I know the good King and Queen sent for you.

Rosencrantz For what purpose, my lord?

Hamlet You'll have to tell me that. But let me entreat you, by the bonds of our fellowship, by the similarity of our ages, by the obligations of our long-standing love—and by whatever's more valuable that a better speaker could urge you to consider—be straight and honest with me as to whether or not you were sent for.

Rosencrantz [*aside to* **Guildenstern**] What will you say?

Hamlet Now, I've got my eye on you. If you love me, don't hold back.

Guildenstern My lord, we were sent for.

Hamlet I'll tell you why. That way, I'll say in advance what you would otherwise have had to reveal to me, so your promise of secrecy to the King and Queen will remain intact. Lately, for reasons I don't understand, I have lost all my sense of happiness, given up exercising as I used to do. Indeed, my mood is so heavy that this lovely dwelling, the earth, seems like nothing but a barren rock to me. This wonderful canopy, the air—look—this splendid overarching sky, this majestic roof decorated with golden fire— why, to me it seems like nothing except a foul and noxious set of vapors. What a masterwork is man: how noble in his ability to reason, how infinite in abilities, how expressive and admirable in his construction and movement, how angelic in his actions, how godlike in his mental powers. The greatest beauty in the world, the most perfect of animals! And yet, to me, what is this pure quintessence of dust? Man delights not me – no, nor woman neither, though by your smiling you seem to say so.

315 **Rosencrantz** My lord, there was no such stuff in my thoughts.

Hamlet Why did ye laugh then, when I said man delights not me?

Rosencrantz To think, my lord, if you delight not in man,
320 what Lenten entertainment the players shall receive from you. We coted them on the way, and hither are they coming to offer you service.

Hamlet He that plays the King shall be welcome – his Majesty shall have tribute of me; the adventurous knight
325 shall use his foil and target; the lover shall not sigh gratis; the humorous man shall end his part in peace; the clown shall make those laugh whose lungs are tickle a th' sear; and the lady shall say her mind freely, or the blank verse shall halt for't. What players are they?

330 **Rosencrantz** Even those you were wont to take such delight in; the tragedians of the city.

Hamlet How chances it they travel? Their residence, both in reputation and profit, was better both ways.

Rosencrantz I think their inhibition comes by the means of
335 the late innovation.

Hamlet Do they hold the same estimation they did when I was in the city? Are they so followed?

Rosencrantz No, indeed are they not.

Hamlet How comes it? Do they grow rusty?

perfection of dust? Man gives me no delight. No, neither does woman, though your smiles seem to imply that.

Rosencrantz My lord, I thought no such thing.

Hamlet Then why did you laugh, when I said man gives me no delight?

Rosencrantz I was thinking, my lord, that if man gives you no delight, what a meager welcome the actors will get from you. On the way here we passed them by, and they are coming here to offer you their services.

Hamlet The one who plays the King will be welcome—I'll pay "his Majesty" tribute. The adventure-seeking knight will use his sword and shield; the lover will not sigh without reward. The eccentric will speak his piece out to the end; the clown will make those who are easily tickled laugh; and the lady will speak her mind without censorship, or else the missing words will cripple the blank verse. Which actors are these?

Rosencrantz The same ones you used to be so fond of—the actors who play tragedies in the city.

Hamlet Why are they touring? Remaining in their home town would be better for their reputation and profits.

Rosencrantz I think they were prohibited from playing at home because of the recent upheavals.

Hamlet Do they have the same high reputation as when I was in the city? Are they still so popular?

Rosencrantz No, indeed, they're not.

Hamlet Why is that? Are they getting stale?

340 **Rosencrantz** Nay, their endeavour keeps in the wonted pace;
but there is, sir, an eyrie of children, little eyases, that cry out
on the top of question, and are most tyrannically clapped
for't. These are now the fashion, and so berattle the common
stages – so they call them – that many wearing rapiers are
345 afraid of goose-quills and dare scarce come thither.

Hamlet What, are they children? Who maintains 'em? How
are they escoted? Will they pursue the quality no longer than
they can sing? Will they not say afterwards, if they should
grow themselves to common players – as it is most like, if
350 their means are no better – their writers do them wrong to
make them exclaim against their own succession?

Rosencrantz Faith, there has been much to do on both sides;
and the nation holds it no sin to tar them to controversy.
There was for a while no money bid for argument unless
355 the poet and the player went to cuffs in the question.

Hamlet Is't possible?

Guildenstern O, there has been much throwing about of
brains.

Hamlet Do the boys carry it away?

360 **Rosencrantz** Ay, that they do, my lord; Hercules and his load
too.

Hamlet It is not very strange; for my uncle is King of
Denmark, and those that would make mouths at him while
my father lived give twenty, forty, fifty, a hundred ducats
365 apiece for his picture in little. 'Sblood, there is something in
this more than natural, if philosophy could find it out.

[*A flourish of trumpets*]

Guildenstern There are the players.

Rosencrantz No, they've kept up their high quality. But there is, sir, a nest of children, little fledglings, who cry out shrilly above the competition, and are most outrageously applauded for it. These child actors are now in fashion. They berate the "common stages" (so they call them), so much that many gentlemen who wear swords are afraid to attend, for fear of the playwrights' goose-quill pens.

Hamlet What, are they children? Who manages them? How are they subsidized? Will they keep up acting only until their high voices change and can no longer sing? If they develop into "common" actors (which seems likely, since acting is all they know how to do), won't they say later that their writers did them wrong by making them attack their own future?

Rosencrantz In truth, there's been much fuss on both sides, and people think it's no sin to keep the controversy going. For a time no play was commissioned unless its plot joined the battle between the children's playwrights and the adult actors.

Hamlet Is that possible?

Guildenstern Oh, much intelligence has been wasted on this issue.

Hamlet Do the boys win out?

Rosencrantz Yes, indeed they do, my lord; they carry off Hercules and his load of the Globe, too.

Hamlet It's not really so strange. My uncle is the King of Denmark, and the people who made faces at him while my father was alive will now pay twenty, forty, fifty, a hundred ducats for his portrait in miniature. By God's blood, there's something about this that's hardly natural, if philosophy could figure it out.

[Fanfare of trumpets]

Guildenstern That must be the players.

Hamlet Gentlemen, you are welcome to Elsinore. Your
hands, come then. The appurtenance of welcome is fashion
370 and ceremony. Let me comply with you in this garb – lest
my extent to the players, which I tell you must show fairly
outwards, should more appear like entertainment than yours.
You are welcome. But my uncle-father and aunt-mother are
deceived.

375 **Guildenstern** In what, my dear lord?

Hamlet I am but mad north-north-west. When the wind is
southerly, I know a hawk from a handsaw.

[*Enter* **Polonius**]

Polonius Well be with you, gentlemen.

Hamlet Hark you, Guildenstern, and you too – at each ear a
380 hearer. That great baby you see there is not yet out of his
swaddling-clouts.

Rosencrantz Happily he's the second time come to them, for
they say an old man is twice a child.

Hamlet I will prophesy he comes to tell me of the players.
385 Mark it. You say right, sir, a Monday morning, 'twas then
indeed.

Polonius My lord, I have news to tell you.

Hamlet My lord, I have news to tell you. When Roscius was
an actor in Rome –

390 **Polonius** The actors are come hither, my lord.

Hamlet Buzz, buzz.

Polonius Upon my honour –

Hamlet *Then came each actor on his ass –*

Hamlet Gentlemen, you are welcome to Elsinore. Come then, shake hands. Custom and ceremony are necessary parts of welcome. Let me follow form with you in this way—so that my courtesy to the players (which I must tell you will look very cordial) won't seem like a better reception than your own. You are welcome. But my uncle-father and aunt-mother are deceived.

Guildenstern In what way, my dear lord?

Hamlet I'm only mad when the wind blows north-by-northwest. When the wind's from the south, I know a hawk from a handsaw.

[**Polonius** *enters*]

Polonius Good day, gentlemen.

Hamlet Listen, Guildenstern. [*To* **Rosencrantz**] And you too. A listener at each ear. That big baby you see there isn't out of his diapers yet.

Rosencrantz Perhaps it's his second time wearing them, since they say an old man is a child for the second time.

Hamlet I predict he's come to tell me about the players. Watch. [*Pretending to be talking about something else*] You're right sir—on Monday morning, it was indeed then.

Polonius My lord, I have news for you.

Hamlet My lord, I have news for *you*. When Roscius was an actor in Rome, in the first century B.C. . . . .

Polonius The actors have come here, my lord.

Hamlet Buzz, buzz.

Polonius Upon my word—

Hamlet [*quoting a ballad*] *Then came each actor on his ass—*

Polonius The best actors in the world, either for tragedy,
395   comedy, history, pastoral, pastoral-comical, historical-
       pastoral, tragical-historical, tragical-comical-historical-
       pastoral, scene individable, or poem unlimited. Seneca
       cannot be too heavy, nor Plautus too light. For the law of
       writ, and the liberty, these are only men.

400 **Hamlet** *O, Jephthah, judge of Israel, what a treasure hadst
       thou!*

     Polonius What a treasure had he, my lord?

     Hamlet Why,

              One fair daughter and no more,
405   *The which he loved passing well.*

     Polonius [*aside*] Still on my daughter.

     Hamlet Am I not i'th'right, old Jephthah?

     Polonius If you call me Jephthah, my lord, I have a daughter
       that I love passing well.

410 **Hamlet** Nay, that follows not.

     Polonius What follows then, my lord?

     Hamlet Why,

              As by lot God wot,

     And then, you know,

415   *It came to pass, as most like it was.*
       The first row of the pious chanson will show you more, for
       look where my abridgement comes.

     [*Enter the Players*]

Polonius   They're the best actors in the world, either for tragedy, comedy, history, pastoral, pastoral-comical, historical-pastoral, tragical-historical, tragical-comical-historical-pastoral, for plays observing the classical rules, or for plays ignoring those rules. Seneca's tragedies aren't too heavy for them, nor Plautus's comedies too light. For sticking to the classics or pushing dramatic boundaries, these are the absolute best men.

Hamlet   [*quoting a ballad again*] *Oh, Jephthah, judge of Israel, what a treasure you had!*

Polonius   What treasure did he have, my lord?

Hamlet   Why,

>*One fair daughter and no more,*
>*For whom he had utmost love.*

Polonius   [*aside*] Always going on about my daughter.

Hamlet   Aren't I right, old Jephthah?

Polonius   Since you call me Jephthah, my lord, then I have a daughter for whom I feel the utmost love.

Hamlet   No, that doesn't follow.

Polonius   Then what does follow, my lord?

Hamlet   Why,

>*As by chance God knew,*

And then, you know,

>*It came to pass as it was bound to.*

The first stanza of the pious song will tell you the rest, for here comes my interruption.

[*The* **Players** *enter*]

You are welcome, masters. Welcome, all – I am glad to see
thee well – Welcome, good friends – O, old friend, why
420 thy face is valanced since I saw thee last. Com'st thou to
beard me in Denmark? – What, my young lady and mistress!
By'r lady, your ladyship is nearer to heaven than when I saw
you last by the altitude of a chopine. Pray God your voice,
like a piece of uncurrent gold, be not cracked within the
425 ring. Masters, you are all welcome. We'll e'en to't like
French falconers, fly at anything we see. We'll have a speech
straight. Come, give us a taste of your quality. Come, a
passionate speech.

1st Player What speech, my good lord?

430 **Hamlet** I heard thee speak me a speech once, but it was
never acted, or if it was, not above once – for the play, I
remember, pleased not the million, 'twas caviare to the
general. But it was, as I received it – and others, whose
judgments in such matters cried in the top of mine – an
435 excellent play, well digested in the scenes, set down with as
much modesty as cunning. I remember one said there were
no sallets in the lines to make the matter savoury, nor no
matter in the phrase that might indict the author of
affection, but called it an honest method, as wholesome as
440 sweet, and by very much more handsome than fine. One
speech in it I chiefly loved; 'twas Aeneas' tale to Dido; and
thereabout of it especially when he speaks of Priam's
slaughter. If it live in your memory, begin at this line – let
me see, let me see –

445 *The rugged Pyrrhus, like th'Hyrcanian beast –*

It is not so. It begins with Pyrrhus –

The rugged Pyrrhus, he whose sable arms,
Black as his purpose, did the night resemble
When he lay couched in the ominous horse,
450 *Hath now this dread and black complexion smear'd*

Welcome, masters. Welcome—all—I'm glad to see you well—
Welcome, good friends. Old friend, you've grown a beard since
I last saw you. Have you come to confront me in Denmark? [*To
a boy actor*] Well, my young lady and mistress! By our lady,
since the last time I saw you your ladyship has grown closer to
heaven—you're taller by the height of a high-heeled shoe! Pray
to God that your voice—like a mangled coin—hasn't cracked to
the point it's breaking. Masters, you are all welcome. We'll jump
to it like French hunters with their falcons, flying at anything we
see. Let's have a speech. Come, give us a taste of your skill.
Come—a passionate speech.

1st Player   Which speech, my lord?

Hamlet   I heard you recite a speech once, but it was never acted.
Or if it was, it was performed no more than once, since as I
recall the play didn't please the masses. For the general public,
it was like caviar—too good for common tastes. But in my
judgment—and in the judgment of others more knowledgeable
than me in such matters—it was an excellent play, well
plotted in its scenes, written with as much economy as skill. I
remember someone said there weren't enough spicy lines to
make the play tasty, and nothing in the language that would
make you accuse the author of affectation. But he said it was an
honorable style, as wholesome as it was delightful, and much
more beautiful than merely showy. It contained one speech
that I especially loved. It was the story the Trojan hero Aeneas
related to Dido, the queen of Carthage, and particularly the
section when he speaks of the slaughter of Priam. If you still
remember it, begin at this line—let me see, let me see—

The rugged Pyrrhus, like a tiger from the Caucasus—

That's not right. It begins with Pyrrhus—

The rugged Pyrrhus, he whose dark armor,
Black as his purpose, resembled the night,
While he lay hidden in the ominous Trojan horse,
Has now smeared this terrifying black complexion

With heraldry more dismal. Head to foot
Now is he total gules, horridly tricked
With blood of fathers, mothers, daughters, sons,
Baked and impasted with the parching streets,
455   That lend a tyrannous and a damned light
To their lord's murder. Roasted in wrath and fire,
And thus o'ersized with coagulate gore,
With eyes like carbuncles, the hellish Pyrrhus
Old grandsire Priam seeks.

460   So proceed you.

Polonius   'Fore God, my lord, well spoken, with good accent and good discretion.

1st Player   Anon he finds him,
Striking too short at Greeks. His antique sword,
465   Rebellious to his arm, lies where it falls,
Repugnant to command. Unequal matched,
Pyrrhus at Priam drives, in rage strikes wide;
But with the whiff and wind of his fell sword
Th'unnerved father falls. Then senseless Ilium,
470   Seeming to feel this blow, with flaming top
Stoops to his base, and with a hideous crash
Takes prisoner Pyrrhus' ear. For lo, his sword,
Which was declining on the milky head
Of reverend Priam, seemed i'th'air to stick;
475   So, as a painted tyrant, Pyrrhus stood,
And like a neutral to his will and matter,
Did nothing.
But as we often see against some storm
A silence in the heavens, the rack stand still,
480   The bold winds speechless, and the orb below
As hush as death, anon the dreadful thunder
Doth rend the region; so after Pyrrhus' pause
Aroused vengeance sets him new awork,
And never did the Cyclops' hammers fall
485   On Mars's armour, forged for proof eterne,

With still more dismaying colors. Head to foot,
Now he is totally red, horribly adorned
With the blood of fathers, mothers, daughters, sons,
Baked and dried with the heat of the torched streets,
Giving a fierce and damned light
To their king's murder. Roasted in fury and fire,
And covered all over with bloody gore,
With eyes like fiery jewels, the hellish Pyrrhus
Seeks old grandfather Priam.

Now, go on.

Polonius Before God, my lord, well recited, with good
intonation and good taste!

1st Player *Soon he finds him*
Striking weakly at Greeks. His ancient sword,
Too heavy for his arm, lies where it falls,
Resisting his command. Unequally matched,
Pyrrhus drives at Priam, strikes wide in rage,
But at the whiff and wind of his cruel sword
The strength-drained father falls. Then the senseless fortress,
Seeming to feel this blow, falls with its top in flames
To the ground, and with a hideous crash
Besieges Pyrrhus's hearing. For lo, his sword,
Which was falling towards the milk-white head
Of aged Priam, seemed to stick in the air.
So, like a tyrant in a painting, Pyrrhus stood,
And, stuck between desire and action,
Did nothing.
But—much as we often see, before some storm,
A calm in the sky, when the clouds stay still,
The strong winds quiet, and the world below
As hushed as death—soon the dreadful thunder
Tears the sky. So, after Pyrrhus's pause,
An aroused sense of vengeance sets him to work again,
And never did the Cyclops' hammers fall
On the war god's armor, forged to last forever,

> With less remorse than Pyrrhus' bleeding sword
> Now falls on Priam.
> Out, out, thou strumpet Fortune! All you gods
> In general synod take away her power,
490 Break all the spokes and fellies from her wheel,
> And bowl the round nave down the hill of heaven
> As low as to the fiends.

Polonius This is too long.

Hamlet It shall to the barber's with your beard! Prithee say
495 on. He's for a jig or a tale of bawdry, or he sleeps. Say on,
come to Hecuba.

1st Player *But who – ah, woe! – had seen the mobled queen –*

Hamlet *The mobled queen?*

Polonius That's good.

500 **1st Player** *Run barefoot up and down, threat'ning the flames*
> *With bisson rheum, a clout upon that head*
> *Where late the diadem stood, and, for a robe,*
> *About her lank and all o'erteemed loins*
> *A blanket, in th'alarm of fear caught up –*
505 *Who this had seen, with tongue in venom steeped,*
> *'Gainst Fortune's state would treason have pronounced.*
> *But if the gods themselves did see her then,*
> *When she saw Pyrrus make malicious sport*
> *In mincing with his sword her husband's limbs,*
510 *The instant burst of clamour that she made,*
> *Unless things mortal move them not at all,*
> *Would have made milch the burning eyes of heaven*
> *And passion in the gods.*

Polonius Look whe'er he has not turned his colour and has
515 tears in's eyes. Prithee no more.

With less pity than Pyrrhus's bloody sword
Now falls on Priam.
Out, out, Fortune, you strumpet! All you gods,
In general conference, take away the power,
Break all the spokes and the rim from her wheel
And bowl the round hub down heaven's hill
As low as the fiends in hell.

Polonius   This is too long.

Hamlet   It needs trimming at a barber's, like your beard! Please go on. He likes a song-and-dance or a dirty tale, otherwise he falls asleep. Keep going—come to the part about Hecuba.

1st Player   *But who—ah, woe—had seen the muffled queen—*

Hamlet   *The muffled queen?*

Polonius   That's good.

1st Player   *Run barefoot, up and down, threatening the flames*
With blinding tears, a scarf upon her head
Where the crown had recently stood, and for a robe,
Around her thin, worn-out pelvis,
A blanket—caught up in the alarm of fright—
Whoever had seen this, with his tongue dripping venom,
Would have declared treason against Fortune's rule.
But if the gods themselves had seen her then—
When she saw Pyrrhus taking malicious joy
In mincing her husband's limbs with his sword—
The wailing that came from her instantly then,
Unless mortal things don't move them at all,
Would have made the burning stars cry milky tears,
And made the gods feel grief.

Polonius   Look how he's changed color and has tears in his eyes. Please, no more.

Hamlet 'Tis well. I'll have these speak out the rest of this
soon. Good my lord, will you see the players well bestowed?
Do you hear, let them be well used, for they are the abstract
and brief chronicles of the time. After your death you were
520   better to have a bad epitaph than their ill report while you
live.

Polonius My lord, I will use them according to their desert.

Hamlet God's bodykins, man, much better. Use every man
after his desert, and who shall scape whipping? Use them
525   after your own honour and dignity: the less they deserve, the
more merit is in your bounty. Take them in.

Polonius Come, sirs.

Hamlet Follow him, friends. We'll hear a play
tomorrow. [*To* **1st Player**] Dost thou hear me, old
530   friend? Can you play *The Murder of Gonzago*?

1st Player Ay, my lord.

Hamlet We'll ha't tomorrow night. You could for a need
study a speech of some dozen or sixteen lines, which I would
set down and insert in't, could you not?

535   **1st Player** Ay, my lord.

Hamlet Very well. [*To the* **Players**] Follow that lord, and
look you mock him not.

[*Exeunt* **Polonius** *and* **Players**]

[*To* **Rosencrantz** *and* **Guildenstern**] My good friends, I'll
leave you till night. You are welcome to Elsinore.

540   **Rosencrantz** Good my lord.

[*Exeunt* **Rosencrantz** *and* **Guildenstern**]

Hamlet   That's good. I'll have you recite the rest of this soon. My good lord, will you see that the actors have good accommodations? Take heed, make sure they're treated well— for they are the recorders and historians of our times. You'd be better off with a bad epitaph after you're dead than you will be if they give a bad report while you're alive.

Polonius   My lord, I will treat them as they deserve.

Hamlet   By the body of Christ, man, much better. If you treat every man as he deserves, who will escape being whipped? Treat them as your honor and dignity require. The less they deserve, the more praiseworthy is your generosity. Take them in.

Polonius   Come, sirs.

Hamlet   Follow him, friends. We'll hear a play tomorrow. [*To* **1st Player**] Listen, old friend, can you perform *The Murder of Gonzago*?

1st Player   Yes, my lord.

Hamlet   We'll have it performed tomorrow night. If necessary, you could memorize a speech of some twelve or sixteen lines, which I would write down and insert into it, couldn't you?

1st Player   Yes, my lord.

Hamlet   Good. [*To the* **Players**] Follow that lord—and see that you don't make fun of him.

[**Polonius** *and the* **Players** *exit*]

[*To* **Rosencrantz** *and* **Guildenstern**] My good friends, I'll leave you until tonight. You are welcome to Elsinore.

Rosencrantz   My good lord.

[**Rosencrantz** *and* **Guildenstern** *exit*]

Hamlet Ay, so God be wi'ye. Now I am alone.
        O, what a rogue and peasant slave am I!
        Is it not monstrous that this player here,
        But in a fiction, in a dream of passion,
545   Could force his soul so to his own conceit
        That from her working all his visage wanned,
        Tears in his eyes, distraction in his aspect,
        A broken voice, and his whole function suiting
        With forms to his conceit? And all for nothing!
550   For Hecuba!
        What's Hecuba to him, or he to Hecuba,
        That he should weep for her? What would he do
        Had he the motive and the cue for passion
        That I have? He would drown the stage with tears,
555   And cleave the general ear with horrid speech,
        Make mad the guilty and appal the free,
        Confound the ignorant, and amaze indeed
        The very faculties of eyes and ears.
        Yet I,
560   A dull and muddy-mettled rascal, peak
        Like John-a-dreams, unpregnant of my cause,
        And can say nothing – no, not for a king,
        Upon whose property and most dear life
        A damned defeat was made. Am I a coward?
565   Who calls me villain, breaks my pate across,
        Plucks off my beard and blows it in my face,
        Tweaks me by the nose, gives me the lie i'th'throat
        As deep as to the lungs? Who does me this?
        Ha!
570   'Swounds, I should take it; for it cannot be
        But I am pigeon-livered and lack gall
        To make oppression bitter, or ere this
        I should ha' fatted all the region kites
        With this slave's offal. Bloody, bawdy villain!
575   Remorseless, treacherous, lecherous, kindless villain!
        Why, what an ass am I! This is most brave,

Hamlet   And so. Good-bye. Now I'm alone. Oh, what a low and base character I am! Isn't it incredible that this actor here, playing a mere piece of fiction, in a dreamed-up passion, could make his soul so convinced by his imagination that it caused him to go pale? That it caused him to have tears in his eyes, distress in his looks, and a broken voice, with the movements of his whole body expressing what he imagines? And all for nothing. For Hecuba! What does Hecuba matter to him, or what does he matter to Hecuba, that should make him weep for her? What would he do if he had the motive and reason for passion that I have? He would drown the stage in tears, and assault the audience's ears with horrifying speeches, drive the guilty insane and terrify the innocent, confuse the ignorant, amaze the very senses of sight and hearing. Yet I—a passive and spiritless rascal—mope like John Dreamer, with no fullness of purpose, unable to speak. No, not even to speak for a king whose property and life were damnably destroyed. Am I a coward? Who calls me a villain, hits me on the head, pulls out my beard and blows it in my face, yanks at my nose, and tells me I lie with every breath? Who says this about me? Ha! By Christ's wounds, I would take it. For I must be chicken-livered, lacking the gall to bitterly resent injustice, or by now I would have fattened all the vultures with this scum's guts. Bloody, lustful villain! Remorseless, treacherous, lecherous, inhuman villain! Why, what an ass I am! This is truly splendid—that I, being the son

That I, the son of a dear father murdered,
Prompted to my revenge by heaven and hell,
Must like a whore unpack my heart with words
580   And fall a-cursing like a very drab,
A scullion! Fie upon't! Foh!
About, my brains. I have heard —   ⑤
That guilty creatures sitting at a play
Have, by the very cunning of the scene,
585   Been struck so to the soul that presently
They have proclaimed their malefactions.
⑤ For murder, though it have no tongue, will speak
With most miraculous organ. I'll have these players
Play something like the murder of my father
590   Before mine uncle. I'll observe his looks;
I'll tent him to the quick. If he but blench,
I know my course. The spirit that I have seen — ⑥
May be a devil, and the devil hath power
T'assume a pleasing shape, yea, and perhaps, ⑥
595   Out of my weakness and my melancholy,
As he is very potent with such spirits,
Abuses me to damn me. I'll have grounds — ⑦
More relative than this. The play's the thing ⑦
Wherein I'll catch the conscience of the King.

[*Exit*]

146

of a dear, murdered father, encouraged by heaven and hell to take revenge, must bare my heart with words like a whore, and resort to cursing like a mere slut, a kitchen maid! A curse upon it! Phew! Get going, my brains. I have heard that guilty creatures, sitting in the audience of a play, have been struck so deeply by the power of a scene that they have immediately confessed their evil deeds. For murder, though it's silenced, will speak through miraculous means. I'll have these actors perform a scene like my father's murder in front of my uncle. I'll watch how he looks; I'll examine him intensely. If he so much as flinches, I'll know what to do. The ghost that I saw may be a devil, and the devil has the power to appear in pleasant forms. Yes, and perhaps, in my weakness and my melancholy mood (since the devil is very powerful in such states), he's deluding me in order to damn me. I'll have stronger evidence than this. The play's the thing with which I'll catch the conscience of the King.

[**Hamlet** *exits*]

Comprehension Check What You Know

1. What does Polonius ask Reynaldo to do for him?

2. What news comes from Norway?

3. Why is Polonius upset with Hamlet?

4. What do the King and Queen ask Rosencrantz and Guildenstern to do?

5. Describe Hamlet's behavior in Scene 2 when he is speaking with the following person or persons: Polonius, Rosencrantz, and Guildenstern.

6. What is Hamlet planning with the Players at the end of Scene 2?

7. What does Hamlet hope to accomplish by the end of Act 2? See Scene 2, lines 590–595, and describe his motives.

Activities & Role-Playing Classes or Informal Groups

You may choose to complete one of the following activities as time permits:

Reading for Rhythm Select a passage of about ten lines from Act 2. Read it silently until you understand it fully. Then practice reading the same passage aloud. When the punctuation notes that you should stop, pause at the end of the line. Then read the passage to the class or your small group so that the meaning comes through clearly to your audience.

Hamlet's Many Faces Find lines in Act 2 that show these characteristics of Hamlet: sneaky, civilized, knows acting and theater, sarcastic, and rude. Then act out these lines with the appropriate motivation. How might Hamlet act sneaky? When is he secretly insulting someone? How might Hamlet's voice sound? What body language will you use to show these aspects of his character?

The Two "Friends" Study Rosencrantz and Guildenstern. Identify the parts of Scene 2 in which they are not speaking lines. Imagine what they are thinking

Jack Ryland as Claudius,
Tom Hulce as Hamlet, and
Franchelle Stewart Dorn as
Gertrude in The
Shakespeare Theatre's pro-
duction of *Hamlet* directed
by Michael Kahn.
Photo by Joan Marcus.

as the other characters are speaking. What is Rosencrantz and Guidenstern's secret? What are they trying to find out about Hamlet? Use these questions as you imagine their secret thoughts. Then write short production notes that explain the thoughts for a specific set of lines or passages. Pair your brief notes with specific lines or text of the play. For example, when Polonius enters the scene, what is Rosencrantz thinking about?

Understanding the Subplot Make a list of all the geographic locations listed in Act 2. Then refer to a map or an atlas to trace the subplot or political events explained in this act. For example, why are Fortinbras's plans important to the King?

Discussion   Classes or Informal Groups

1. Review lines 379–386 in Scene 2. Discuss how the behavior of the characters (Hamlet, Rosencrantz, Guildenstern) changes when Polonius enters the room. Is this hurtful or playful behavior? What clues can you find in Hamlet's speech to explain how he acts?

2. Polonius is busy in Act 2. Discuss the motions and emotions of this character.

3. Early in Scene 2, the Queen expressed her theory about Hamlet's behavior. Discuss her views and whether or not the other characters are listening to her.

Suggestions for Writing   Improve Your Skills

1. Write a prediction of the upcoming play that Hamlet is planning with the players. How do you think the King and Queen will react?

2. Write captions for the photos and images that appear in Acts 1 and 2.

3. Think of any of the brief quotes by or about one of the characters. Then write a sentence or two explaining how each quotation is important to the events in the play.

4. Translate Hamlet's soliloquy (private speech) at the end of Act 2. Retell or rewrite this speech into good modern English. Try to retain the emotions and meaning of the original text.

5. To understand Hamlet, you must make inferences about him. Draw conclusions about Hamlet based on the information given by other characters. Identify actions, thoughts, words, and appearance. When Ophelia describes Hamlet's behavior, what do you infer about Hamlet? From this evidence, write a character sketch of Hamlet.

All the World's a Stage Introduction

What is Hamlet's plan? The Ghost demanded revenge for the poisoning of King Hamlet, but so far Hamlet seems to have done little about his father's murder. Still, Hamlet is acting very strangely. Polonius thinks the prince has gone insane because of his love for Ophelia. Gertrude and Claudius still seek peace in their court, but Hamlet won't reveal what's wrong.

Then a company of traveling actors arrives at Elsinore. For Hamlet, the actors spark a plan to test the ghost's story—and also test Claudius. Meanwhile, Hamlet is carefully watched—by Polonius and by Rosencrantz and Guildenstern. In Elsinore, the characters watch, wait, guess, and spy.

What's in a Name? Characters

One of Shakespeare's greatest talents is his ability to create complex characters. Even his "bad guys" possess appealing qualities. Based on what you've seen so far of Claudius, is he a villain or a misunderstood brother of a dead king? Is he a good or bad husband? A good or bad king? If you hadn't heard the Ghost's accusation, would you trust him?

During Act 3, the audience begins to see unexpected other "sides" of characters' personalities. "Bad" characters show that they have consciences, appealing somewhat to our sympathy. Hamlet's behavior tests how we think about the prince. Overall, would you classify him as a good guy or a bad guy? If you were an ordinary member of the Danish court, would you like or trust Hamlet?

COME WHAT MAY Things to Watch For

Hamlet's audience sees that several characters seem to be playing "roles" as they hide what they really think, know, or feel. Then in Act 2, *real* actors, the traveling players, arrive at the Danish court. This is your chance to check out the many meanings of "acting."

Shakespeare makes the audience connect our everyday performance as "ourselves" and the profession of play-acting. What does it take to "act" well? Each of us has many roles: brother, sister, daughter, son, friend, and so on. Do they distort who we really are or want to become? Characters in *Hamlet* also play many roles:

- Hamlet: prince, son, nephew, lover
- Gertrude: queen, mother, wife, widow
- Claudius: king, uncle, husband, brother
- Ophelia: sister, daughter, lover

In fact, no main character has only one role to play. As you read, consider how well the characters "play" their roles as prince, queen, adviser, son, friends.

All Our Yesterdays **Historical and Social Context**

"Taking the show on the road" was common for performers in England at Shakespeare's time. Although travel was difficult, companies traveled as a group during the summer or all year long.

Earlier in the century small troupes traveled throughout the country performing folk and religious plays. By the time of *Hamlet*, many actors preferred to stay near London. Some players traveled overseas. For example, English actors performed in the Danish town of Helsingør during the 1580s. There they would have seen the Kronborg fortress—the inspiration for *Hamlet*'s castle.

The Play's the Thing **Staging**

"To be, or not to be. . . ." These well-known words open Hamlet's most famous *soliloquy*. In a soliloquy, a person is talking to himself or herself.

In a soliloquy, you may learn about the thinking behind a character's actions, or you may learn the answers to some of your questions, such as: Why did he say that to her? Why is he acting that way? You might also find some clues about the plot. In Act 1, Hamlet's long speech that begins "O that this too too solid flesh would melt" (1.2.131) is another example of a soliloquy. So is Claudius's speech in Act 3 (3.3.39–75), which he gives while he tries to pray.

Act 3 also features a *dumb show*. In a dumb show, actors mimed a "plot summary" before the actual play began.

My Words Fly Up **Language**

To convince the court he is mad, Hamlet makes his speech confusing, rude, and full of double meanings. Ophelia correctly tells Hamlet his remarks are "Still better, and worse." His words are "better" because they play so wittily. They are "worse" because they hurt, confuse, and offend.

Ophelia is often the target of Hamlet's rude words and actions. When he tells her to go to a "nunnery," he uses a term that meant "convent" but that may also have been slang for "brothel." Even modern-day audiences can easily detect the sexual suggestions (or "country matters") of Hamlet's request to "lie" in Ophelia's "lap." Today's audiences may miss the possible reference to sexual parts in the discussion of "nothing" that follows, however.

Note the contrast between Hamlet's speech with Rosencrantz and Guildenstern and how he speaks with Horatio. Hamlet uses his "mad" words to toy with his spying old friends, but Horatio seems to get the "straight talk."

Act III

Scene I

Enter **King, Queen, Polonius, Ophelia, Rosencrantz, Guildenstern.**

King And can you by no drift of conference
Get from him why he puts on this confusion,
Grating so harshly all his days of quiet
With turbulent and dangerous lunacy?

5 **Rosencrantz** He does confess he feels himself distracted,
But from what cause he will by no means speak.

Guildenstern Nor do we find him forward to be sounded,
But with a crafty madness keeps aloof
When we would bring him on to some confession
10 Of his true state.

Queen   Did he receive you well?

Rosencrantz Most like a gentleman.

Guildenstern But with much forcing of his disposition.

Rosencrantz Niggard of question, but of our demands
15 Most free in his reply.

Queen   Did you assay him
To any pastime?

Rosencrantz Madam, it so fell out that certain players
We o'erraught on the way. Of these we told him,
20 And there did seem in him a kind of joy

The **King, Queen, Polonius, Ophelia, Rosencrantz,** *and* **Guildenstern** *enter.*

King   And can't you find out in conversation why he's acting in this confused way, disrupting his quiet state with stormy and dangerous madness?

Rosencrantz   He admits he feels disturbed, but he won't say why by any means.

Guildenstern   Nor have we found that he's willing to be questioned. He's crafty in his madness, and he avoids answering when we try to get him to confide in us about what's really wrong.

Queen   Did he greet you courteously?

Rosencrantz   Very cordially.

Guildenstern   But with forced interest.

Rosencrantz   Stingy with his words, but he answered our questions freely.

Queen   Did you try to engage his interest in any activities?

Rosencrantz   Madam, it happened that we came upon a certain troupe of players on our way. We told him about them and he seemed to feel pleased about that. They are here at court,

To hear of it. They are here about the court,
And, as I think, they have already order
This night to play before him.

Polonius   'Tis most true,
25   And he beseeched me to entreat your Majesties
To hear and see the matter.

King With all my heart; and it doth much content me
To hear him so inclined.
Good gentlemen, give him a further edge,
30   And drive his purpose into these delights.

Rosencrantz We shall, my lord.

[*Exeunt* **Rosencrantz** *and* **Guildenstern**]

King   Sweet Gertrude, leave us too,
For we have closely sent for Hamlet hither
That he, as 'twere by accident, may here
35   Affront Ophelia.
Her father and myself, lawful espials,
Will so bestow ourselves that, seeing unseen,
We may of their encounter frankly judge,
And gather by him, as he is behaved,
40   If't be th'affliction of his love or no
That thus he suffers for.

Queen   I shall obey you.
And for your part, Ophelia, I do wish
That your good beauties be the happy cause
45   Of Hamlet's wildness; so shall I hope your virtues
Will bring him to his wonted way again,
To both your honours.

Ophelia   Madam, I wish it may.

[*Exit* **Queen**]

and I believe they've already been commissioned to perform for him tonight.

Polonius That's very true. And he requested that I ask your Majesties to hear and see the play.

King With all my heart. I'm very pleased to hear he's so inclined. Good gentlemen, encourage his enthusiasm, and direct his interest toward these pleasures.

Rosencrantz We will, my lord.

[**Rosencrantz** *and* **Guildenstern** *exit*]

King My sweet Gertrude, leave us too. We conspired to send for Hamlet, so that he can confront Ophelia here, as if by accident. Her father and I, eavesdropping, will hide ourselves so that we can look on without being seen. That way we can judge the true nature of their encounter. From his behavior, we'll gather whether he's suffering from the pains of love or not.

Queen I'll obey you. As for you, Ophelia, I hope that your fair charms are the happy cause of Hamlet's madness. And I also hope that your virtues will bring him back to normal, for both your sakes.

Ophelia Madam, I hope so too.

[*The* **Queen** *exits*]

Polonius Ophelia, walk you here. Gracious, so please you,
50   We will bestow ourselves. Read on this book,
        That show of such an exercise may colour
        Your loneliness. We are oft to blame in this,
        'Tis too much proved, that with devotion's visage
        And pious action we do sugar o'er
55   The devil himself.

King [*aside*]   O, 'tis too true.
        How smart a lash that speech doth give my conscience!
        The harlot's cheek, beautied with plast'ring art,
        Is not more ugly to the thing that helps it
60   Than is my deed to my most painted word.
        O heavy burden!

Polonius I hear him coming. Let's withdraw, my lord.

[*Exeunt* **King** *and* **Polonius**]

[*Enter* **Hamlet**]

Hamlet To be, or not to be, that is the question:
        Whether 'tis nobler in the mind to suffer
65   The slings and arrows of outrageous fortune,
        Or to take arms against a sea of troubles
        And by opposing end them. To die – to sleep,
        No more; and by a sleep to say we end
        The heart-ache and the thousand natural shocks
70   That flesh is heir to: 'tis a consummation
        Devoutly to be wished. To die, to sleep;
        To sleep, perchance to dream – ay, there's the rub:
        For in that sleep of death what dreams may come,
        When we have shuffled off this mortal coil,
75   Must give us pause – there's the respect
        That makes calamity of so long life.
        For who would bear the whips and scorns of time,
        The oppressor's wrong, the proud man's contumely,

Polonius   Ophelia, walk here. [*To the* **King**] Your Grace, with your permission, we'll conceal ourselves. [*To* **Ophelia** *again, giving her a religious book*] Read this book, so you seem to be engaged in religious contemplation. It's too often been found that we're guilty in this way. We make displays of devotion and pious acts in order to sweetly disguise the devil himself.

King   [*aside*] Oh, that's too true. What a sharp pain that speech gives to my conscience! A whore's painted face, made beautiful with makeup, is hardly more ugly to the cosmetics helping it than my deeds seem ugly to my falsely beautiful words. Oh, this is a heavy burden!

Polonius   I hear him coming. Let's hide, my lord.

[*The* **King** *and* **Polonius** *hide*]

[**Hamlet** *enters*]

Hamlet   To be—or not to be. That is the question. Is it more noble to suffer stoically from the blows and injuries of a whimsical fortune, or to do battle against a sea of troubles, ending them by opposing them? To die . . . to die is to sleep, no more. And we say that we end the heartache and the body's thousand infirmities with a sleep. That's an outcome one could wish for devoutly: to die, to sleep. To sleep, and then perhaps to dream—yes, that's the hitch! For the dreams that may come while we sleep the sleep of death, after we've cast off the turmoil of mortal life—those dreams must make us hesitate. That's the thought that makes us endure suffering for so long. Since who would bear the world's cruelty and indifference—the tyrant's abuse, the proud man's

The pangs of despised love, the law's delay,
80 The insolence of office, and the spurns
That patient merit of the unworthy takes,
When he himself might his quietus make
With a bare bodkin? Who would fardels bear,
To grunt and sweat under a weary life,
85 But that the dread of something after death,
The undiscovered country, from whose bourn
No traveller returns, puzzles the will,
And make us rather bear those ills we have
Than fly to others that we know not of?
90 Thus conscience does make cowards of us all,
And thus the native hue of resolution
Is sicklied o'er with the pale cast of thought,
And enterprises of great pitch and moment
With this regard their currents turn awry
95 And lose the name of action. Soft you now,
The fair Ophelia! Nymph, in thy orisons
Be all my sins remembered.

Ophelia   Good my lord,
How does your honour for this many a day?

100 **Hamlet**   I humbly thank you, well.

Ophelia My lord, I have remembrances of yours
That I have longed long to redeliver.
I pray you now receive them.

Hamlet   No, not I.
105 I never gave you aught.

Ophelia My honoured lord, you know right well you did,
And with them words of so sweet breath composed
As made the things more rich. Their perfume lost,
Take these again; for to the noble mind
110 Rich gifts wax poor when givers prove unkind.
There, my lord.

rude arrogance, the pangs of unrequited love, the slowness of justice, the insolence of those in power, and the insults that good humble people suffer from unworthy people— when he could settle his account himself with a dagger? Who would bear burdens, grunting and sweating under the weight of his weary life, if it weren't for the fear of something after death, the undiscovered country from whose borders no traveler returns? That fear paralyzes our wills and makes us prefer bearing the burdens we have, rather than flying toward other burdens we know nothing about. And so thinking turns us all into cowards, and so the naturally healthy color of our wills becomes sickly-looking with the pallor of pondering too much. This is how plans of the greatest importance go off course and fail to be enacted. But hush—the lovely Ophelia! Nymph, let my sins be remembered in your prayers.

Ophelia My good lord, how have you been these past days?

Hamlet I humbly thank you, well.

Ophelia My lord, I have some tokens of yours that I have wanted to return for a long time. Please receive them now.

Hamlet No, not I. I never gave you anything.

Ophelia My honored lord, you know very well you did, and along with them came words written with such sweetness that they made the gifts all the more precious. Now that their sweet perfume has faded, take these again. To people with noble minds, generous gifts become worthless when the givers become uncaring. There, my lord.

Hamlet Ha, ha! Are you honest?

Ophelia My lord?

Hamlet Are you fair?

115 **Ophelia** What means your lordship?

Hamlet That if you be honest and fair, your honesty should admit no discourse to your beauty.

Ophelia Could beauty, my lord, have better commerce than with honesty?

120 **Hamlet** Ay, truly; for the power of beauty will sooner transform honesty from what it is to a bawd than the force of honesty can translate beauty into his likeness. This was sometime a paradox, but now the time gives it proof. I did love you once.

125 **Ophelia** Indeed, my lord, you made me believe so.

Hamlet You should not have believed me; for virtue cannot so inoculate our old stock but we shall relish of it. I loved you not.

Ophelia I was the more deceived.

130 **Hamlet** Get thee to a nunnery. Why wouldst thou be a breeder of sinners? I am myself indifferent honest, but yet I could accuse me of such things that it were better my mother had not borne me. I am very proud, revengeful, ambitious, with more offences at my beck than I have thoughts to put 135 them in, imagination to give them shape, or time to act them in. What should such fellows as I do crawling between earth and heaven? We are arrant knaves all; believe none of us. Go thy ways to a nunnery. Where's your father?

Ophelia At home, my lord.

140 **Hamlet** Let the doors be shut upon him, that he may play the fool nowhere but in's own house. Farewell.

Hamlet Hah! Are you chaste?

Ophelia My lord?

Hamlet Are you beautiful?

Ophelia What does your lordship mean?

Hamlet That if you are both chaste and beautiful, your chastity should prevent familiar dealings with your beauty.

Ophelia Could beauty, my lord, have better dealings than with chastity?

Hamlet Yes, surely. For the power of beauty will change chastity into whorishness faster than the force of chastity can transform beauty into something like itself. In the past this belief was unthinkable, but now our times have shown that it's true. I loved you once.

Ophelia Indeed, my lord, you made me believe that was true.

Hamlet You should not have believed me. No amount of virtue grafted onto sin will change its basic nature. I didn't love you.

Ophelia Then I was all the more fooled.

Hamlet Go and enter a convent. Why would you want to give birth to sinners? I'm fairly virtuous myself. Yet I could still accuse myself of such things that would make it better if my mother had never had me. I am very proud, revengeful, and ambitious, with more bad qualities than I have thoughts to contain them, imagination to give them form, or time in which to act. What business do scoundrels like me have crawling between earth and heaven? We're all utter cads; don't believe any of us. Go on, go your own way to a convent. Where's your father?

Ophelia At home, my lord.

Hamlet Lock him in, so he can only play the fool in his own house. Farewell.

Ophelia O, help him, you sweet heavens!

Hamlet If thou dost marry, I'll give thee this plague for thy
dowry: be thou as chaste as ice, as pure as snow, thou shalt
145 not escape calumny. Get thee to a nunnery, farewell. Or if
thou wilt needs marry, marry a fool; for wise men know well
enough what monsters you make of them. To a nunnery, go;
and quickly too. Farewell.

Ophelia Heavenly powers, restore him!

150 **Hamlet** I have heard of your paintings well enough. God
hath given you one face and you make yourselves another.
You jig, you amble, and you lisp, you nickname God's
creatures, and make your wantonness your ignorance. Go to,
I'll no more on't, it hath made me mad. I say we will have
155 no more marriages. Those that are married already, all but
one, shall live; the rest shall keep as they are. To a nunnery,
go.

[*Exit*]

Ophelia O, what a noble mind is here o'erthrown!
The courtier's, soldier's, scholar's, eye, tongue, sword,
160 Th'expectancy and rose of the fair state,
The glass of fashion and the mould of form,
Th'observed of all observers, quite, quite down!
And I, of ladies most deject and wretched,
That sucked the honey of his music vows,
165 Now see that noble and most sovereign reason
Like sweet bells jangled out of tune and harsh,
That unmatched form and feature of blown youth
Blasted with ecstasy. O woe is me
T'have seen what I have seen, see what I see.

[*Enter* **King** *and* **Polonius**]

Ophelia Oh, sweet heaven, help him!

Hamlet If you marry, I'll give you this curse for your dowry: you can be as chaste as ice and pure as snow, and still you won't escape scandal. Go and enter a convent, farewell. Or if you must marry, marry a fool. Wise men know well enough how you turn them into cuckolds. To a convent—go—and quickly, too. Farewell.

Ophelia May heaven's powers cure him!

Hamlet I've heard all about your makeup. God gave you one face and you make yourself another. You dance, you lisp, you use precious language, and you pretend you're too ignorant to know what you're doing. Enough; I won't take it anymore; it's made me mad. I say we'll have no more marriages. Those who are married already—all except one—shall stay married. The rest shall stay as they are. Go to a convent.

[**Hamlet** *exits*]

Ophelia Oh, what a noble mind is lost here! His looks, speech, and skill of a courtier, soldier, and scholar; the hope and ornament of the kingdom he made lovely; the mirror of noble style and the model of courtly behavior; the center of all attention—completely, completely destroyed! And I—the most miserable and sorrowing of women, who feasted on the honey of his sweetly spoken vows—I now see his noble and surpassingly powerful mind all jangled like sweet bells ringing harshly out of tune. That unmatched example of blooming youth is blighted with madness. Oh, such woe has befallen me—that I have seen what I have seen, that I see what I see now!

[*The* **King** *and* **Polonius** *enter*]

170 **King** Love! His affections do not that way tend,
    Nor what he spake, though it lacked form a little,
    Was not like madness. There's something in his soul
    O'er which his melancholy sits on brood,
    And I do doubt the hatch and the disclose
175   Will be some danger; which for to prevent,
    I have in quick determination
    Thus set it down: he shall with speed to England
    For the demand of our neglected tribute.
    Haply the seas and countries different,
180   With variable objects, shall expel
    This something-settled matter in his heart,
    Whereon his brains still beating puts him thus
    From fashion of himself. What think you on't?

Polonius It shall do well. But yet do I believe
185   The origin and commencement of his grief
    Sprung from neglected love. How now, Ophelia!
    You need not tell us what Lord Hamlet said,
    We heard it all. My lord, do as you please,
    But if you hold it fit, after the play
190   Let his queen-mother all alone entreat him
    To show his grief: let her be round with him,
    And I'll be placed, so please you, in the ear
    Of all their conference. If she find him not,
    To England send him; or confine him where
195   Your wisdom best shall think.

King   It shall be so.
    Madness in great ones must not unwatched go.

                                        [*Exeunt*]

King Love! His emotions aren't inclined that way. And what he said—though it lacked form a little—was not like madness. His melancholy mood is brooding over something that's in his soul, and I fear that danger will be the result. To prevent this, I have just made up my mind that he will be sent to England immediately, to demand the payment of the tribute they still owe us for protection. Perhaps the sea travel and the change of scene will rid him of this strange matter that has settled in his heart and that obsesses his mind, making him act so unlike himself. What do you think?

Polonius That will work well. But I still believe that his grief arose from unrequited love. [*To* **Ophelia**] Well now, Ophelia! You don't need to tell us what Lord Hamlet said; we heard it all. [*To the* **King**] My lord, do as you wish. But, if you will consent to this, after the play let his mother the queen privately ask him to reveal the nature of his grief. Let her be blunt with him, and with your permission I'll be hidden somewhere where I can hear all of their conversation. If she can't discover what's upsetting him, send him to England. Or confine him wherever in your wisdom you think best.

King It shall be so. Madness in the great must be watched.

[*They exit*]

Act III

Scene II

Enter **Hamlet** *and the* **Players.**

Hamlet Speak the speech, I pray you, as I pronounced it to
you, trippingly on the tongue; but if you mouth it as many of
your players do, I had as lief the town-crier spoke my lines.
Nor do not saw the air too much with your hand, thus, but
5   use all gently; for in the very torrent, tempest, and, as I may
say, whirlwind of your passion, you must acquire and beget
a temperance that may give it smoothness. O, it offends me
to the soul to hear a robustious periwig-pated fellow tear a
passion to tatters, to very rags, to split the ears of the
10   groundlings, who for the most part are capable of nothing
but inexplicable dumb-shows and noise. I would have such
a fellow whipped for o'erdoing Termagant. It out-Herods
Herod. Pray you avoid it.

1st Player I warrant your honour.

15   **Hamlet** Be not too tame neither, but let your own discretion
be your tutor. Suit the action to the word, the word to the
action, with this special observance, that you o'erstep not the
modesty of nature. For anything so o'erdone is from the
purpose of playing, whose end, both at the first and now,
20   was and is to hold as 'twere the mirror up to nature; to show
virtue her feature, scorn her own image, and the very age
and body of the time his form and pressure. Now this

Hamlet *enters with the* **Players.**

Hamlet Please speak the speech as I recited it to you, in an easy, natural way. But if you declaim it bombastically the way many actors do these days, I'd just as soon have the town crier speak my lines. And don't gesticulate too violently with your hand, like this, but use more moderate gestures. Even in the very torrent, tempest, and (so to speak) whirlwind of your passionate portrayal, you must cultivate a restraint that will make it seem effortlessly natural. Oh, it offends me to my core when I hear some over-the-top ham tear a passion to shreds, tear it to rags even, just to deafen the standing spectators in the pit, who for the most part can only appreciate idiotic mime shows and noise. I would have a fellow like that whipped for overdoing even the most villainous character. It out-evils Evil Itself. Please avoid that.

1st Player I guarantee it, your honor.

Hamlet But don't be too tame, either. Let your discretion guide you. Make your movements fit with the words you speak, and the words fit with your movements. Follow this stipulation: don't overstep the bounds of what's natural. Anything overdone in this way contradicts the purpose of acting—the point of which, both traditionally and today, is to mirror reality. It must faithfully reflect virtuous qualities, expose what deserves scorn, and portray our time's current state of affairs through dramatic form and expression. Now if this is

overdone, or come tardy off, though it makes the unskilful
laugh, cannot but make the judicious grieve, the censure of
25   the which one must in your allowance o'erweigh a whole
theatre of others. O, there be players that I have seen
play – and heard others praise, and that highly – not to
speak it profanely, that neither having th'accent of
Christians, nor the gait of Christian, pagan, nor man, have
30   so strutted and bellowed that I have thought some of
Nature's journeymen had made men, and not made them
well, they imitated humanity so abominably.

1st Player   I hope we have reformed that indifferently with
us, sir.

35   **Hamlet**   O reform it altogether. And let those that play your
clowns speak no more than is set down for them; for there be
of them that will themselves laugh, to set on some quantity
of barren spectators to laugh too, though in the meantime
some necessary question of the play be then to be
40   considered. That's villainous, and shows a most pitiful
ambition in the fool that uses it. Go make you ready.

[*Exeunt* **Players**]

[*Enter* **Polonius, Rosencrantz,** *and* **Guildenstern**]

How now, my lord? Will the King hear this piece of work?

Polonius   And the Queen too, and that presently.

Hamlet   Bid the players make haste.

[*Exit* **Polonius**]

45   Will you two help to hasten them?

Rosencrantz   Ay, my lord.

overacted or poorly acted, it might make the unsophisticated audience members laugh. But the more discerning spectators will moan in grief—and you must value the judgment of even one such spectator over a whole theaterful of the unsophisticated types. Oh, I've seen some actors perform— and I've heard some people praise them, and highly—who, not to be blasphemous, neither speak nor move like Christians, pagans, or any other human beings. Instead, they strut and bellow so much that I thought they must be cast-offs and freaks of nature—that's how abominably they imitated humanity.

1st Player I hope that's been corrected reasonably well with us, sir.

Hamlet Oh, correct it completely. And make sure your actors specializing in clown roles stick to the script. Some of these professional clowns laugh themselves, in order to start a few idiots in the audience laughing too, even though in the meantime some important part of the play is lost. That's reprehensible, and it shows a pathetic ambition on the part of the fool who does it. Go, get yourselves ready.

[*The* **Players** *exit*]

[**Polonius, Rosencrantz,** *and* **Guildenstern** *enter*]

Well now, my lord, will the King attend this play?

Polonius And the Queen too, at once.

Hamlet Tell the actors to hurry.

[**Polonius** *exits*]

Will you two help get them to hurry up?

Rosencrantz Yes, my lord.

[*Exeunt* **Rosencrantz** *and* **Guildenstern**]

Hamlet What ho, Horatio!

[*Enter* **Horatio**]

Horatio Here, sweet lord, at your service.

Hamlet Horatio, thou art e'en as just a man
50   As e'er my conversation coped withal.

Horatio O my dear lord!

Hamlet   Nay, do not think I flatter,
       For what advancement may I hope from thee
       That no revenue hast but thy good spirits
55   To feed and clothe thee? Why should the poor be flattered?
       No, let the candied tongue lick absurd pomp,
       And crook the pregnant hinges of the knee
       Where thrift may follow fawning. Dost thou hear?
       Since my dear soul was mistress of her choice,
60   And could of men distinguish her election,
       Hath sealed thee for herself; for thou hast been
       As one, in suff'ring all, that suffers nothing,
       A man that Fortune's buffets and rewards
       Hast ta'en with equal thanks; and blest are those
65   Whose blood and judgment are so well co-mingled
       That they are not a pipe for Fortune's finger
       To sound what stop she please. Give me that man
       That is not passion's slave, and I will wear him
       In my heart's core, ay, in my heart of hearts,
70   As I do thee. Something too much of this.
       There is a play tonight before the King:
       One scene of it comes near the circumstance
       Which I have told thee of my father's death.
       I prithee, when thou seest that act afoot,
75   Even with the very comment of thy soul
       Observe my uncle. If his occulted guilt

[**Rosencrantz** *and* **Guildenstern** *exit*]

Hamlet [*calling out*] Horatio!

[**Horatio** *enters*]

Horatio Here, sweet lord! At your service.

Hamlet Horatio, you're as principled as any man with whom I've ever talked.

Horatio Oh, my dear lord!

Hamlet No, don't think I'm flattering you. What advantage can I hope to gain from you, who have no assets except your good spirits to keep you fed and clothed? Why would anyone flatter the poor? No, let flatterers sweet talk and suck up to greatness, and bend the joints of their always-willing knees, where there's a real payoff for fawning. You hear me? Ever since I could make up my own mind and could distinguish the differences among people, I've chosen you as a soul mate. For you have seemed to suffer nothing, even though you've suffered so much. You have taken bad luck and good fortune with equal composure. And those people are blessed whose temperament and judgment are so well adjusted that Fortune can't play them at will, like a panpipe. Give me a man who's not a slave to passion, and I'll take him firmly to heart—indeed, to my heart of hearts—as I do you. But enough of that. Tonight, a play will be performed before the King. One of its scenes is very similar to the circumstances of my father's death, which I told you about. When you see that part performed, please use your highest powers of concentration and observation to watch my uncle. If his

Do not itself unkennel in one speech,
It is a damned ghost that we have seen,
And my imaginations are as foul
80 As Vulcan's stithy. Give him heedful note;
For I mine eyes will rivet to his face,
And after we will both our judgments join
In censure of his seeming.

Horatio   Well, my lord.
85 If he steal aught the whilst this play is playing
And scape detecting, I will pay the theft.

Hamlet They are coming to the play. I must be idle.
Get you a place.

[*Enter* **King, Queen, Polonius, Ophelia, Rosencrantz,
Guildenstern,** *and the other Lords attendant, with the
King's Guard carrying torches*]

King How fares our cousin Hamlet?

90 **Hamlet** Excellent, i'faith, of the chameleon's dish. I eat the
air, promise-crammed. You cannot feed capons so.

King I have nothing with this answer, Hamlet. These words
are not mine.

Hamlet No, nor mine now. [*To* **Polonius**] My lord, you
95 played once i'th'university, you say?

Polonius That did I, my lord, and was accounted a good
actor.

Hamlet What did you enact?

Polonius I did enact Julius Caesar. I was killed i'th'Capitol.
100 Brutus killed me.

Hamlet It was a brute part of him to kill so capital a calf
there. Be the players ready?

secret guilt doesn't break into view during one particular speech, then the ghost we've seen is a damned devil, and my suspicions are as foul as the pit of hell. Watch him carefully, and for my part I'll keep my eyes riveted on his face. Afterwards, we'll compare our opinions to judge how he acted.

Horatio   Yes, my lord. If he gets away with anything while the play is being performed that escapes being detected, I'll pay for it.

Hamlet   They're coming to the play. I must start acting crazy. Get yourself a seat.

[*The* **King** *and* **Queen** *enter, with* **Polonius, Ophelia, Rosencrantz, Guildenstern,** *and other Lords and Attendants, accompanied by Guards carrying torches*]

King   How is our kinsman Hamlet?

Hamlet   Excellent, indeed. I eat the same food they say chameleons do. I eat the air [*he puns on* heir], full of empty promises. You can't feed and stuff chickens like that.

King   I can't make anything of that answer, Hamlet. Those words have nothing to do with me.

Hamlet   No, and now they're not mine either. [*To* **Polonius**] My lord, you performed once at the university, didn't you say?

Polonius   Indeed I did, my lord, and was considered a good actor.

Hamlet   What role did you play?

Polonius   I played Julius Caesar. I was killed in the Capitol. Brutus killed me.

Hamlet   What a dumb brute he was to kill such a capital fool there! Are the players ready?

Rosencrantz Ay, my lord, they stay upon your patience.

Queen Come hither, my dear Hamlet, sit by me.

105 **Hamlet** No, good mother, here's metal more attractive.

[*Turns to* **Ophelia**]

Polonius [*aside to the* **King**] O ho! Do you mark that?

Hamlet [*lying down at* **Ophelia**'s *feet*] Lady, shall I lie in your lap?

Ophelia No, my lord.

110 **Hamlet** I mean, my head upon your lap.

Ophelia Ay, my lord.

Hamlet Do you think I meant country matters?

Ophelia I think nothing, my lord.

Hamlet That's a fair thought to lie between maids' legs.

115 **Ophelia** What is, my lord?

Hamlet Nothing.

Ophelia You are merry, my lord.

Hamlet Who, I?

Ophelia Ay, my lord.

120 **Hamlet** O God, your only jig-maker! What should a man do but be merry? For look you how cheerfully my mother looks and my father died within's two hours.

Ophelia Nay, 'tis twice two months, my lord.

Hamlet So long? Nay then, let the devil wear black, for I'll
125 have a suit of sables. O heavens, die two months ago and not forgotten yet! Then there's hope a great man's memory may outlive his life half a year. But by'r lady he must build

Rosencrantz Yes, my lord, they're waiting till you're ready.

Queen Come here, my dear Hamlet, sit by me.

Hamlet No, good mother, here's someone more attractive.

[*He turns toward* **Ophelia**]

Polonius [*aside to the* **King**] Oho! Did you hear that?

Hamlet [*lying down at* **Ophelia**'s *feet*] Lady, shall I lie in your lap?

Ophelia No, my lord.

Hamlet I mean, with my head in your lap.

Ophelia Yes, my lord.

Hamlet Did you think I meant something indecent?

Ophelia I thought nothing, my lord.

Hamlet That's a fine thought to lie between a young lady's legs.

Ophelia What is, my lord?

Hamlet Nothing.

Ophelia You are merry, my lord.

Hamlet Who, me?

Ophelia Yes, my lord.

Hamlet Oh God—your best song-and-dance man! What else should a man do except be merry? Look how cheerful my mother looks, with my father dead for less than two hours.

Ophelia No, it's been four months, my lord.

Hamlet So long? Well then, let the devil wear black, for I'll wear a suit of fine furs. Oh, heaven, died two months ago and not forgotten yet! Then there's hope a great man might be remembered for half a year after his death. But, by our

churches then, or else shall he suffer not thinking on, with
the hobby-horse, whose epitaph is, *For O, for O, the*
130   *hobby-horse is forgot.*

[*The trumpets sound. A dumb-show follows*]

Enter a **King** *and a* **Queen,** *very lovingly, the* **Queen**
*embracing him and he her. She kneels, and makes show of
protestation unto him. He takes her up, and declines his head
upon her neck. He lies him down upon a bank of flowers. She,
seeing him asleep, leaves him. Anon comes in another* **Man,**
*takes off his crown, kisses it, pours poison in the sleeper's ears,
and leaves him. The* **Queen** *returns, finds the* **King** *dead,
makes passionate action. The* **Poisoner** *with some Three or
Four comes in again. They seem to condole with her. The dead
body is carried away. The* **Poisoner** *woos the* **Queen** *with gifts.
She seems harsh awhile, but in the end accepts his love.*

[*Exeunt*]

Ophelia   What means this, my lord?

Hamlet   Marry, this is miching mallecho. It means mischief.

Ophelia   Belike this show imports the argument of the play.

[*Enter* **Prologue**]

Hamlet   We shall know by this fellow. The players cannot
135   keep counsel: they'll tell all.

Lady, he'll have to leave his money for the building of churches, or else he'll be forgotten, along with the hobbyhorses in the old country dances. Their epitaph is repeated in an old ballad: *For oh, for oh, the hobbyhorse is forgotten.*

[*The trumpets sound, followed by a play performed in pantomime. Two actors enter, playing a king and queen who appear to be very loving. The* **Player Queen** *embraces the* **Player King** *and he embraces her. She kneels, pantomiming a display of love for him. He helps her up and lays his head upon her shoulder. Then he lies down on a row of flowers. She sees that he is asleep and leaves. Soon after that, another* **Man** *enters. He removes the* **Player King**'s *crown, kisses it, and pours poison in the sleeping* **Player King**'s *ears. The* **Player Queen** *returns, finds the* **Player King** *dead, and pantomimes passionate grief. Then the* **Poisoner** *enters again, with three or four other actors. They appear to mourn with the* **Player Queen.** *The dead body is carried away. The* **Poisoner** *woos the* **Player Queen** *with gifts. For a while she seems to reject him, but in the end she accepts his love.*]

[*The* **Players** *exit*]

Ophelia   What does this mean, my lord?

Hamlet   Surely, this is sneaking skullduggery. It means mischief.

Ophelia   Probably this show foretells the plot of the play.

[*The* **Prologue,** *an actor who traditionally introduces the play, enters*]

Hamlet   This fellow will let us know. The actors can't keep a secret; they'll tell all.

Ophelia Will he tell us what this show meant?

Hamlet Ay, or any show that you will show him. Be not you ashamed to show, he'll not shame to tell you what it means.

140 **Ophelia** You are naught, you are naught. I'll mark the play.

Prologue *For us and for our tragedy,*
Here stooping to your clemency,
We beg your hearing patiently. [*Exit*]

Hamlet Is this a prologue, or the posy of a ring?

145 **Ophelia** 'Tis brief, my lord.

Hamlet As woman's love.

[*Enter the* **Player King** *and* **Queen**]

Player King *Full thirty times hath Phoebus' cart gone round*
Neptune's salt wash and Tellus' orbed ground,
And thirty dozen moons with borrowed sheen
150 *About the world have times twelve thirties been*
Since love our hearts and Hymen did our hands
Unite commutual in most sacred bands.

Player Queen *So many journeys may the sun and moon*
Make us again count o'er ere love be done.
155 *But woe is me, you are so sick of late,*
So far from cheer and from your former state,
That I distrust you. Yet though I distrust,
Discomfort you, my lord, it nothing must;
For women's fear and love hold quantity,
160 *In neither aught, or in extremity.*
Now what my love is, proof hath made you know,
And as my love is sized, my fear is so.
Where love is great, the littlest doubts are fear;
Where little fears grow great, great love grows there.

Ophelia   Will he tell us what the dumb show meant?

Hamlet   Yes, or any other show you'd like to show him. If you're not ashamed to show him, he won't be ashamed to tell you what it's for.

Ophelia   You are wicked, very wicked. I'll watch the play.

Prologue   *For us, and for our tragedy,*
We bow to ask your pardon
And beg you to hear us patiently. [*Exit*]

Hamlet   Is this a prologue, or a short motto inscribed inside a ring?

Ophelia   It's brief, my lord.

Hamlet   As a woman's love.

[*The* **Player King** *and* **Player Queen** *enter*]

Player King   *For thirty years the sun god has gone round*
The sea god's salty water and earth goddess's globe of ground.
And thirty dozen moons, with their reflected shine,
Have gone around the world for twelve-times-thirty times
Since love joined our hearts and marriage our hands,
Uniting them in wedlock's sacred bonds.

Player Queen   *I hope as many trips by sun and moon*
Will be counted again, before our love's done.
But woe is me—you've been so sick of late,
So lacking in cheer and changed from your old state,
That I worry about you. But though I feel afraid,
You must not let that upset you, my lord.
For women, fear and love are related:
There's nothing to either, or both are too inflated.
How much I love you has been proved to you,
And as my love's measured, so my fear is too.
Where love is great, the smallest worries become fears.
Where small worries grow great, great love grows there.

165   **Player King** *Faith, I must leave thee, love, and shortly too:*
        My operant powers their functions leave to do;
        And thou shalt live in this fair world behind,
        Honoured, beloved; and haply one as kind
        For husband shalt thou –

170   **Player Queen**   *O confound the rest.*
        Such love must needs be treason in my breast.
        In second husband let me be accurst;
        None wed the second but who killed the first.

  Hamlet [*aside*] That's wormwood.

175   **Player Queen** *The instances that second marriage move*
        Are base respects of thrift, but none of love.
        A second time I kill my husband dead,
        When second husband kisses me in bed.

  Player King *I do believe you think what now you speak;*
180   *But what we do determine, oft we break.*
        Purpose is but the slave to memory,
        Of violent birth but poor validity,
        Which now, the fruit unripe, sticks on the tree,
        But fall unshaken when they mellow be.
185   *Most necessary 'tis that we forget*
        To pay ourselves what to ourselves is debt.
        What to ourselves in passion we propose,
        The passion ending, doth the purpose lose.
        The violence of either grief or joy
190   *Their own enactures with themselves destroy.*
        Where joy most revels grief doth most lament;
        Grief joys, joy grieves, on slender accident.
        This world is not for aye, nor 'tis not strange
        That even our loves should with our fortunes change,
195   *For 'tis a question left us yet to prove,*
        Whether love lead fortune or else fortune love.
        The great man down, you mark his favourite flies;
        The poor advanced makes friends of enemies;

Player King   *Faith, love, I must leave you, and very soon, too.*
   My faculties don't function as they used to do.
   You'll stay behind here in this beautiful world,
   Honored and beloved. With good fortune, you'll find
   A husband just as kind, whom you'll—

Player Queen   *Oh, don't say the rest!*
   Such love as that would be treason in my breast.
   If I take a second husband, let me be cursed:
   No one marries twice, unless she's killed the first.

Hamlet   [*aside*] That tastes bitter.

Player Queen   *The reasons for second marriages*
   Aren't for love, but just base advantages.
   I'd be killing again my husband who's dead
   If a second husband kissed me in bed.

Player King   *I feel you believe what you have just said.*
   But often we break the promises we've made.
   Our intentions rely upon our memory:
   They're strong at first, but lack longevity,
   Like unripe fruit that hangs firmly on the tree
   Until it mellows and falls, too easily.
   It's necessary that we should forget
   To honor these resolutions, these self-owed debts.
   In the heat of strong passion, we often intend
   Things that lose their purpose when the passion ends.
   Both grief and joy are violent emotions,
   And in their very violence, they're prone to self-destruction.
   Where joy is happiest, grief feels the most pain:
   Grief joys, joy grieves, for the slightest reason.
   This world won't last forever, and it's not strange
   That changes in our fortunes should cause our love to change.
   For this is a problem we still haven't solved:
   Does love make our fate, or fate determine love?
   When the great man falls, watch how his luck flees.
   When the poor man rises, he befriends old enemies.

181

And hitherto doth love on fortune tend:
200   *For who not needs shall never lack a friend,*
And who in want a hollow friend doth try
Directly seasons him his enemy.
But orderly to end where I begun,
Our wills and fates do so contrary run
205   *That our devices still are overthrown:*
Our thoughts are ours, their ends none of our own.
So think thou wilt no second husband wed,
But die thy thoughts when thy first lord is dead.

Player Queen *Nor earth to me give food, nor heaven light,*
210   *Sport and repose lock from me day and night,*
To desperation turn my rust and hope,
An anchor's cheer in prison be my scope,
Each opposite, that blanks the face of joy,
Meet what I would have well and it destroy,
215   *Both here and hence pursue me lasting strife,*
If, once a widow, ever I be a wife.

Hamlet If she should break it now.

Player King *'Tis deeply sworn. Sweet, leave me here awhile.*
My spirits grow dull, and fain I would beguile
220   *The tedious day with sleep.*

Player Queen   *Sleep rock thy brain,*
And never come mischance between us twain.

                                  [Exit. He sleeps]

Hamlet Madam, how like you this play?

Queen The lady doth protest too much, methinks.

225 **Hamlet** Oh, but she'll keep her word.

King Have you heard the argument? Is there no offence in 't?

Hamlet No, no, they do but jest – poison in jest. No offence i'th'world.

And so it seems love must follow fortune in the end,
Since the man who needs nothing never lacks friends,
But a man who turns to a false friend in need
Quickly changes that friend to his enemy.
But to end up neatly where I began:
Our wills and our fates are in such opposition
That our plans are continually overthrown.
Our thoughts are ours, but their outcomes aren't our own.
You think a second man and you won't wed,
But that thought will die when your first husband's dead.

Player Queen *May earth refuse me food and heaven light;*
Keep pleasure and rest locked away, day and night;
Turn my hope and my trust into desperation;
Make my comforts no more than a hermit's in prison,
May grief, which turns the joyful face pale,
Destroy all desires that I hope will turn out well;
Here and henceforward, curse me with strife
If, once a widow, I should ever be a wife.

Hamlet If she breaks her promise now!

Player King *A deeply sworn vow. Sweet, leave me here awhile.*
I'm feeling fatigued, and I'd like to lull
The tiring day with sleep.

Player Queen   *May sleep lull your thoughts,*
And may bad luck never divide us.

[*The **Player Queen** exits. The **Player King** sleeps*]

Hamlet Madam, how do you like the play?

Queen The lady protests her love too much, I think.

Hamlet Oh, but she'll keep her word.

King Do you know the plot? Is there anything offensive in it?

Hamlet No, no, they only jest—there's no actual poisoning.
They commit no offense at all.

King What do you call the play?

230 **Hamlet** *The Mousetrap* – marry, how tropically! This play is
the image of a murder done in Vienna; Gonzago is the
Duke's name, his wife Baptista; you shall see anon. 'Tis a
knavish piece of work, but what o'that? Your Majesty, and
we that have free souls, it touches us not. Let the galled jade
235 wince, our withers are unwrung.

[*Enter* **Lucianus**]

This is one Lucianus, nephew to the King.

Ophelia You are as good as a chorus, my lord.

Hamlet I could interpret between you and your love if I
could see the puppets dallying.

240 **Ophelia** You are keen, my lord, you are keen.

Hamlet It would cost you a groaning to take off my edge.

Ophelia Still better, and worse.

Hamlet So you must take your husbands. Begin, murderer.
Leave thy damnable faces and begin. Come, the croaking
245 raven doth bellow for revenge.

Lucianus *Thoughts black, hands apt, drugs fit, and time
agreeing,*
Confederate season, else no creature seeing,
Thou mixture rank, of midnight weeds collected,
250 *With Hecate's band thrice blasted, thrice infected,*
Thy natural magic and dire property
On wholesome life usurps immediately.

[*Pours the poison in the sleeper's ears*]

King   What's the play called?

Hamlet   *The Mousetrap.* Indeed, what a tricky play on words! This play depicts a murder that occurred in Vienna. The Duke is named Gonzago. His wife is Baptista. You'll see soon. It's a naughty little play, but what of it? Your Majesty—and those of us with clear consciences—it's nothing to us. Let the whipped horse wince; our hides are unscathed.

[*An actor playing the character* **Lucianus** *enters*]

That's Lucianus, the king's nephew.

Ophelia   You're as informative as a Greek chorus, my lord.

Hamlet   I could relate the action between you and your lover, like a puppet-master, if I saw you both in motion.

Ophelia   You are sharp, my lord, you are sharp.

Hamlet   You'd be moaning with work to take off my edge.

Ophelia   Still one better—and still worse.

Hamlet   That's how you take in your husbands—for better, for worse. [*To the actor playing* **Lucianus**] Begin, murderer. Stop making those damnable faces and begin. Come— [*he misquotes a line from an older play*] "The croaking raven bellows for revenge."

Lucianus   *Black thoughts, skilled hands, strong drugs, and time
      agree.
The time is my ally; no other creature sees.
Foul mixture of poisonous weeds I've collected,
Three times cursed by witchcraft, three times infected,
Your natural magic and dreadful properties
Destroy the healthy life immediately.*

[*He pours the poison in the* **Player King's** *ears*]

Hamlet He poisons him i'th'garden for his estate. His name's
Gonzago. The story is extant, and written in very choice
255 Italian. You shall see anon how the murderer gets the love of
Gonzago's wife.

Ophelia The King rises.

Hamlet What, frighted with false fire?

Queen How fares my lord?

260 **Polonius** Give o'er the play.

King Give me some light. Away.

Polonius Lights, lights, lights.

[*Exeunt all but* **Hamlet** *and* **Horatio**]

Hamlet *Why, let the strucken deer go weep,*
The hart ungalled play;
265 *For some must watch while some must sleep,*
Thus runs the world away.

Would not this, sir, and a forest of feathers, if the rest of my
fortunes turn Turk with me, with two Provincial roses on
my razed shoes, get me a fellowship in a cry of players?

270 **Horatio** Half a share.

Hamlet A whole one, I.
For thou dost know, Oh Damon dear,
This realm dismantled was
Of Jove himself, and now reigns here
275 *A very, very – pajock.*

Horatio You might have rhymed.

Hamlet He poisons him in the garden for his money. His name's Gonzago. The story is in print and is written in very good Italian. You'll soon see how the murderer gets the love of Gonzago's wife.

Ophelia The king's standing up.

Hamlet What—frightened by blanks?

Queen [*to* **King Claudius**] Are you all right, my lord?

Polonius Stop the play.

King Bring me some light. Go!

Polonius Lights! Lights! Bring lights!

[*All exit except* **Hamlet** *and* **Horatio**]

Hamlet *Why, let the wounded deer go weep,*
The buck, unhurt, shall play;
Some must keep watch, while some must sleep,
So the world goes its way.

[*Referring to the play and its effect*] If my luck turned bad on me, wouldn't this get me a partnership with a company of actors, with feathers on my hat and French-style roses on my fancy shoes?

Horatio Half a share in partnership.

Hamlet A whole one!
For you must know, oh Damon dear,
This realm abandoned was
By Jove himself, and now here reigns
A very, very—peacock.

Horatio You could have rhymed. [*He means that* **Hamlet** *could have said "ass," rather than "peacock," to make a half-rhyme with "was"*]

Hamlet Oh good Horatio, I'll take the ghost's word for a
thousand pound. Didst perceive?

Horatio Very well, my lord.

280 **Hamlet** Upon the talk of the poisoning?

Horatio I did very well note him.

Hamlet Ah ha! Come, some music; come, the recorders.
For if the King like not the comedy,
Why then, belike he likes it not, perdie.

285 Come, some music.

[*Enter* **Rosencrantz** *and* **Guildenstern**]

Guildenstern Good my lord, vouchsafe me a word with you.

Hamlet Sir, a whole history.

Guildenstern The King, sir –

Hamlet Ay, sir, what of him?

290 **Guildenstern** Is in his retirement marvellous distempered.

Hamlet With drink, sir?

Guildenstern No, my lord, with choler.

Hamlet Your wisdom should show itself more richer to
signify this to the doctor, for, for me to put him to his
295 purgation would perhaps plunge him into more choler.

Guildenstern Good my lord, put your discourse into some
frame, and start not so wildly from my affair.

Hamlet I am tame, sir. Pronounce.

Guildenstern The Queen your mother, in most great
300 affliction of spirit, hath sent me to you.

Hamlet You are welcome.

Hamlet Oh, good Horatio, I'll bet a thousand pounds the ghost is telling the truth. Did you see?

Horatio Very well, my lord.

Hamlet When they talked about poisoning?

Horatio I watched him very closely.

Hamlet Aha! Come, let's have some music. Come, the recorders!
If the King dislikes the comedy
Then it seems he dislikes it, most certainly.

Come, some music.

[**Rosencrantz** *and* **Guildenstern** *enter*]

Guildenstern My good lord, let me have a word with you.

Hamlet Sir, you may have a whole history.

Guildenstern The King, sir—

Hamlet Yes, sir, what about him?

Guildenstern He's in his room, in a highly upset state.

Hamlet From drinking, sir?

Guildenstern No, my lord, from anger.

Hamlet You'd be much wiser to tell this to the doctor. Any medicine that I prescribed him would probably make him feel worse.

Guildenstern My good lord, keep your words in context, and don't stray so wildly off the topic.

Hamlet I've restrained myself, sir. Go ahead.

Guildenstern Your mother, the Queen, is suffering great distress and has sent me to you.

Hamlet You are welcome.

Guildenstern Nay, good my lord, this courtesy is not of the right breed. If it shall please you to make me a wholesome answer, I will do your mother's commandment; if not, your
305   pardon and my return shall be the end of my business.

Hamlet Sir, I cannot.

Rosencrantz What, my lord?

Hamlet Make you a wholesome answer. My wit's diseased. But sir, such answer as I can make, you shall command – or
310   rather, as you say, my mother. Therefore no more, but to the matter. My mother, you say –

Rosencrantz Then thus she says: your behaviour hath struck her into amazement and admiration.

Hamlet O wonderful son, that can so astonish a mother!
315   But is there no sequel at the heels of this mother's admiration? Impart.

Rosencrantz She desires to speak with you in her closet ere you go to bed.

Hamlet We shall obey, were she ten times our mother. Have
320   you any further trade with us?

Rosencrantz My lord, you once did love me.

Hamlet And do still, by these pickers and stealers.

Rosencrantz Good my lord, what is your cause of distemper? You do surely bar the door upon your own liberty if you
325   deny your griefs to your friend.

Hamlet Sir, I lack advancement.

Rosencrantz How can that be, when you have the voice of the King himself for your succession in Denmark?

Hamlet Ay, sir, but while the grass grows – the proverb is
330   something musty.

Guildenstern   No, my good lord, these polite responses are hardly courteous. If you will consent to give me a reasonable answer, I'll fulfill your mother's instructions. If not, your permission to leave and my return to her will end my errand.

Hamlet   Sir, I cannot.

Rosencrantz   Cannot what, my lord?

Hamlet   Make you a reasonable answer. My mind's diseased. But, sir, I'll give you whatever answer I can, at your bidding—or rather, as you say, at my mother's bidding. Therefore, enough of that; let's get back to the subject. My mother, you say—

Rosencrantz   She says this: Your behavior has astonished and bewildered her.

Hamlet   What an amazing son, to astonish his mother that way! But is there no follow-up to this mother's astonishment? Tell the rest.

Rosencrantz   She wishes to speak with you in her room, before you go to bed.

Hamlet   We'll obey, even if she were our mother ten times over. Do you have any further business with us?

Rosencrantz   My lord, you were fond of me once.

Hamlet   And still am, by these hands.

Rosencrantz   My good lord, what's causing your disorder? You shut the door against your own cure if you won't tell your troubles to a friend.

Hamlet   Sir, I can't get ahead.

Rosencrantz   How can that be, when the King of Denmark himself has made you the heir to the throne?

Hamlet   Yes, sir, but "While the grass grows, the horse starves." The old proverb's a little stale.

[*Enter the* **Players** *with recorders*]

Oh, the recorders. Let me see one. To withdraw with you, why do you go about to recover the wind of me, as if you would drive me into a toil?

Guildenstern Oh my lord, if my duty be too bold, my love is
335 too unmannerly.

Hamlet I do not well understand that. Will you play upon this pipe?

Guildenstern My lord, I cannot.

Hamlet I pray you.

340 **Guildenstern** Believe me, I cannot.

Hamlet I do beseech you.

Guildenstern I know no touch of it, my lord.

Hamlet It is as easy as lying. Govern these ventages with your fingers and thumb, give it breath with your mouth, and
345 it will discourse most eloquent music. Look you, these are the stops.

Guildenstern But these cannot I command to any utterance of harmony. I have not the skill.

Hamlet Why, look you now, how unworthy a thing you
350 make of me. You would play upon me, you would seem to know my stops, you would pluck out the heart of my mystery, you would sound me from my lowest note to the top of my compass; and there is much music, excellent voice, in this little organ, yet cannot you make it speak. Why, do
355 you think I am easier to be played on than a pipe? Call me what instrument you will, though you can fret me, you cannot play upon me.

[*Enter* **Polonius**]

[*The* **Players** *enter, carrying recorders*]

Oh, the recorders. Let me see one. Just between you and me, why do you keep maneuvering around me, as if you wanted to drive me into a trap?

Guildenstern Oh my lord, if I'm being too presumptuous with you, it's because my love makes me act inappropriately.

Hamlet I don't understand that. Will you play something on this recorder?

Guildenstern I can't, my lord.

Hamlet Please.

Guildenstern Believe me, I can't.

Hamlet I beg you.

Guildenstern I don't know how to play it, my lord.

Hamlet It's as easy as lying. Manipulate the stops with your fingers and thumb, blow into it through your mouth, and it will make very melodious music. See? Here are the stops.

Guildenstern But I can't make them sound tuneful. I don't have the skill.

Hamlet Why now, look how little you think of me. You want to play upon me, you seem to know how to work my stops, you want to pull out the heart of my secrets, you want to sound me out, from my lowest to my highest note. And there's a great deal of music, an excellent sound, in this little instru-ment—but you can't make it speak. Why, do you think you can play me more easily than you can play a pipe? Call me whatever instrument you like, you can handle me, but you can't play me.

[**Polonius** *enters*]

God bless you, sir.

Polonius My lord, the Queen would speak with you, and
360   presently.

Hamlet Do you see yonder cloud that's almost in shape of a
    camel?

Polonius By th'mass and 'tis like a camel indeed.

Hamlet Methinks it is like a weasel.

365 **Polonius** It is backed like a weasel.

Hamlet Or like a whale.

Polonius Very like a whale.

Hamlet Then I will come to my mother by and by. [*Aside*]
    They fool me to the top of my bent. I will come by and by.

370 **Polonius** I will say so.

[*Exit* **Polonius**]

Hamlet 'By and by' is easily said. Leave me, friends.

[*Exeunt all but* **Hamlet**]

'Tis now the very witching time of night,
When churchyards yawn and hell itself breathes out
Contagion to this world. Now could I drink hot blood,
375   And do such bitter business as the day
Would quake to look on. Soft, now to my mother.
O heart, lose not thy nature. Let not ever
The soul of Nero enter this firm bosom;
Let me be cruel, not unnatural.
380   I will speak daggers to her, but use none.
My tongue and soul in this be hypocrites:
How in my words somever she be shent,
To give them seals never, my soul, consent.

[*Exit*]

God bless you, sir.

Polonius My lord, the Queen wishes to speak with you, and at once.

Hamlet Do you see that cloud over there that's shaped almost like a camel?

Polonius By heaven, it is indeed like a camel.

Hamlet I think it's like a weasel.

Polonius It has a back like a weasel.

Hamlet Or like a whale.

Polonius Very like a whale.

Hamlet Then I'll visit my mother right away. [*Aside*] They make me play the fool to the limit of my tolerance. [*To* **Polonius**] I'll come right away.

Polonius I'll say so.

[**Polonius** *exits*]

Hamlet "Right away" is easily said. Leave me, friends.

[*All exit except* **Hamlet**]

It's now the witches' time of night, when graves in cemeteries open, and hell itself breathes foul, contagious airs into the world. Now I could drink hot blood, and perform acts so terrible that the day would shudder to look at them. Enough—now I'll go to my mother. Oh heart, don't lose your natural affection. Don't ever let the soul of Nero, who killed his mother, enter this firm chest. Let me be cruel, but not inhuman. My words will be like daggers, but I won't use a real dagger. In this respect, my words and my soul won't match each other. However my words may chastise her, my soul must never let those words be backed up with deeds.

[**Hamlet** *exits*]

Act III

Scene III

Enter **King, Rosencrantz,** *and* **Guildenstern.**

King I like him not; nor stands it safe with us
To let his madness range. Therefore prepare you.
I your commission will forthwith dispatch,
And he to England shall along with you.
5   The terms of our estate may not endure
Hazard so near us as doth hourly grow
Out of his brows.

Guildenstern   We will ourselves provide.
Most holy and religious fear it is
10   To keep those many many bodies safe
That live and feed upon your Majesty.

Rosencrantz The single and peculiar life is bound
With all the strength and armour of the mind
To keep itself from noyance; but much more
15   That spirit upon whose weal depends and rests
The lives of many. The cease of majesty
Dies not alone, but like a gulf doth draw
What's near it with it. Or it is a massy wheel
Fixed on the summit of the highest mount,
20   To whose huge spokes ten thousand lesser things
Are mortised and adjoined, which when it falls,
Each small annexment, petty consequence,
Attends the boist'rous ruin. Never alone
Did the King sigh, but with a general groan.

The **King, Rosencrantz,** *and* **Guildenstern** *enter.*

King I don't like how he's acting, and it isn't safe for us to let him wander freely while he's mad. Therefore, get yourselves ready. I'll have your commission written up immediately, and he'll be sent to England, along with you. In my position as King, I can't tolerate the danger from the threats and plots growing incessantly in his mind.

Guildenstern We'll get ready. It's a holy and sacred obligation to protect those countless people whose daily lives rely on your Majesty.

Rosencrantz The private individual finds it instinctively necessary to defend himself from harm by using all his strength of mind. This is even more the case for that lord who has many other lives depending upon his welfare. The death of a king is not an isolated death. Like a whirlpool, it draws in whatever is near it. Or it's like a massive wheel that's affixed to the summit of the highest mountain and that has ten thousand lesser things attached to its huge spokes— so that when it falls, each small appendage and minor hanger-on takes part in the calamitous wreck. The King doesn't so much as sigh alone; when he sighs, it's as if the whole country did, too.

25   **King** Arm you, I pray you, to this speedy voyage,
      For we will fetters put about this fear
      Which now goes too free-footed.

   Rosencrantz   We will haste us.

             [*Exeunt* **Rosencrantz** *and* **Guildenstern**]

    [*Enter* **Polonius**]

   Polonius My lord, he's going to his mother's closet.
30   Behind the arras I'll convey myself
      To hear the process. I'll warrant she'll tax him home,
      And as you said – and wisely was it said –
      'Tis meet that some more audience than a mother,
      Since nature makes them partial, should o'erhear
35   The speech of vantage. Fare you well, my liege.
      I'll call upon you ere you go to bed,
      And tell you what I know.

   King   Thanks, dear my lord.

                        [*Exit* **Polonius**]

      Oh, my offence is rank, it smells to heaven;
40   It hath the primal eldest curse upon't –
      A brother's murder! Pray can I not,
      Though inclination be as sharp as will,
      My stronger guilt defeats my strong intent,
      And, like a man to double business bound,
45   I stand in pause where I shall first begin,
      And both neglect. What if this cursed hand
      Were thicker than itself with brother's blood,
      Is there not rain enough in the sweet heavens
      To wash it white as snow? Whereto serves mercy
50   But to confront the visage of offence?
      And what's in prayer but this twofold force,
      To be forestalled ere we come to fall

King   Please prepare yourselves, then, for this imminent voyage. We'll chain this fear that now runs loose.

Rosencrantz   We'll hurry.

[**Rosencrantz** *and* **Guildenstern** *exit*]

[**Polonius** *enters*]

Polonius   My lord, he's going to his mother's room. I'll conceal myself behind the tapestry curtain and eavesdrop on what's going on. I bet she'll rebuke him severely. And, as you said— and wisely—it's appropriate that someone other than a mother should also listen to what's said, since mothers are naturally partial to their children's point of view. Good-bye, my liege. I'll visit you before you go to bed, and tell you what I've found out.

King   Thanks, my dear lord.

[**Polonius** *exits*]

Oh, my crime is foul. It smells to heaven. It has the ancient curse of Cain upon it—a brother's murder! As much as I yearn to, I cannot pray. My guilt is even stronger and defeats my inclinations. Like a man who needs to do two things at once, I stop the minute I begin, and don't do either one. What if this cursed hand of mine was thickened with a coating of my brother's blood—is there enough rain in the sweet heavens to wash the hand white as snow? What's mercy for, except to look sin in the face? And what is there in prayer except this double strength: to stop us before we fall into sin

Or pardoned being down? Then I'll look up.
My fault is past. But oh, what form of prayer
55   Can serve my turn? 'Forgive me my foul murder'?
That cannot be, since I am still possessed
Of those effects for which I did the murder –
My crown, mine own ambition, and my queen.
May one be pardoned and retain th'offence?
60   In the corrupted currents of this world
Offence's gilded hand may shove by justice,
And oft 'tis seen the wicked prize itself
Buys out the law. But 'tis not so above:
There is no shuffling, there the action lies
65   In his true nature, and we ourselves compelled
Even to the teeth and forehead of our faults
To give in evidence. What then? What rests?
Try what repentance can. What can it not?
Yet what can it, when one cannot repent?
70   O wretched state! O bosom black as death!
O limed soul, that struggling to be free
Art more engaged! Help, angels! Make assay.
Bow, stubborn knees; and heart with strings of steel,
Be soft as sinews of the new-born babe.
75   All may be well. [*He kneels*]

[*Enter* **Hamlet**]

Hamlet Now might I do it pat, now he is a-praying.
And now I'll do't. [*Draws his sword*]
               And so he goes to heaven;
And so am I revenged. That would be scanned:
80   A villain kills my father, and for that
I, his sole son, do this same villain send
To heaven.
Why, this is hire and salary, not revenge.
He took my father grossly, full of bread,
85   With all his crimes broad blown, as flush as May;

or to pardon us once we've fallen? So I'll look up. My sin is in the past. But oh, what kind of prayer can plead my case? "Forgive me my foul act of murder"? That can't be, since I still possess those things for which I committed the murder— my crown, my own ambition, and my queen. Can one be pardoned for a crime and yet keep its results? In the corrupt ways of the world, the bribing hands of the guilty can push justice aside, and often the riches gained by the crime itself are used to buy out the law. But that's not true in heaven. There you can't escape by tricks; there we are charged with the full truth of our crimes and forced to give evidence against our own sins, with no holding back. What then? What options are left? See what repentance can do. What *can't* it do? And yet, what can it do if one can't repent? Oh, what a wretched state I'm in! Oh heart as black as death! Oh, my soul is trapped, caught like a bird in lime—the more it struggles to break free, the more it's entangled! Help, angels! Try. Bend in prayer, stubborn knees. And heart with strings of steel, be as soft as the sinews of a newborn baby. All may still be well.

[*He kneels*]

[**Hamlet** *enters*]

Hamlet   Now I could do it easily, now while he's praying. And now I'll do it. [*He draws his sword*] And so he goes to heaven? And so I take revenge? That needs to be examined: a villain kills my father, for which I—my father's only son— send this same villain to heaven. Why, this is hired service, not revenge. He killed my father when my father was gorged with pleasures, not purged of them, when my father's sins were in full bloom and profuse as flowers in May. And who,

And how his audit stands who knows save heaven?
But in our circumstance and course of thought
'Tis heavy with him. And am I then revenged,
To take him in the purging of his soul,
90 When he is fit and seasoned for his passage?
No.
Up, sword, and know thou a more horrid hent:
When he is drunk asleep, or in his rage,
Or in th'incestuous pleasure of his bed,
95 At game a-swearing, or about some act
That has no relish of salvation in't,
Then trip him, that his heels may kick at heaven
And that his soul may be as damned and black
As hell, whereto it goes. My mother stays.
100 This physic but prolongs thy sickly days.

[*Exit*]

King My words fly up, my thoughts remain below.
Words without thoughts never to heaven go.

[*Exit*]

except heaven, knows how his reckoning stands? But to our perspective here on earth, his case looks bad. So then am I revenged if I kill this man while he's purging his sins, when he's ripe and ready to go to heaven? No. My sword, return to your sheath, and wait to be seized at a more horrible time: when he's dead drunk or raging in passion, or in the midst of incestuous pleasures in bed, or swearing while gambling, or performing some act that involves no trace of salvation. Then I'll trip him so his heels kick up, backward toward heaven, while his soul is damned as black as the hell it goes to. My mother is waiting for me. This prayer merely prolongs your sinful life.

[**Hamlet** *exits*]

King My words fly upward, but my thoughts stay here below. Insincere words will never reach heaven.

[*The* **King** *exits*]

Act III

Scene IV

Enter **Queen** *and* **Polonius**.

Polonius   He will come straight. Look you lay home to him,
Tell him his pranks have been too broad to bear with
And that your Grace hath screened and stood between
Much heat and him. I'll silence me even here.
5   Pray you be round.

Queen   I'll warrant you, fear me not.
Withdraw, I hear him coming.

[**Polonius** *hides behind the arras*]

[*Enter* **Hamlet**]

Hamlet   Now, mother, what's the matter?

Queen   Hamlet, thou hast thy father much offended.

10   **Hamlet**   Mother, you have my father much offended.

Queen   Come, come, you answer with an idle tongue.

Hamlet   Go, go, you question with a wicked tongue.

Queen   Why, how now, Hamlet?

Hamlet   What's the matter now?

15   **Queen**   Have you forgot me?

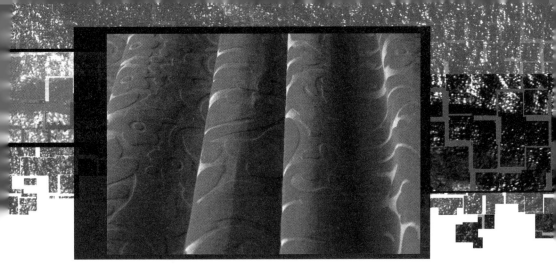

The **Queen** *and* **Polonius** *enter.*

Polonius He'll come right away. Make sure that you hit home with him. Tell him his antics have been too incorrigible to be tolerated, and that your Grace has protected and screened him from taking the heat of others' anger. [*Beginning to hide behind the tapestry*] I'll hide myself here. Please be direct!

Queen You can rely on me. Hide: I hear him coming.

[**Polonius** *hides behind the tapestry*]

[**Hamlet** *enters*]

Hamlet Now, mother, what's the matter?

Queen Hamlet, you have greatly offended your father.

Hamlet Mother, *you* have greatly offended my father.

Queen Come, come. You answer foolishly.

Hamlet Go, go. You question wickedly.

Queen [*rebuking him*] Hamlet!

Hamlet What's the matter now?

Queen Have you forgotten who you're speaking to?

Hamlet   No, by the rood, not so.
You are the Queen, your husband's brother's wife,
And, would it were not so, you are my mother.

Queen   Nay, then I'll set those to you that can speak.

20   **Hamlet**   Come, come, and sit you down, you shall not budge.
You go not till I set you up a glass
Where you may see the inmost part of you.

Queen   What wilt thou do? Thou wilt not murder me?
Help, ho!

25   **Polonius**   [*behind the arras*]   What ho! Help!

Hamlet   How now? A rat! Dead for a ducat, dead.

                     [*He thrusts his rapier through the arrras*]

Polonius   [*behind*]   Oh, I am slain.

Queen   O me, what hast thou done?

30   **Hamlet**   Nay, I know not.
Is it the King?

          [*He lifts up the arras and discovers* **Polonius,** *dead*]

Queen   Oh what a rash and bloody deed is this!

Hamlet   A bloody deed. Almost as bad, good mother,
As kill a king and marry with his brother.

Queen   As kill a king?

35   **Hamlet**   Ay, lady, it was my word.
Thou wretched, rash, intruding fool, farewell.
I took thee for thy better. Take thy fortune:
Thou find'st to be too busy is some danger.
Leave wringing of your hands. Peace, sit you down,
40   And let me wring your heart; for so I shall

Hamlet No, by the cross, I haven't. You are the Queen, your husband's brother's wife, and—if only it wasn't true!—you are my mother.

Queen Well, then, I'll go get people who can talk to you.

Hamlet Come, come. Sit down; you won't budge. You're not going until I show you the reflection of your innermost self.

Queen What are you going to do? You won't murder me, will you? Help, help!

Polonius [*behind the tapestry*] Help! Somebody help!

Hamlet What's this? A rat! Dead, I'll wager, dead!

[*He thrusts his sword through the tapestry*]

Polonius [*behind the tapestry*] Oh, I'm dying!

Queen Oh God, what have you done?

Hamlet I don't know. Is it the King?

[*He pulls back the tapestry and discovers the dead body of* **Polonius**]

Queen Oh, what a heedless, bloody deed!

Hamlet A bloody deed. Almost as bad, good mother, as to kill a king and marry his brother.

Queen As kill a king?

Hamlet Yes, my lady, that's what I said. [*To* **Polonius***'s corpse*] You cursed, thoughtless, intruding fool—farewell. I mistook you for the King. Accept your bad luck. You've learned that it's dangerous not to mind your own business. [*To the* **Queen**] Stop wringing your hands. Quiet; sit down and let me wring your heart. Because I'll do that, assuming your heart

If it be made of penetrable stuff,
If damned custom have not brazed it so,
That it be proof and bulwark against sense.

Queen What have I done, that thou dar'st wag thy tongue
45   In noise so rude against me?

Hamlet   Such an act
That blurs the grace and blush of modesty,
Calls virtue hypocrite, takes off the rose
From the fair forehead of an innocent love
50   And sets a blister there, makes marriage vows
As false as dicers' oaths. O, such a deed
As from the body of contraction plucks
The very soul, and sweet religion makes
A rhapsody of words. Heaven's face does glow
55   O'er this solidity and compound mass
With tristful visage, as against the doom,
Is thought-sick at the act.

Queen   Ay me, what act
That roars so loud and thunders in the index?

60 **Hamlet** Look here upon this picture, and on this,
The counterfeit presentment of two brothers.
See what a grace was seated on this brow;
Hyperion's curls, the front of Jove himself,
An eye like Mars, to threaten and command,
65   A station like the herald Mercury
New-lighted on a heaven-kissing hill;
A combination and a form indeed
Where every god did seem to set his seal
To give the world assurance of a man.
70   This was your husband. Look you now what follows.
Here is your husband, like a mildewed ear
Blasting his wholesome brother. Have you eyes?
Could you on this fair mountain leave to feed
And batten on this moor? Ha, have you eyes?

can be pierced, assuming wicked habits haven't made it so shameless that it's armored and fortified against all reason.

Queen What have I done, that you should dare to use your tongue with such loud, rude words against me?

Hamlet You've done such an act that it makes innocence seem shameless, calls virtue a hypocrite, blisters the clear complexion of innocent love; makes marriage vows as false as gamblers' promises. Oh, a deed that steals the heart from solemn contracts, and turns holy vows into a series of meaningless words! Heaven's face blushes over this gross, compounded world with a sorrowful expression, as sad as at Doomsday, sickened by the thought of what you've done.

Queen Woe is me; what have I done that spells out my doom so thunderously?

Hamlet [*Showing her two miniature portraits, one worn in a locket by* **Hamlet** *and one by the* **Queen**] Look at this portrait here, and at this one. These are the portraits of two brothers. Look at what grace resided in this face: the curls of a sun god; the noble forehead of the deity Jove himself; eyes like the war god's, to threaten and command; a stance like Mercury, the heavenly herald, just alighting on the top of a heaven-reaching hill. Indeed, all the gods seemed to stamp their impressions on him, to show the world a perfect man. Now look what follows. Here is your husband—like a mildewed fungus, infecting his healthy brother. Can't you see? How could you stop feeding on this lovely mountain to gorge on this barren swamp? Hah, can't you see? You can't

75   You cannot call it love; for at your age
The heyday in the blood is tame, it's humble,
And waits upon the judgment, and what judgment
Would step from this to this? Sense sure you have,
Else could you not have motion; but sure that sense
80   Is apoplexed, for madness would not err,
Nor sense to ecstasy was ne'er so thralled
But it reserved some quantity of choice
To serve in such a difference. What devil was't
That thus hath cozened you at hoodman-blind?
85   Eyes without feeling, feeling without sight,
Ears without hands or eyes, smelling sans all,
Or but a sickly part of one true sense
Could not so mope. Oh shame, where is thy blush?
Rebellious hell,
90   If thou canst mutine in a matron's bones,
To flaming youth let virtue be as wax
And melt in her own fire; proclaim no shame
When the compulsive ardour gives the charge,
Since frost itself as actively doth burn
95   And reason panders will.

Queen   Oh, Hamlet, speak no more.
Thou turn'st my eyes into my very soul,
And there I see such black and grained spots
As will not leave their tinct.

100 **Hamlet**   Nay, but to live
In the rank sweat of an enseamed bed,
Stewed in corruption, honeying and making love
Over the nasty sty!

Queen   Oh speak to me no more.
105   These words like daggers enter in my ears.
No more, sweet Hamlet.

Hamlet   A murderer and a villain,
A slave that is not twentieth part the tithe

call it love. At your age, passion is tamed, it's manageable and heedful of judgment. And what kind of judgment would step from this to this? Your senses must function, or you couldn't even move. But surely those senses are paralyzed. Because madness wouldn't go that far wrong. And the senses couldn't be so insanely enthralled that they didn't retain some power of choice to detect these obvious differences. What devil tricked you at blindman's-bluff—leaving you with the sense of sight but not touch, touch but not sight, hearing but not touch or sight, the sense of smell but nothing else? Even a weak part of one working sense could not have blundered so aimlessly! Oh, shame, why aren't you blushing? Unruly hell, if you can make middle-aged women lose control of themselves, then for hot-blooded young people virtue should be like sealing wax, melting in a candle's flame. Don't condemn the young when they're overcome by passion, since cold-blooded old people burn just as hot, and reason surrenders to lust.

Queen Oh, Hamlet, don't say any more. You've forced me to look deep into my soul, and there I see such black, ingrained stains of guilt, which won't go away.

Hamlet No, but for you to live in the filthy sweat of a greasy bed, soaked in corruption, debauching and making love in that nasty pigsty!

Queen Oh, please don't say any more. These words pierce my ears like daggers. No more, sweet Hamlet.

Hamlet A murderer and a villain, scum who's not worth the twentieth part of a tenth of your former husband, a parody of

Of your precedent lord, a vice of kings,
110   A cutpurse of the empire and the rule,
That from a shelf the precious diadem stole
And put it in his pocket –

Queen   No more.

Hamlet   A king of shreds and patches –

[*Enter* **Ghost**]

115   Save me and hover o'er me with your wings,
You heavenly guards! What would your gracious figure?

Queen   Alas, he's mad.

Hamlet   Do you not come your tardy son to chide,
That, lapsed in time and passion, lets go by
120   Th'important acting of your dread command?
Oh say.

Ghost   Do not forget. This visitation
Is but to whet thy almost blunted purpose.
But look, amazement on thy mother sits.
125   Oh step between her and her fighting soul.
Conceit in weakest bodies strongest works.
Speak to her, Hamlet.

Hamlet   How is it with you, lady?

Queen   Alas, how is't with you,
130   That you do bend your eye on vacancy,
And with th'incorporal air do hold discourse?
Forth at your eyes your spirits wildly peep,
And, as the sleeping soldiers in th'alarm,
Your bedded hair, like life in excrements,
135   Start up and stand on end. Oh, gentle son,
Upon the heat and flame of thy distemper
Sprinkle cool patience. Whereon do you look?

kings, a petty thief of realm and reign, who stole the precious
crown from a shelf and put it in his pocket—

Queen No more.

Hamlet A king of rags and patches—

[*The* **Ghost** *enters*]

Save me and hover above me with guarding wings, you
heavenly angels! [*To the* **Ghost**] What do you want, gracious
lord?

Queen [*she cannot see the* **Ghost**] Alas, he's mad.

Hamlet Haven't you come to scold your tardy son, who has let
time go by and passion slip away, neglecting to follow your
fearful orders? Oh, tell me.

Ghost Do not forget. This visit is only to sharpen your almost-
dulled sense of purpose. But look, your mother is bewildered.
Oh, intercede between her and her struggling conscience.
Imagination is strongest in the weak. Speak to her, Hamlet.

Hamlet How are you, lady?

Queen Alas, how are you—what makes you stare at emptiness
and talk to the thin air? Your stare wildly, and your smooth
hair stands on end like soldiers awakened by an alarm, as if it
were alive. Oh gentle son, sprinkle cool patience on the heat
and fire of your disorder. What are you looking at?

Hamlet On him, on him! Look you how pale he glares.
His form and cause conjoined, preaching to stones,
140 Would make them capable. Do not look upon me,
Lest with this piteous action you convert
My stern effects. Then what I have to do
Will want true colour – tears perchance for blood.

Queen To whom do you speak this?

145 **Hamlet** Do you see nothing there?

Queen Nothing at all; yet all that is I see.

Hamlet Nor did you nothing hear?

Queen No, nothing but ourselves.

Hamlet Why, look you there, look how it steals away.
150 My father, in his habit as he lived!
Look where he goes even now out at the portal.

[*Exit* **Ghost**]

Queen This is the very coinage of your brain.
This bodiless creation ecstasy
Is very cunning in.

155 **Hamlet** Ecstasy?
My pulse as yours doth temperately keep time,
And makes as healthful music. It is not madness
That I have uttered. Bring me to the test,
And I the matter will re-word, which madness
160 Would gambol from. Mother, for love of grace,
Lay not that flattering unction to your soul,
That not your trespass but my madness speaks.
It will but skin and film the ulcerous place,
Whiles rank corruption, mining all within,
165 Infects unseen. Confess yourself to heaven,
Repent what's past, avoid what is to come;
And do not spread the compost on the weeds

Hamlet At him, at him! Look how palely he glares. The combination of his looks and his cause would make stones listen to his words. [*To the* **Ghost**] Don't look at me, in case that pitiable action distracts me from my stern obligation. Then my actions will seem unconvincing—tears instead of blood.

Queen Who are you saying this to?

Hamlet Don't you see anything there?

Queen Nothing at all—yet I see all that there is to see.

Hamlet You didn't hear anything, either?

Queen No, nothing but you and me.

Hamlet Why, look there—look how it steals away! My father, in the clothes he wore when alive! Look where he's going out now through the door!

[*The* **Ghost** *exits*]

Queen This is something made up in your brain. Madness is very skillful in creating such hallucinations.

Hamlet Madness? My pulse beats just as evenly as yours; its music is just as healthy. What I've said isn't madness. Put me to the test, and I'll say exactly the same thing, which madness would avoid. Mother, for love of grace, don't give your soul that flattering balm, believing that it's not your transgression but my madness speaking. That will only cover the ulcer with skin and membrane, while foul corruption will work under the surface and infect invisibly. Confess your sins to heaven, repent the past, avoid what is to come, don't make the weeds grow fatter by spreading manure on them.

To make them ranker. Forgive me this my virtue;
For in the fatness of these pursy times
170   Virtue itself of vice must pardon beg,
Yea, curb and woo for leave to do him good.

Queen Oh Hamlet, thou hast cleft my heart in twain.

Hamlet Oh throw away the worser part of it
And live the purer with the other half.
175   Good night. But go not to my uncle's bed.
Assume a virtue if you have it not.
That monster, custom, who all sense doth eat
Of habits devil, is angel yet in this,
That to the use of actions fair and good
180   He likewise gives a frock or livery
That aptly is put on. Refrain tonight,
And that shall lend a kind of easiness
To the next abstinence, the next more easy;
For use almost can change the stamp of nature,
185   And either curb the devil or throw him out
With wondrous potency. Once more, good night,
And when you are desirous to be blest,
I'll blessing beg of you. For this same lord
I do repent; but heaven hath pleased it so,
190   To punish me with this and this with me,
That I must be their scourge and minister.
I will bestow him, and will answer well
The death I gave him. So, again, good night.
I must be cruel only to be kind.
195   Thus bad begins, and worse remains behind.
One word more, good lady.

Queen   What shall I do?

Hamlet Not this, by no means, that I bid you do:
Let the bloat King tempt you again to bed,
200   Pinch wanton on your cheek, call you his mouse,
And let him, for a pair of reechy kisses,

Forgive me for making this reminder of virtue. In the grossness of these morally flabby times, virtue itself must beg for vice's pardon. Indeed, it must bow and scrape for permission to do vice good.

Queen Oh, Hamlet, you've cut my heart in two.

Hamlet Oh, throw away the worse part of it, and live that much more purely with the other half. Good night. But don't go to my uncle's bed. Act virtuous even if you aren't. That monster, custom, which consumes natural feelings, is a devil in that it establishes bad habits. But it's also like an angel, because it makes the habitual practice of acting good become natural and instinctive. Stay away tonight, and that will give a kind of ease to the next abstinence, and the next will be easier still. Habit can almost change nature, and either tame the devil or throw him out with wondrous power. Once more, good night. And when you long to be blessed yourself, I'll ask for your blessing. As for this lord [*meaning* **Polonius**], I repent. It has pleased heaven to punish me with his death and to punish him through me, making me its scourge and agent. I'll dispose of him, and I'll pay well for killing him. So, again, good night. I must be cruel in order to be kind. And so things are begun badly and the worse is still to come. One more word, good lady.

Queen What do you want me to do?

Hamlet Don't, by any means, do these things: let the bloated king tempt you to bed again, pinch your cheek lecherously, call you his "mouse," and let him—for a couple of filthy

Or paddling in your neck with his damned fingers,
Make you to ravel all this matter out
That I essentially am not in madness,
205   But mad in craft. 'Twere good you let him know,
For who that's but a queen, fair, sober, wise,
Would from a paddock, from a bat, a gib,
Such dear concernings hide? Who would do so?
No, in despite of sense and secrecy,
210   Unpeg the basket on the house's top,
Let the birds fly, and like the famous ape,
To try conclusions, in the basket creep,
And break your own neck down.

Queen Be thou assured, if words be made of breath,
215   And breath of life, I have no life to breathe
What thou hast said to me.

Hamlet I must to England, you know that?

Queen   Alack,
I had forgot. 'Tis so concluded on.

220 **Hamlet** There's letters sealed, and my two schoolfellows,
Whom I will trust as I will adders fanged –
They bear the mandate, they must sweep my way
And marshal me to knavery. Let it work;
For 'tis the sport to have the engineer
225   Hoist with his own petard, and't shall go hard
But I will delve one yard below their mines
And blow them at the moon. Oh, 'tis most sweet
When in one line two crafts directly meet.
This man shall set me packing.
230   I'll lug the guts into the neighbouring room.
Mother, good night indeed. This counsellor
Is now most still, most secret, and most grave,
Who was in life a foolish prating knave.
Come, sir, to draw toward an end with you.
235   Good night, mother.

[*Exit dragging in* **Polonius**. *The* **Queen** *remains*]

kisses, or for fondling your neck with his damned fingers—
make you unravel the truth: that I'm not really mad, but
pretending to be. [*Sarcastically*] You really should tell him,
for how could a mere queen—beautiful, dignified, wise—
conceal such matters of deep concern from a toad, a bat, a
tomcat? Who would do such a thing? No, forget about sense
and caution. Let the cat out of the bag, let the birds fly the
coop. Copy the legendary ape that climbed into the cage just
to see if he could fly out of it, and break your own neck in the
process.

Queen Be assured that if words are made out of breath and
breath is the product of life, I hardly have life to breathe a
word of what you've said to me.

Hamlet I have to go to England, you know that?

Queen Alas, I'd forgotten. It's been decided.

Hamlet The royal letters are sealed, and my two school-
mates—whom I'll trust like I trust snakes with fangs—they've
gotten their orders. They must accompany me and lead me
into some villainy. So be it: it's amusing to watch the bomb-
maker get blown sky high by his own weapon, but watch out
in case I dig a yard under their land mines and blow them as
high as the moon. Oh, it's sweet when two schemes head for
each other on a collision course! [*Indicating* **Polonius**] This
man will ensure that I'm sent packing. I'll lug the guts into
the room next door. Mother, at last good night. This
councilor is now so still, so secret, and so grave. In life he
was a prattling, foolish villain. Come, sir, to finish my
business with you. Good night, mother.

[**Hamlet** *exits, dragging* **Polonius**'s *body*]

Comprehension   **Check What You Know**

1. In Scene 1, what information do Rosencrantz and Guildenstern give the King and Queen about Hamlet? Is the information accurate? Why or why not?

2. In the soliloquy in Scene 1 that begins "To be or not to be," what questions does Hamlet ask about death and dying? List some answers he gives about why we should live or die.

3. Review the conversations between Hamlet and Ophelia. How does Hamlet treat her? How does she react?

4. Describe the events in Hamlet's play performed by the players in Scene 2. What do the characters do?

5. How does the King react to Hamlet's play?

6. In Scene 3, what do Rosencrantz and Guildenstern say about why the King should be protected?

7. What emotions does Hamlet exhibit when he is speaking with his mother in Scene 4? What does he feel he needs to tell her? What does he ask her to do?

8. What happens to Polonius? Why?

Activities & Role-Playing   **Classes or Informal Groups**

A Close Call As a group, imagine that you are staging a production of *Hamlet*. Discuss how you would present the action in Scene 3 when Hamlet finds the

©Robbie Jack/CORBIS

King trying to pray. Would the King pace or stand still before he kneels? Would he close his eyes? Where would you position the King and Hamlet on the stage? How close would Hamlet come to Claudius before leaving the stage?

Play Within a Play As a group, role-play Hamlet's play in Scene 2. Take the parts of the Player Queen, the Player King, the Man/Poisoner, and the Prologue. Then match each character from Hamlet's play to the real play, *Hamlet*.

Discussion Classes or Informal Groups

1. Discuss Hamlet's actions and behavior in this act. What likeable qualities does he display? What do you find in him that is cruel or clever?

2. Discuss Ophelia's character in Acts 1–3. Then, as a group, chart the characteristics of her character: strengths, weaknesses, and other qualities. Revisit the chart and add items to it after you have read Acts 4 and 5. Could Ophelia have behaved or reacted differently to change her situation?

3. Compare the King's and Queen's reactions to Hamlet's play in Scene 2. How are they similar? How are they different from each other?

4. Do you think Polonius deserved his fate? Explain your answer.

Suggestions for Writing Improve Your Skills

1. In Scene 1, Hamlet tells Ophelia why she should go to a "nunnery." Suppose Ophelia told you about her conversation with Hamlet. Write a paragraph telling Ophelia whether you agree or disagree with Hamlet's suggestion. Before you write, ask yourself these questions: Is Hamlet fair to Ophelia? Is he fair in his opinions about women? How do his feelings about his mother affect his words to Ophelia?

2. Review Rosencrantz's remarks in lines 12–24 of Scene 3. Identify the two main images he uses to describe the death of a king, and write two or three sentences explaining how the images are similar. Pay attention to ideas of size, movement, and relation of small to larger parts.

3. Photocopy the King's speech before he tries to pray (Scene 3, lines 39–75). Mark any places where he seems to change his mind or start arguing with himself. Write a paragraph that explains why the King is experiencing such a dilemma.

4. Review Scene 4 and write a sentence or two that explains the Queen's interpretation of Hamlet's behavior, his feelings about his father, and his feelings about being sent to England.

All the World's a Stage Introduction

The trap has sprung. Claudius's guilty reaction to the play pushes the tension even further. Hamlet feels he has the proof he needs to trust the Ghost and to take revenge. But Claudius is clever and extremely dangerous, and Hamlet has made some serious mistakes. He did not kill King Claudius while he seemed to be praying, saying that he didn't want Claudius to go to heaven. Then, after being too cautious, Hamlet rashly killed Polonius by mistake. Now, Claudius has an excuse to punish his enemy.

What's in a Name? Characters

In Act 4, you meet Fortinbras, Prince of Norway. We have already heard about this young man. At the beginning of the play, he threatened to invade Denmark. He wanted to reclaim land that his father had lost in battle to the Danes. After some successful negotiations, Fortinbras seemed to give up his plan to attack the Danish kingdom. But Hamlet notices that Fortinbras still is eager to spring into action. In Act 4, Scene 4, Hamlet comments on the contrast between Fortinbras's action and his own delay.

Shakespeare doesn't tell us how old Hamlet is (though he'll give us a hint in Act 5), but it's easy to think of the prince as fairly young. We never forget that he is someone's son, so it is his duty to clean up the mess caused by his elders. In *Hamlet,* the "younger generation" dominates Act 4: Fortinbras marches to new battles. Laertes and Ophelia react to the death of Polonius. And Hamlet continues to plot his revenge.

COME WHAT MAY Things to Watch For

Claudius is a powerful king. Since Denmark defeated England in previous military conflicts, Claudius can make "requests" of the English ruler that are sure to be followed. Still, some may wonder why Claudius is King of Denmark at all. Why didn't Hamlet inherit the throne?

In Elsinore, the Danish ruler is elected by the court's senior councilors. Although Claudius has a legitimate claim to the throne, his rule still had to be approved by the senior members of the court. On the other hand, the Danish *people* can only "vote" by force. In Act 4, they begin to wonder if they should have a new man on the throne.

Shakespeare wrote very carefully about kings. He defended their right to rule, but he showed how pride and corruption led to their fall from power. Shakespeare himself lived under the stable rule of Elizabeth I and James I. These monarchs avoided the type of civil war that had troubled England for years before them. But violence and threats were still a constant part of life, and both Elizabeth and James had to sidestep plots against their lives.

During Shakespeare's time, the person on the throne demanded absolute obedience from the common people. Religious and family structures proved useful as models for this type of power. The people believed that the monarch (king or queen) had special powers from God. They were also taught to think of their king like a father. In Act 4, Claudius speaks about a king's God-given right to rule. But is he a good father figure? Is he a good ruler for Denmark?

All Our Yesterdays Historical and Social Context

Shakespeare puts together many events that seem to take very little time. In Act 4, Hamlet's journey seems to occur with modern-day speed, but actual travel in Shakespeare's England involved great time, effort, and danger. On land, people journeyed long distances on foot or by horse. They traveled on muddy roads and stayed in inns that offered poor service and bad food. Highway robbery often took place on these roads—making the idea of a trip a dangerous one.

At sea, travelers feared shipwrecks and pirates. They often sailed on ships called *privateers*. Privateers were privately owned ships that were authorized by their governments to harass the ships of other nations. One of England's best-known commanders of privateers was Francis Drake, the famous explorer.

The Play's the Thing Staging

How frightened would you be? You are facing about one thousand soldiers at the Danish seacoast. And they are ready to fight *you*, the enemy! The key here is to use your imagination. On the Elizabethan stage, this scene might include four or five players in military dress. They might be carrying prop swords and a drum and banner on a bare stage.

The benefits of artificial stage lighting and scenery help create theatrical entertainment today. Shakespeare's audiences didn't have these aids, so they needed to be alert to entrances and exits, clues in dialogue, and costume changes to follow his rapid changes of scene.

My Words Fly Up Language

One scene that is a standout in Act 4 features Ophelia's grief. Her sorrow and madness change her appearance and words. Her songs and speech include off-color puns, and the flowers and herbs she gives people had symbolic meanings. Rosemary represented remembrance. Pansies symbolized love (but their name also sounds like the French word *pensées,* meaning "thoughts"). Fennel stood for flattery. Columbines were for unchaste or ungrateful behavior. Rue, called the "herb of grace," symbolized repentance. Daisies meant lying and faithlessness. Violets were for the faithful.

223

Act IV

Scene I

To the **Queen,** *enter* **King,** *with* **Rosencrantz** *and* **Guildenstern.**

King There's matter in these sighs, these profound heaves,
You must translate. 'Tis fit we understand them.
Where is your son?

Queen Bestow this place on us a little while.

[*Exeunt* **Rosencrantz** *and* **Guildenstern**]

5   Ah, my good lord, what have I seen tonight!

King What, Gertrude, how does Hamlet?

Queen Mad as the sea and wind when both contend
Which is the mightier. In his lawless fit,
Behind the arras hearing something stir,
10   Whips out his rapier, cries 'A rat, a rat,'
And in this brainish apprehension kills
The unseen good old man.

King   Oh heavy deed!
It had been so with us had we been there.
15   His liberty is full of threats to all –
To you yourself, to us, to everyone.
Alas, how shall this bloody deed be answered?
It will be laid to us, whose providence
Should have kept short, restrained, and out of haunt

The **King, Rosencrantz,** *and* **Guildenstern** *enter, visiting the* **Queen** *in her room.*

King There's something in these sighs, these sobs of yours: you must translate. It's right that we should understand their meaning. Where's your son?

Queen Leave us alone for a while.

[**Rosencrantz** *and* **Guildenstern** *exit*]

Ah, my good lord—the things I've seen tonight!

King There now, Gertrude. How is Hamlet?

Queen As mad as the sea and the wind when they fight to prove which one's mightier. In his mad fit, hearing something stir behind the tapestry, he whipped out his sword, crying, "A rat, a rat!," and in this crazy delusion he killed the hidden, good old man.

King Oh, dreadful act! [*Using the royal "we" to mean "I"*] It would have happened to us if we'd been there. His freedom deeply threatens us all: you yourself, us, everyone. Alas, how shall we explain this bloody deed? It will be blamed on us. We should have had the foresight to keep this mad young

20　　This mad young man. But so much was our love,
　　　We would not understand what was most fit,
　　　But like the owner of a foul disease,
　　　To keep it from divulging, let it feed
　　　Even on the pith of life. Where is he gone?

25　**Queen**　To draw apart the body he hath killed,
　　　O'er whom his very madness, like some ore
　　　Among a mineral of metals base,
　　　Shows itself pure: he weeps for what is done.

　　　King　Oh, Gertrude, come away!
30　　The sun no sooner shall the mountains touch
　　　But we will ship him hence; and this vile deed
　　　We must with all our majesty and skill
　　　Both countenance and excuse. Ho, Guildenstern!

　　　[*Enter* **Rosencrantz** *and* **Guildenstern**]

　　　Friends both, go join you with some further aid.
35　　Hamlet in madness hath Polonius slain,
　　　And from his mother's closet hath he dragged him.
　　　Go seek him out: speak fair, and bring the body
　　　Into the chapel. I pray you haste in this.

　　　[*Exeunt* **Rosencrantz** *and* **Guildenstern**]

　　　Come, Gertrude, we'll call up our wisest friends,
40　　And let them know both what we mean to do
　　　And what's untimely done. So, haply, slander,
　　　Whose whisper o'er the world's diameter,
　　　As level as the cannon to his blank,
　　　Transports his poisoned shot, may miss our name
45　　And hit the woundless air. O come away,
　　　My soul is full of discord and dismay.

　　　　　　　　　　　　　　　　　　　　[*Exeunt*]

man on a short leash, restrained and isolated. But we loved him so much that we refused to see what needed to be done. Like someone with a terrible disease who wants to keep it secret, we let this feed on life itself. Where did he go?

Queen To take away the corpse he killed, over which his very madness shows its purity, like some vein of gold in a mine of base metals. He weeps for what's been done.

King Oh Gertrude, come away! We'll send him away as soon as the sunrise shows over the mountains, and we'll have to use all our authority and skill to excuse and put a good face on this horrible deed. [*Calling*] Guildenstern!

[**Rosencrantz** *and* **Guildenstern** *enter*]

Friends, go get help. In his madness, Hamlet has killed Polonius and dragged the body away from his mother's room. Go and find him. Humor him, and bring the body to the chapel. Please hurry.

[**Rosencrantz** *and* **Guildenstern** *exit*]

Come, Gertrude. We'll summon our wisest friends, and we'll let them know both what we intend to do and what's unfortunately already been done. That way, with luck, it's possible that slanderous rumor, whose whisper sends its deadly shot all through the world as surely as the cannon hits its target, might miss us and hit the invulnerable air. Oh, come away. My soul is full of uneasiness and fear.

[*The* **King** *and* **Queen** *exit*]

Act IV

Scene II

Enter **Hamlet.**

Hamlet Safely stowed.   [*Calling within*]
What noise? Who calls on Hamlet? Oh, here they come!

[*Enter* **Rosencrantz** *and* **Guildenstern**]

Rosencrantz What have you done, my lord, with the dead
body?

5 **Hamlet** Compounded it with dust, whereto 'tis kin.

Rosencrantz Tell us where 'tis, that we may take it thence
and bear it to the chapel.

Hamlet Do not believe it.

Rosencrantz Believe what?

10 **Hamlet** That I can keep your counsel and not mine own.
Besides, to be demanded of a sponge – what replication
should be made by the son of a king?

Rosencrantz Take you me for a sponge, my lord?

Hamlet Ay, sir, that soaks up the King's countenance, his
15 rewards, his authorities. But such officers do the King best
service in the end: he keeps them, like an ape, in the corner
of his jaw; first mouthed, to be last swallowed. When he

Hamlet *enters.*

Hamlet   Safely hidden. [*Voices are heard, calling him*] What's that? Who's calling me? Oh, here they come!

[**Rosencrantz** *and* **Guildenstern** *enter*]

Rosencrantz   My lord, what have you done with the dead body?

Hamlet   Mixed it with its relative, dust.

Rosencrantz   Tell us where it is, so we can take it away and carry it to the chapel.

Hamlet   Don't believe it.

Rosencrantz   Believe what?

Hamlet   That I can keep your secrets and not my own. Besides, to be interrogated by a sponge—what answer can the son of a king give?

Rosencrantz   Do you take me for a sponge, my lord?

Hamlet   Yes, sir, one that soaks up the King's favors, his rewards, his power. But such helpers do serve the King best in the end. He's like an ape, putting them in his mouth first but swallowing them last, keeping them tucked away in the corner of his jaw. When he needs the information you've

needs what you have gleaned, it is but squeezing you and, sponge, you shall be dry again.

20 **Rosencrantz** I understand you not, my lord.

Hamlet I am glad of it. A knavish speech sleeps in a foolish ear.

Rosencrantz My lord, you must tell us where the body is and go with us to the King.

25 **Hamlet** The body is with the King, but the King is not with the body. The King is a thing –

Guildenstern A thing, my lord?

Hamlet Of nothing. Bring me to him.

[*Exeunt*]

found out, all he has to do is squeeze you and—sponge—
you'll be dry again.

Rosencrantz I don't understand you, my lord.

Hamlet I'm glad. A slippery speech sounds meaningless to
a fool.

Rosencrantz My lord, you must tell us where the body is and
come with us to the King.

Hamlet The body is with the King, but the King isn't with the
body. The King is a thing—

Guildenstern A thing, my lord?

Hamlet Of no importance. Bring me to him.

[*They exit*]

Act IV

Scene III

Enter the **King** *and two or three Lords.*

King   I have sent to seek him and to find the body.
How dangerous is it that this man goes loose!
Yet must not we put the strong law on him:
He's loved of the distracted multitude,
5   Who like not in their judgment but their eyes,
And where 'tis so, th'offender's scourge is weighed,
But never the offence. To bear all smooth and even,
This sudden sending him away must seem
Deliberate pause. Diseases desperate grown
10   By desperate appliance are relieved,
Or not at all.

[*Enter* **Rosencrantz, Guildenstern,** *and others*]

How now, what hath befallen?

Rosencrantz   Where the dead body is bestowed, my lord,
We cannot get from him.

15   **King**   But where is he?

Rosencrantz   Without, my lord, guarded, to know your
pleasure.

King   Bring him before us.

Rosencrantz   Ho! Bring in the lord.

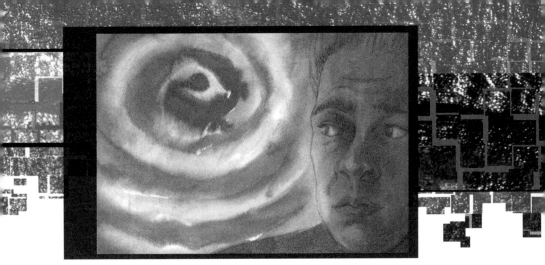

The **King** *and two or three Lords enter.*

King I have sent people to look for him and find the body. How dangerous it is that this man runs loose! But we can't put him under arrest. He's loved by the fickle public—whose approval is based on appearances, not reason. When that's the case, people ponder the offender's punishment, never the offence. To keep everything calm and under control, our suddenly sending him away must seem like a well-considered decision. Critical diseases are cured by drastic treatments, or not cured at all.

[**Rosencrantz, Guildenstern,** *and others enter*]

Well now, what happened?

Rosencrantz We can't get him to say where the dead body is, my lord.

King But where is he?

Rosencrantz Outside, my lord, under guard, awaiting your wishes.

King Bring him to us.

Rosencrantz Bring in the lord!

[*Enter* **Hamlet** *with guards*]

20 **King** Now, Hamlet, where's Polonius?

Hamlet At supper.

King At supper? Where?

Hamlet Not where he eats, but where he is eaten. A certain
convocation of politic worms are e'en at him. Your worm is
25 your only emperor for diet: we fat all creatures else to fat us,
and we fat ourselves for maggots. Your fat king and your
lean beggar is but variable service – two dishes, but to one
table. That's the end.

King Alas, alas.

30 **Hamlet** A man may fish with the worm that hath eat of a
king, and eat of the fish that hath fed of that worm.

King What dost thou mean by this?

Hamlet Nothing but to show you how a king may go a
progress through the guts of a beggar.

35 **King** Where is Polonius?

Hamlet In heaven. Send thither to see. If your messenger
find him not there, seek him i'th'other place yourself. But if
indeed you find him not within this month, you shall nose
him as you go up the stairs into the lobby.

40 **King** [*to some Attendants*] Go seek him there.

Hamlet He will stay till you come.

[*Exeunt Attendants*]

King Hamlet, this deed, for thine especial safety –
Which we do tender, as we dearly grieve
For that which thou hast done – must send thee hence
45 With fiery quickness. Therefore prepare thyself.

[**Hamlet** *enters, guarded*]

King Now Hamlet, where's Polonius?

Hamlet At supper.

King At supper? Where?

Hamlet Not where he eats, but where he's eaten. A certain assembly of shrewd worms are going at him right now. Your worm is the king of eaters: we fatten all creatures to fatten ourselves, and we fatten ourselves for maggots to eat. Your fat king and your skinny beggar are just different courses— two dishes, but served to the same table. That's the end.

King Alas, alas.

Hamlet A man can go fishing with the worm that's dined off a king, and then eat the fish that ate the worm.

King What do you mean by that?

Hamlet Nothing, just to show you how a king may take a royal journey through a beggar's guts.

King Where's Polonius?

Hamlet In heaven. Send for him there. If your messenger can't find him there, look for him in the other place yourself. But if you don't find him within the month, you'll smell him as you go up the stairs into the lobby.

King [*to some Attendants*] Go look for him there.

Hamlet He'll wait until you come.

[*The Attendants exit*]

King Because of this deed, Hamlet, for your own safety— which we hold just as dearly as we grieve deeply over what you've done—we must send you away with the utmost speed. Therefore, make your preparations. The ship is ready,

The bark is ready, and the wind at help,
Th'associates tend, and everything is bent
For England.

Hamlet For England?

50 **King** Ay, Hamlet.

Hamlet Good.

King So is it, if thou knew'st our purposes.

Hamlet I see a cherub that sees them. But come, for
England. Farewell, dear mother.

55 **King** Thy loving father, Hamlet.

Hamlet My mother. Father and mother is man and wife,
man and wife is one flesh; so my mother. Come, for
England.

[*Exit*]

King Follow him at foot. Tempt him with speed aboard,
60   Delay it not. I'll have him hence tonight.
        Away! For everything is sealed and done
        That else leans on th'affair. Pray you make haste.

[*Exeunt all but the* **King**]

And England, if my love thou hold'st at aught –
As my great power thereof may give thee sense,
65   Since yet thy cicatrice looks raw and red
After the Danish sword, and thy free awe
Pays homage to us – thou mayst not coldly set
Our sovereign process, which imports at full,
By letters conjuring to that effect,
70   The present death of Hamlet. Do it, England;
For like the hectic in my blood he rages,
And thou must cure me. Till I know 'tis done,
Howe'er my haps, my joys were ne'er begun.

[*Exit*]

and the wind is favorable. Your associates are waiting, and everything is set to go to England.

Hamlet   To England?

King   Yes, Hamlet.

Hamlet   Good.

King   So it is, if you knew my intentions.

Hamlet   I see a cherub that sees them. But come: off to England. Farewell, dear mother.

King   Your loving *father,* Hamlet.

Hamlet   My mother. Father and mother are man and wife, man and wife are one flesh. So—my mother. Come, off to England.

[**Hamlet** *exits*]

King   Follow at his heels. Get him on board quickly; don't delay. I want him gone by tonight. Go! Everything relating to this affair has been signed and sealed. Make haste.

[*All exit except the* **King**]

Now, King of England, if you value my favor at all—and my great power will remind you of its worth, since your country's scars haven't healed from the wound Denmark gave it in war, and you pay tribute money because of your fear—you may not disregard our sovereign command. It is fully stated in letters giving instructions for Hamlet's immediate death. Do it, England. He rages against me like a persistent fever, and you must cure me. Until I know it's been done, whatever my fortunes may be, my joy cannot begin.

[**King** *exits*]

Act IV

Scene IV

*Enter **Fortinbras** with his army marching over the stage.*

Fortinbras Go, Captain, from me greet the Danish king.
Tell him that by his licence Fortinbras
Craves the conveyance of a promised march
Over his kingdom. You know the rendezvous.
5   If that his Majesty would aught with us,
We shall express our duty in his eye;
And let him know so.

Captain   I will do't, my lord.

Fortinbras Go softly on.

*[Exeunt all but the **Captain**]*

*[Enter **Hamlet, Rosencrantz, Guildenstern** and others]*

10   **Hamlet** Good sir, whose powers are these?

Captain They are of Norway, sir.

Hamlet How purposed, sir, I pray you?

Captain Against some part of Poland.

Hamlet Who commands them, sir?

15   **Captain** The nephew to old Norway, Fortinbras.

Fortinbras, *the King of Norway's nephew, marches over the stage with his army, including a* **Captain.**

Fortinbras Captain, go bring my greetings to the Danish king. Tell him that, as he has agreed, Fortinbras requests safe conduct for his army's planned march through the Danish kingdom. You know the rendezvous. If his Majesty wishes to speak with us, we'll pay our respects to him in person. Let him know that.

Captain I will, my lord.

Fortinbras March on, slowly.

[*All exit except the* **Captain**]

[**Hamlet, Rosencrantz,** *and* **Guildenstern** *enter with Attendants*]

Hamlet Good sir, whose forces are these?

Captain They're from Norway, sir.

Hamlet Where are they headed, sir?

Captain They're headed for some part of Poland.

Hamlet Who's commanding them, sir?

Captain The old King of Norway's nephew, Fortinbras.

Hamlet Goes it against the main of Poland, sir,
Or for some frontier?

Captain Truly to speak, and with no addition,
We go to gain a little patch of ground
20 That hath in it no profit but the name.
To pay five ducats – five – I would not farm it;
Nor will it yield to Norway or the Pole
A ranker rate should it be sold in fee.

Hamlet Why, then the Polack never will defend it.

25 **Captain** Yes, it is already garrisoned.

Hamlet Two thousand souls and twenty thousand ducats
Will not debate the question of this straw!
This is th'imposthume of much wealth and peace,
That inward breaks, and shows no cause without
30 Why the man dies. I humbly thank you, sir.

Captain God be wi'you, sir.

[*Exit*]

Rosencrantz   Will't please you go, my lord?

Hamlet I'll be with you straight. Go a little before.

[*Exeunt all but* **Hamlet**]

How all occasions do inform against me,
35 And spur my dull revenge! What is a man
If his chief good and market of his time
Be but to sleep and feed? A beast, no more.
Sure he that made us with such large discourse,
Looking before and after, gave us not
40 That capability and godlike reason
To fust in us unused. Now whether it be
Bestial oblivion, or some craven scruple

Hamlet Are they going to battle against all of Poland, or some frontier?

Captain To speak frankly and plainly, we go to conquer a little patch of ground that's not worth getting except for its name. I wouldn't rent it for five ducats a year, not five. It wouldn't go for a higher rate even if Norway or Poland sold it outright.

Hamlet Why, then the Polish king will never defend it.

Captain Yes, it's already garrisoned.

Hamlet Two thousand men and twenty thousand ducats will hardly be enough to settle this trivial thing! This is an abscess of wealth and peace: it bursts internally, so death seems to happen with no apparent cause. I humbly thank you, sir.

Captain God be with you, sir.

[*The* **Captain** *exits*]

Rosencrantz Are you ready to go, my lord?

Hamlet I'll be with you right away. Go ahead a bit.

[*All exit except* **Hamlet**]

How all circumstances accuse me and stir up my sluggish revenge! What is a man, if his life's only purpose is to sleep and eat? An animal, nothing more. Surely the God who created us with such powers of understanding, of memory and foresight, didn't give us that power and godlike reason for it to grow moldy in us, unused. Whether it's because of animal forgetfulness, or some cowardly reservation caused

Of thinking too precisely on th'event –
A thought which, quartered, hath but one part wisdom
45 And ever three parts coward – I do not know
Why yet I live to say this thing's to do,
Sith I have cause, and will, and strength, and means
To do't. Examples gross as earth exhort me,
Witness this army of such mass and charge,
50 Led by a delicate and tender prince,
Whose spirit, with divine ambition puffed,
Makes mouths at the invisible event,
Exposing what is mortal and unsure
To all that fortune, death, and danger dare,
55 Even for an eggshell. Rightly to be great
Is not to stir without great argument,
But greatly to find quarrel in a straw
When honour's at the stake. How stand I then,
That have a father killed, a mother stained,
60 Excitements of my reason and my blood,
And let all sleep, while to my shame I see
The imminent death of twenty thousand men
That, for a fantasy and trick of fame,
Go to their graves like beds, fight for a plot
65 Whereon the numbers cannot try the cause,
Which is not tomb enough and continent
To hide the slain? O, from this time forth
My thoughts be bloody or be nothing worth.

[*Exit*]

by thinking too hard about the consequences (the kind of thinking that, upon examination, turns out to be one part wisdom and three parts cowardice), I don't know why I still live with this thing still not done. Examples as plain as day inspire me. Witness this large and costly army, led by a fine and youthful prince whose spirit, inflated by divine ambition, makes faces at what can't be foreseen. He risks life and limb, facing all that fate, death, and danger dare against him—and all for nothing, an eggshell. To be truly great is not to stir only when there's a great cause, but to find a quarrel in a trivial thing when honor is at stake. How can I stand here, then, and do nothing—with a father killed, a mother defiled, motives urged by reason and passion? And at the same time I see, to my shame, the imminent death of twenty thousand men who go to their graves like they're going to their beds, for a whim and a token of glory. They fight for a piece of land that's not big enough to hold the two fighting armies, that's not large enough to bury all the casualties. Oh, from now on, let my thoughts be bloody, or they are worth nothing.

[Hamlet *exits*]

Act IV

Scene V

Enter **Queen, Horatio,** *and a* **Gentleman**.

Queen I will not speak with her.

Gentleman   She is importunate,
　　Indeed distract. Her mood will needs be pitied.

Queen What would she have?

5 **Gentleman** She speaks much of her father, says she hears
　　There's tricks i'th'world, and hems, and beats her heart;
　　Spurns enviously at straws; speaks things in doubt
　　That carry but half sense. Her speech is nothing,
　　Yet the unshaped use of it doth move
10　The hearers to collection. They aim at it,
　　And botch the words up fit to their own thoughts,
　　Which, as her winks and nods and gestures yield them,
　　Indeed would make one think there might be thought,
　　Though nothing sure, yet much unhappily.

15 **Horatio** 'Twere good she were spoken with, for she may
　　　strew
　　Dangerous conjectures in ill-breeding minds.

Queen Let her come in.

[*Exit* **Gentleman**]

The **Queen, Horatio,** *and a* **Gentleman** *enter.*

Queen I won't speak with her.

Gentleman She's insistent; indeed distracted. Her mood calls for pity.

Queen What does she want?

Gentleman She speaks a great deal about her father, says she hears the world's full of deceptive tricks, and coughs, and beats her chest; takes offence at little things; makes obscure remarks that hardly make sense. Her words are nonsense, but they're so incoherent that they prompt her listeners to guess what she means. They try to figure it out and patch her words together to fit the way they think. Considering how suggestive her winks and nods and gestures are, one could indeed think they might have some meaning—nothing sure, but seeming to mean something very unfortunate.

Horatio She ought to be spoken to, or she might spread dangerous rumors in slanderous minds.

Queen Let her in.

[*The* **Gentleman** *exits*]

[*Aside*] To my sick soul, as sin's true nature is,
20 Each toy seems prologue to some great amiss.
So full of artless jealousy is guilt,
It spills itself in fearing to be spilt.

[*Enter* **Ophelia**]

Ophelia Where is the beauteous Majesty of Denmark?

Queen How now, Ophelia?

25 **Ophelia** [*sings*] *How should I your true love know*
From another one?
By his cockle hat and staff
And his sandal shoon.

Queen Alas, sweet lady, what imports this song?

30 **Ophelia** Say you? Nay, pray you mark.

He is dead and gone, lady,
He is dead and gone;
At his head a grass-green turf,
At his heels a stone.

35 O ho!

Queen Nay, but Ophelia –

Ophelia Pray you mark.
[*Sings*] *White his shroud as the mountain snow –*

[*Enter* **King**]

Queen Alas, look here, my lord.

40 **Ophelia** *Larded with sweet flowers*
Which bewept to the grave did not go
With true-love showers.

[*Aside*] To my sick soul, as is always true with sin, each trivial thing seems to foreshadow some great calamity. Guilt is so full of suspicion that its very paranoia gives it away.

[**Ophelia** *enters*]

Ophelia Where is the beautiful Queen of Denmark?

Queen How are you, Ophelia?

Ophelia [*singing from a popular song*]

How will I know your true love
    From another one I might choose?
By his cockleshell hat and staff
    And his sandal shoe.

Queen Alas, sweet lady, what's the meaning of this song?

Ophelia What did you say? No, listen.

He is dead and gone, lady,
    He is dead and gone;
At his head is grass-green turf,
    At his heels a stone.

Oh!

Queen No, but Ophelia—

Ophelia Now listen. [*She sings*]

His shroud was as white as the mountain snow—

[*The* **King** *enters*]

Queen Alas, my lord, look!

Ophelia *Dressed up with sweet flowers*
        Which didn't go tearfully to the grave
        With true-love showers.

King How do you, pretty lady?

Ophelia Well, good 'ild you. They say the owl was a baker's
45   daughter. Lord, we know what we are, but know not what
we may be. God be at your table.

King Conceit upon her father.

Ophelia Pray let's have no words of this, but when they ask
you what it means, say you this:

50   *Tomorrow is Saint Valentine's day,*
All in the morning betime,
And I a maid at your window,
To be your Valentine.
Then up he rose, and donned his clothes,
55   *And dupped the chamber door,*
Let in the maid that out a maid
Never departed more.

King Pretty Ophelia –

Ophelia Indeed, without an oath, I'll make an end on't.

60   *By Gis and by Saint Charity,*
Alack and fie for shame!
Young men will do't if they come to't –
By Cock, they are to blame.
Quoth she, 'Before you tumbled me,
65   *You promised me to wed.'*

He answers,

'So would I'a done, by yonder sun,
And thou hadst not come to my bed.'

King How long hath she been thus?

70 **Ophelia** I hope all will be well. We must be patient. But I
cannot choose but weep to think they would lay him

King How are you, pretty lady?

Ophelia God reward you, I'm well. They say the baker's daughter got turned into an owl, for being so stingy. Lord, we know what we are, but we don't know what we may be. May God be at your table.

King Brooding over her father.

Ophelia Let's not talk about this anymore, but when they ask you what it means, say this:

Tomorrow is Saint Valentine's day,
  Early in morning-time,
And I a girl at your window,
  To be your Valentine.
Then up he rose, and put on his clothes,
  And opened the bedroom door.
He let in the virgin, who as virgin again
  Never departed more.

King Pretty Ophelia—

Ophelia Indeed, I'll finish it without swearing an oath.

By Jesus and by Charity
  Alas and oh what shame!
Young men will do it, if they come to it,
  By Cock, they are to blame.
She said: "Before you slept with me,
  You promised we'd be wed."

He answers,

"By yonder sun, I would have done,
If you hadn't come to my bed!"

King How long has she been like this?

Ophelia I hope all will be well. We must be patient. But I can't help crying when I think of how they laid him in the cold

i'th'cold ground. My brother shall know of it. And so I
thank you for your good counsel. Come, my coach. Good
night, ladies, good night. Sweet ladies, good night, good
75 night.

[*Exit* **Ophelia**]

King Follow her close; give her good watch, I pray you.

[*Exit* **Horatio**]

O, this is the poison of deep grief: it springs
All from her father's death.
O Gertrude, Gertrude,
80 When sorrows come, they come not single spies,
But in battalions, First, her father slain;
Next, your son gone, and he most violent author
Of his own just remove; the people muddied,
Thick and unwholesome in their thoughts and whispers
85 For good Polonius' death – and we have done but greenly
In hugger-mugger to inter him; poor Ophelia
Divided from herself and her fair judgment,
Without the which we are pictures, or mere beasts;
Last, and as much containing as all these,
90 Her brother is in secret come from France,
Feeds on this wonder, keeps himself in clouds,
And wants not buzzers to infect his ear
With pestilent speeches of his father's death;
Wherein necessity, of matter beggared,
95 Will nothing stock our person to arraign
In ear and ear. O my dear Gertrude, this,
Like to a murd'ring-piece, in many places
Gives me superfluous death. [*A noise within*]
                    Attend!

100 **Queen** Alack, what noise is this?

ground. My brother will hear about it! And so I thank you for your good advice. Come, my coach. Good night, ladies, good night. Sweet ladies, good night, good night.

[**Ophelia** *exits*]

King Follow her closely and please watch her carefully.

[**Horatio** *exits*]

Oh, this is the poison that comes from deep grief. It all springs from her father's death. Oh Gertrude, Gertrude—when sorrows come, they don't come alone, like scouts sent out by an army; instead, they come in battalions. First, her father killed. Next, your son gone, and the violent cause of his own just removal. The people are agitated: they are confused and suspicious in their thoughts and whispers about good Polonius's death. And we behaved like a naive fool in secretly burying him so hastily. Poor Ophelia, lost to her better self and judgment, without which we are shadows or mere animals! Last but hardly least, her brother has come back in secret from France. He broods over this astonishing turn of events, keeps himself aloof, and has plenty of gossips to buzz and infect his ear with poisonous rumors about his father's death. Needing to build up their gossip but lacking facts, they won't hesitate to accuse our royal person in everyone's ears. Oh, my dear Gertrude, this is like a cannon loaded with shot that scatters randomly—it kills me over and over. [*A noise is heard offstage*] Guard!

Queen Oh, no, what noise is that?

King Where are my Switzers? Let them guard the door.

[*Enter a* **Messenger**]

What is the matter?

Messenger   Save yourself, my lord.
    The ocean, overpeering of his list,
105 Eats not the flats with more impetuous haste
    Than young Laertes, in a riotous head,
    O'erbears your officers. The rabble call him lord,
    And, as the world were now but to begin,
    Antiquity forgot, custom not known –
110 The ratifiers and props of every word –
    They cry, 'Choose we! Laertes shall be king.'
    Caps, hands, and tongues applaud it to the clouds,
    'Laertes shall be king, Laertes king.'

Queen How cheerfully on the false trail they cry.
115 O, this is counter, you false Danish dogs. [*A noise within*]

King The doors are broke.

[*Enter* **Laertes** *with Followers*]

Laertes Where is this King? Sirs, stand you all without.

Followers No, let's come in.

Laertes   I pray you give me leave.

120 **Followers** We will, we will.

Laertes I thank you. Keep the door.

[*Exeunt Followers*]

                      Oh thou vile King,
  Give me my father.

King Where are my Swiss guards? Have them guard the door.

[*A* **Messenger** *enters*]

What's the matter?

Messenger Save yourself, my lord. Not even a tidal wave floods the plains with more violent speed than young Laertes overcomes your soldiers with his treasonous band of rebels. The mob calls him their lord. As if the world were just now about to begin and as if all traditions and customs (which should justify and underlie our every word) were forgotten and unknown, they cry, "We'll choose! Laertes shall be king!" They throw their caps in the air, clap, and cheer. Their applause reaches to the sky: "Laertes shall be king, Laertes for king!"

Queen How happily they bark up the wrong tree. Oh, this is the wrong way, you false Danish dogs! [*A noise is heard off-stage*]

King They've broken down the doors.

[**Laertes** *enters with his rebel followers*]

Laertes Where is this King? [*To his followers*] Sirs, wait outside.

Followers No, let's come in.

Laertes Let me take care of this.

Followers We will, we will.

Laertes Thank you. Guard the door.

[*His followers exit*]

Oh vile king! Give me my father.

Queen Calmly, good Laertes.

125 **Laertes** That drop of blood that's calm proclaims me bastard,
    Cries cuckold to my father, brands the harlot
    Even here between the chaste unsmirched brow
    Of my true mother.

    King   What is the cause, Laertes,
130   That thy rebellion looks so giant-like?
    Let him go, Gertrude. Do not fear our person.
    There's such divinity doth hedge a king
    That treason can but peep to what it would,
    Acts little of his will. Tell me, Laertes,
135   Why thou art thus incensed. Let him go, Gertrude.
    Speak, man.

    Laertes Where is my father?

    King   Dead.

    Queen   But not by him.

140 **King** Let him demand his fill.

    Laertes How came he dead? I'll not be juggled with.
    To hell, allegiance! Vows to the blackest devil!
    Conscience and grace, to the profoundest pit!
    I dare damnation. To this point I stand,
145   That both the worlds I give to negligence,
    Let come what comes, only I'll be revenged
    Most throughly for my father's death.

    King   Who shall stay you?

    Laertes My will, not all the world's.
150   And for my means, I'll husband them so well,
    They shall go far with little.

    King   Good Laertes,
    If you desire to know the certainty
    Of your dear father, is't writ in your revenge

Queen Calm down, good Laertes. [*She tries to restrain him*]

Laertes If one drop of my blood stays calm, it's the drop that proves I'm illegitimate, cries that my father was cheated on, and brands my faithful mother's chaste, unstained face with the mark of a whore.

King Laertes, what has prompted you to incite this massive rebellion? Let him go, Gertrude. Do not fear for our welfare. A king is shielded by his divine right to rule—it protects him, like a hedge. Treason can only look over this hedge at what it wants to have; it can't really act on its desires. Tell me, Laertes, why you're so incensed. Speak, man.

Laertes Where's my father?

King Dead.

Queen But not killed by him. [*She means the* **King**]

King Let him ask whatever he wants.

Laertes How did he die? I won't be tricked. To hell with loyalty! I'll swear allegiance to the blackest devil! Conscience and grace can go to the bottomless pit! I'm not afraid of being damned. Neither this world nor the next means anything to me any more. Whatever else happens, I'll be completely revenged for my father's death.

King Who's going to stop you?

Laertes No one in the world; I'll only stop when my will is accomplished. As for my means, I'll make such good use of them that a little will go a long way.

King Good Laertes, if you want to know the truth about your dear father, does that also mean that your plot for revenge

155   That, swoopstake, you will draw both friend and foe,
    Winner and loser?

Laertes None but his enemies.

King   Will you know them then?

Laertes To his good friends thus wide I'll ope my arms,
160   And, like the kind life-rend'ring pelican,
    Repast them with my blood.

King   Why, now you speak
    Like a good child and a true gentleman.
    That I am guiltless of your father's death
165   And am most sensibly in grief for it,
    It shall as level to your judgment 'pear
    As day does to your eye.

    [*A noise within.* **Ophelia** *is heard singing*]

                  Let her come in.

Laertes How now, what noise is that?

    [*Enter* **Ophelia**]

170   O heat, dry up my brains! Tears seven times salt
    Burn out the sense and virtue of mine eye.
    By heaven, thy madness shall be paid with weight
    Till our scale turn the beam. O rose of May!
    Dear maid, kind sister, sweet Ophelia!
175   O heavens, is't possible a young maid's wits
    Should be as mortal as an old man's life?
    Nature is fine in love, and where 'tis fine
    It sends some precious instance of itself
    After the thing it loves.

180 **Ophelia** [*sings*] *They bore him bare-faced on the bier,*
                     And in his grave rained many a tear –

    Fare you well, my dove.

will affect friend and foe alike, winner and loser, all the cards swept off the table?

Laertes Only his enemies.

King Would you like to know who they are?

Laertes I'll open my arms this wide to his good friends, and I'll nurture them with my own blood, like the legendary pelican.

King Why, now you're talking like a good child and a true gentleman. That I am innocent of your father's death, and that I feel great grief about it, will be made as plain as day to you.

[*Noise is heard from offstage.* **Ophelia** *is heard singing*]

Let her in.

Laertes What's that noise?

[**Ophelia** *enters*]

Oh heat, burn up my brains! Let my tears grow so salty that they scald the sight from my eye! By heaven, your madness will be revenged, and more. Oh rose of May! Dear maid, my kind sister, sweet Ophelia! Oh heavens, is it possible a young girl's sanity should be as mortal as an old man's life? Love refines nature, and when it's refined it sends some precious token of itself to the grave, following the thing it loves.

Ophelia [*singing*]

They bore him, bare-faced, on the bier,
And into his grave there rained many tears—

Farewell, my dove.

Laertes Hadst thou thy wits and didst persuade revenge,
It could not move thus.

185 **Ophelia** You must sing *A-down a-down*, and you *Call him a-down-a*. O, how the wheel becomes it! It is the false steward
that stole his master's daughter.

Laertes This nothing's more than matter.

Ophelia There's rosemary, that's for remembrance – pray
190 you, love, remember. And there is pansies, that's for
thoughts.

Laertes A document in madness: thoughts and remembrance
fitted.

Ophelia There's fennel for you, and columbines. There's rue
195 for you. And here's some for me. We may call it herb of
grace o'Sundays. You must wear your rue with a difference.
There's a daisy. I would give you some violets, but they
withered all when my father died. They say he made a good
end.

200 [*Sings*] *For bonny sweet Robin is all my joy.*

Laertes Thought and affliction, passion, hell itself
She turns to favour and to prettiness.

Ophelia [*sings*] *And will he not come again?*
And will he not come again?
205 *No, no, he is dead,*
Go to thy death-bed,
He never will come again.
His beard was as white as snow,
All flaxen was his poll.
210 *He is gone, he is gone,*
And we cast away moan.
God a mercy on his soul.

And of all Christian souls. God be wi'you.

[*Exit*]

Laertes If you made a case for revenge while you were sane, it could not be more persuasive.

Ophelia [*addressing various others*] You must sing *A-down a-down,* and then you sing *Call him a-down-a.* Oh, it's a fitting refrain! You know the one about the lying handyman and his master's daughter.

Laertes This nonsense is more compelling than sense.

Ophelia [*distributing flowers to the others on stage*] There's rosemary, that's for remembrance. Please, love, remember. And there's pansies, that's for thoughts.

Laertes A lesson from madness: thoughts and remembrance go together.

Ophelia There's fennel for you, and columbines. There's rue for you. And here's some for me. On Sundays we call it "herb of grace." You must wear your rue like a family coat of arms. There's a daisy. I would give you some violets, but they all withered when my father died. They say he died well. [*Singing*] *For lovely sweet Robin is all my joy.*

Laertes She turns misery and suffering, passion, hell itself into pretty and graceful things.

Ophelia [*singing*]

And won't he come again?
And won't he come again?
  No, no, he is dead.
  Go to your death-bed,
He'll never come again.
His beard was white as snow,
His hair was fair and full.
  He is gone, he is gone,
  And we moan in vain.
God have mercy on his soul.

And on all Christian souls. God be with you.

[**Ophelia** *exits*]

Laertes Do you see this, o God?

215 **King** Laertes, I must commune with your grief,
Or you deny me right. Go but apart,
Make choice of whom your wisest friends you will,
And they shall hear and judge 'twixt you and me.
If by direct or by collateral hand
220 They find us touched, we will our kingdom give,
Our crown, our life, and all that we call ours
To you in satisfaction; but if not,
Be you content to lend your patience to us,
And we shall jointly labour with your soul
225 To give it due content.

Laertes   Let this be so.
His means of death, his obscure funeral –
No trophy, sword, nor hatchment o'er his bones,
No noble rite, nor formal ostentation –
230 Cry to be heard, as 'twere from heaven to earth,
That I must call't in question.

King   So you shall.
And where th'offence is, let the great axe fall.
I pray you go with me.

[*Exeunt*]

Laertes God, are you watching this?

King Laertes, don't deny my right to share your grief. Go off and select the wisest of all your friends, and they'll sit in judgment between you and me. If they find that we [*the royal "we"*] are either directly implicated or guilty as an accessory in this affair, we will pay you with our kingdom, our crown, our life, and all that we own. But, if not, be content to be patient with us, and we will work cooperatively with your own soul to bring it satisfaction.

Laertes Let that be so. The way he died, his secret funeral—no memorial, no display of swords, no coat of arms above his grave to mark his bones; no rites of nobility; no formal ceremonies—all these cry out to be heard as loudly as if heaven itself was calling to earth. I must have an explanation.

King So you shall. And let the axe fall on those who are guilty. Please come with me.

[*They exit*]

Act IV

Scene VI

Enter **Horatio** *and a Servant.*

Horatio What are they that would speak with me?

Servant Seafaring men, sir. They say they have letters for you.

Horatio Let them come in.   *[Exit Servant]*

5   I do not know from what part of the world
I should be greeted, if not from Lord Hamlet.

[Enter **Sailors***]*

1st Sailor God bless you, sir.

Horatio Let him bless thee too.

1st Sailor He shall, sir, and please him. There's a letter for
10   you, sir. It came from th'ambassador that was bound for
England – if your name be Horatio, as I am let to know it
is.

Horatio *[reads the letter]* *Horatio, when thou shalt have
overlooked this, give these fellows some means to the King. They*
15   *have letters for him. Ere we were two days old at sea, a pirate of
very warlike appointment gave us chase. Finding ourselves too
slow of sail, we put on a compelled valour, and in the grapple
I boarded them. On the instant they got clear of our ship, so I
alone became their prisoner. They have dealt with me like*

Horatio *and a* **Servant** *enter.*

Horatio   Who are these men who want to speak with me?

Servant   Sailors, sir. They say they have letters for you.

Horatio   Let them in.   [*The* **Servant** *exits*]

I don't know where in the world I'd be getting letters from, unless it's from Lord Hamlet.

[**Sailors** *enter*]

1st Sailor   God bless you, sir.

Horatio   And you too.

1st Sailor   He shall, sir, if that's his will. Here's a letter for you, sir. It came from the ambassador who was going to England—if your name is Horatio, as I've been told.

Horatio   [*reading the letter*] *Horatio, when you've looked over this, arrange for these fellows to meet with the King. They have letters for him. Less than two days into our sea journey, a well-armed pirate ship pursued us. Finding we were too slow, we were forced to fight them, and in the battle I boarded their ship. Just then they got clear of our ship, so I became their only prisoner. They have dealt with me like*

20   *thieves of mercy. But they knew what they did: I am to do a*
turn for them. Let the King have the letters I have sent, and
repair thou to me with as much speed as thou wouldest fly
death. I have words to speak in thine ear will make thee dumb;
yet are they much too light for the bore of the matter. These
25   *good fellows will bring thee where I am. Rosencrantz and*
Guildenstern hold their course for England; of them I have
much to tell thee. Farewell.

    He that thou knowest thine,
      Hamlet.

30   Come, I will give you way for these your letters,
And do't the speedier that you may direct me
To him from whom you brought them.

                                     [*Exeunt*]

*merciful thieves. But they knew what they were doing: I have
to do them a favor. Let the King have the letters I sent, and
meet me as quickly as you would flee from death. I have
words to speak in your ear that will make you dumbstruck,
but even those words will be too weak for this heavy matter.
These good fellows will bring you to where I am.
Rosencrantz and Guildenstern are still headed for England; I
have much to tell you about them. Farewell. Yours, Hamlet.*

[*To the* **Sailors**] Come on. I'll give you access to deliver these
letters, and do it all the more quickly so that you can take me
to the man who gave them to you.

[*They exit*]

Act IV

Scene VII

Enter the **King** *and* **Laertes.**

King Now must your conscience my acquittance seal,
And you must put me in your heart for friend,
Sith you have heard, and with a knowing ear,
That he which hath your noble father slain
5   Pursued my life.

Laertes   It well appears. But tell me
Why you proceeded not against these feats,
So crimeful and so capital in nature,
As by your safety, wisdom, all things else
10   You mainly were stirred up.

King   O, for two special reasons,
Which may to you perhaps seem much unsinewed,
But yet to me they are strong. The Queen his mother
Lives almost by his looks, and for myself –
15   My virtue or my plague, be it either which –
She's so conjunctive to my life and soul
That, as the star moves not but in his sphere,
I could not but by her. The other motive
Why to a public count I might not go
20   Is the great love the general gender bear him,
Who, dipping all his faults in their affection,
Work like the spring that turneth wood to stone,
Convert his gyves to graces; so that my arrows,
Too slightly timbered for so loud a wind,
25   Would have reverted to my bow again,
But not where I had aimed them.

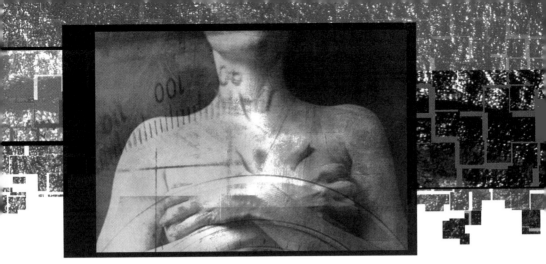

The **King** *and* **Laertes** *enter.*

King Now your conscience must confirm my innocence, and you must take me to heart as your friend, since you have heard and understood well that the man who killed your father also wanted to kill me.

Laertes It does seem so. But tell me why you didn't take action against these deeds—which were of such a criminal and serious nature. For you were greatly prompted to do so, in consideration of your safety, your wisdom, and everything else.

King Oh, for two special reasons, which may seem very weak to you, but to me are very strong. The Queen, his mother, practically lives just to look at him, and as for me—whether it's my blessing or my curse—she's so much a part of my life and soul that I can't make a move without her, just as a star can only move in its fixed orbit. The other reason why I couldn't indict Hamlet publicly is the great love the common people have for him. They're like the stream that turns wood into shiny stone; they affectionately turn all his faults into virtues and his criminality into honor. My accusations, like arrows, are too light for such a wind. They would have turned back and hit me, not where I'd aimed them.

Laertes And so have I a noble father lost,
A sister driven into desp'rate terms,
Whose worth, if praises may go back again,
30   Stood challenger on mount of all the age
For her perfections. But my revenge will come.

King Break not your sleeps for that. You must not think
That we are made of stuff so flat and dull
That we can let our beard be shook with danger
35   And think it pastime. You shortly shall hear more.
I loved your father, and we love ourself,
And that, I hope, will teach you to imagine –

[*Enter a* **Messenger** *with letters*]

Messenger These to your Majesty, this to the Queen.

King From Hamlet! Who brought them?

40 **Messenger** Sailors, my lord, they say. I saw them not.
They were given me by Claudio. He received them
Of him that brought them.

King   Laertes, you shall hear them.
Leave us.

[*Exit* **Messenger**]

45 [*Reads*] *High and mighty, you shall know I am set naked on*
your kingdom. Tomorrow shall I beg leave to see your kingly
eyes, when I shall, first asking your pardon, thereunto recount
the occasion of my sudden and more strange return.
                    Hamlet.

50   What should this mean? Are all the rest come back?
Or is it some abuse, and no such thing?

Laertes Know you the hand?

Laertes   And therefore I have lost a noble father, and my sister is driven into a state of madness—she whose worth, if I may praise her as she was, stood so high it challenged the ages for perfection. But my revenge will come.

King   Don't lose any sleep about that. [*Using the royal "we"*] You must not think we're made of such flat, dull stuff that we can let ourselves be threatened and take it as a joke. You'll hear more soon. I loved your father, as we love ourself, and that, I hope, will start you thinking—

[*A* **Messenger** *enters, bringing letters*]

Messenger   These are for your Majesty, this is to the Queen.

King   From Hamlet! Who brought them?

Messenger   Sailors, my lord, so they say. I didn't see them. Claudio gave them to me. He got them from the man who brought them.

King   Laertes, you shall hear them. Leave us.

[*The* **Messenger** *exits*]

[*Reading*] *High and mighty Majesty, this is to let you know that I've been put ashore in your kingdom, poor and unprotected. Tomorrow I will ask permission to see your kingly eyes—when I shall, after begging your leave, recount to you how my sudden and strange return came to pass. Hamlet.*

What does this mean? Did all the others come back? Or is it some trick, a ruse?

Laertes   Do you recognize the handwriting?

King   'Tis Hamlet's character.
  'Naked' –
55 And in a postscript here he says 'Alone'.
  Can you devise me?

Laertes I am lost in it, my lord. But let him come.
  It warms the very sickness in my heart
  That I shall live and tell him to his teeth,
60 'Thus diest thou.'

King   If it be so, Laertes –
  As how should it be so, how otherwise? –
  Will you be ruled by me?

Laertes   Ay, my lord,
65 So you will not o'errule me to a peace.

King To thine own peace. If he be now returned,
  As checking at his voyage, and that he means
  No more to undertake it, I will work him
  To an exploit, now ripe in my device,
70 Under the which he shall not choose but fall;
  And for his death no wind of blame shall breathe,
  But even his mother shall uncharge the practice
  And call it accident.

Laertes   My lord, I will be ruled,
75 The rather if you could devise it so
  That I might be the organ.

King   It falls right.
  You have been talked of since your travel much,
  And that in Hamlet's hearing, for a quality
80 Wherein they say you shine. Your sum of parts
  Did not together pluck such envy from him
  As did that one, and that, in my regard,
  Of the unworthiest siege.

Laertes   What part is that, my lord?

King It's Hamlet's. "Poor and unprotected"—and in a post-script here he says, "Alone." Can you explain this to me?

Laertes I'm lost, my lord. But let him come. It warms my sick heart to think that I will live and tell him to his face, "Now you will die."

King [*referring to the letter*] If this is true, Laertes—and how *can* it be true, but then how can it be otherwise?—will you do as I tell you?

Laertes Yes, my lord, so long as you don't force me to make peace.

King I'll help you make peace with yourself. If he has now returned, detouring from his voyage because he intends not to finish it, I will manipulate him into an undertaking I've already thought about. It's bound to bring about his downfall, and his death won't cause a whisper of accusation. Even his mother won't believe it's a plot; she'll call it an accident.

Laertes My lord, I'll comply, especially if you can arrange it so that I might be the instrument.

King So it shall be. Since you went to France, you've been much discussed, and in Hamlet's hearing, regarding a skill they say you shine in. All your other talents combined didn't incite such envy in him as that one did, though in my opinion it was the least important of your qualities.

Laertes What skill is that, my lord?

85 **King** A very riband in the cap of youth –
Yet needful too; for youth no less becomes
The light and careless livery that it wears
Than settled age his sables and his weeds
Importing health and graveness. Two months since
90 Here was a gentleman of Normandy –
I have seen myself, and served against, the French,
And they can well on horseback, but this gallant
Had witchcraft in't. He grew unto his seat,
And to such wondrous doing brought his horse
95 As he had been incorpsed and demi-natured
With the brave beast. So far he topped my thought
That I in forgery of shapes and tricks
Come short of what he did.

Laertes   A Norman was't?

100 **King** A Norman.

Laertes Upon my life, Lamond.

King   The very same.

Laertes I know him well. He is the brooch indeed
And gem of all the nation.

105 **King** He made confession of you,
And gave you such a masterly report
For art and exercise in your defence,
And for your rapier most especial,
That he cried out 'twould be a sight indeed
110 If one could match you. The scrimers of their nation
He swore had neither motion, guard, nor eye,
If you opposed them. Sir, this report of his
Did Hamlet so envenom with his envy
That he could nothing do but wish and beg
115 Your sudden coming o'er, to play with you.
Now out of this –

Laertes   What out of this, my lord?

King A little frivolity, a very ribbon in the cap of youthfulness—but necessary, too, for youth is no less suited to its carefree, light style than middle age is suited to its sable robes and garments, which signify its concern for comfort and dignified prosperity. Two months ago a gentleman from Normandy was here. I myself have seen and fought against the French, and they're good equestrians, but this gallant young man was a magician on horseback. He was rooted to his saddle, and he got his splendid horse to perform such amazing tricks that it seemed they were all one body, half-man and half-beast. He so far exceeded my expectations that any tricks or actions I could imagine fell short of what he did.

Laertes He was a Norman?

King A Norman.

Laertes I'd bet my life it was Lamond.

King The very same.

Laertes I know him well. He is indeed his nation's jewel and ornament.

King He confessed his admiration for you, and gave you such a marvelous report regarding your skill and practice with your sword—and especially with your rapier—declaring that if you ever met your match, that would really be something to see. He swore that French fencers couldn't beat you for agility, defense, or marksmanship. Sir, this report of his made Hamlet so green with envy that he could do nothing except wish and beg for your immediate return, so that he could fence with you. Now, from this—

Laertes What can come out of this, my lord?

King Laertes, was your father dear to you?
Or are you like the painting of a sorrow,
120 A face without a heart?

Laertes   Why ask you this?

King Not that I think you did not love your father,
But that I know love is begun by time,
And that I see, in passages of proof,
125 Time qualifies the spark and fire of it.
There lives within the very flame of love
A kind of wick or snuff that will abate it;
And nothing is at a like goodness still;
For goodness, growing to a pleurisy,
130 Dies in his own too-much. That we would do,
We should do when we would: for this 'would' changes
And hath abatements and delays as many
As there are tongues, are hands, are accidents,
And then this 'should' is like a spendthrift sigh
135 That hurts by easing. But to the quick of th'ulcer:
Hamlet comes back; what would you undertake
To show yourself your father's son in deed
More than in words?

Laertes   To cut his throat i'th'church.

140 **King** No place indeed should murder sanctuarize;
Revenge should have no bounds. But good Laertes,
Will you do this, keep close within your chamber;
Hamlet, returned, shall know you are come home;
We'll put on those shall praise your excellence,
145 And set a double varnish on the fame
The Frenchman gave you; bring you, in fine, together,
And wager o'er your heads. He, being remiss,
Most generous, and free from all contriving,
Will not peruse the foils, so that with ease –
150 Or with a little shuffling – you may choose
A sword unbated, and in a pass of practice
Requite him for your father.

King Laertes, was your father dear to you? Or are you like a painting of sorrow, just a heartless face?

Laertes Why are you asking me this?

King Not that I think you didn't love your father, but I know love begins at a certain time, and I've learned from experience that time also weakens love's spark and fire. Inside love's very flame, there exists a kind of wick or snuff that will extinguish it. Nothing stays good in the same way all the time. Goodness grows like an inflammation, then dies of its own excess. What we want to do we should do immediately, because the resolution "I will" soon changes and lessens and gets delayed many times—as many times as there are tongues, hands, and accidents to cause these alterations. And then the words "I shall" are like a sigh (which they say draws blood out of the heart)—they hurt at the same time they give relief. But to get to the point of all this: Hamlet has returned. What would you do to show that you are your father's son, in deeds instead of words?

Laertes I'd cut his throat in the church.

King Indeed, murder should have no place of sanctuary; revenge should have no bounds. But, good Laertes, if you wish to do this, then stay in your room. Hamlet, returned, will know that you've come home. [*Using the royal "we"*] We'll arrange for some people to praise your skill, doubling the luster of the reputation the Frenchman gave you, and finally we'll bring you and Hamlet together in a match, with bets made on both of you. Being ingenuous, generous-minded, and free of conniving, Hamlet won't examine the foils. That way you can easily (or with a little subterfuge) choose a sword without a button to blunt its point. Then, with a skillful thrust, you can pay him back for your father.

Laertes   I will do't.
And for that purpose, I'll anoint my sword.
155   I bought an unction of a mountebank
So mortal that but dip a knife in it,
Where it draws blood, no cataplasm so rare,
Collected from all simples that have virtue
Under the moon, can save the thing from death
160   That is but scratched withal. I'll touch my point
With this contagion, that if I gall him slightly,
It may be death.

King   Let's further think of this,
Weigh what convenience both of time and means
165   May fit us to our shape. If this should fail,
And that our drift look through our bad performance,
'Twere better not assayed. Therefore this project
Should have a back or second that might hold
If this did blast in proof. Soft, let me see.
170   We'll make a solemn wager on your cunnings –
I ha't!
When in your motion you are hot and dry –
As make your bouts more violent to that end –
And that he calls for drink, I'll have prepared him
175   A chalice for the nonce, whereon but sipping,
If he by chance escape your venomed stuck,
Our purpose may hold there. But stay; what noise?

[*Enter* **Queen**]

Queen One woe doth tread upon another's heel,
So fast they follow. Your sister's drowned, Laertes.

180   **Laertes** Drowned? O, where?

Queen There is a willow grows aslant the brook
That shows his hoary leaves in the glassy stream.
There with fantastic garlands did she come

Laertes I'll do it. And for that purpose, I'll poison my sword. I bought an ointment from a quack doctor that's so lethal all you have to do is dip a knife in it, and wherever that knife draws blood (no matter how excellent the antidote, even if it's collected from all the strongest medicinal herbs available), nothing can save the thing from death that's been so much as scratched by it. I'll put this poison on the point of my rapier, so that if I wound him only slightly, he'll die.

King Let's think about this some more, and determine what's the best time and way for us to act our parts. If this should fail, and our real intentions show through our bad performances, it would be better we didn't try it at all. Therefore this project should have a secondary or backup plan that will work in case this one blows up on us. Now wait, let me see. We'll make a serious bet on your respective skills. . . . I've got it! When you become hot and thirsty from your exertion—so make your bouts all the more violent with that purpose—and he asks for a drink, I'll have a goblet ready for him for that occasion. At that point he'll only have to sip it for us to accomplish our purpose, in case he's avoided your poisoned thrust. But wait, what's that noise?

[*The* **Queen** *enters*]

Queen One sorrow tramples another, they follow each other so fast. Your sister has drowned, Laertes.

Laertes Drowned? Oh, where?

Queen There's a willow that slants over the brook, showing its silvery leaves in the reflecting water. She went there with fanciful garlands made from buttercups, nettles, daisies, and

Of crow-flowers, nettles, daisies, and long purples,
185   That liberal shepherds give a grosser name,
But our cold maids do dead men's fingers call them.
There on the pendent boughs her coronet weeds
Clamb'ring to hang, an envious sliver broke,
When down her weedy trophies and herself
190   Fell in the weeping brook. Her clothes spread wide,
And mermaid-like awhile they bore her up,
Which time she chanted snatches of old tunes,
As one incapable of her own distress,
Or like a creature native and indued
195   Unto that element. But long it could not be
Till that her garments, heavy with their drink,
Pulled the poor wretch from her melodious lay
To muddy death.

Laertes   Alas, then she is drowned.

200 **Queen** Drowned, drowned.

Laertes Too much of water hast thou, poor Ophelia,
And therefore I forbid my tears, But yet
It is our trick; nature her custom holds,
Let shame say what it will. [*Weeps*] When these are gone,
205   The woman will be out. Adieu, my lord,
I have a speech o'fire that fain would blaze
But that this folly douts it.

[*Exit*]

King   Let's follow, Gertrude.
How much I had to do to calm his rage.
210   Now fear I this will give it start again.
Therefore, let's follow.

[*Exeunt*]

purple orchids (which our free-spoken shepherds give an obscene name, while our chaste maidens call them "dead men's fingers"). As she climbed up to hang her crowns of weeds on the overhanging boughs, a spiteful branch broke off, and down she and her flowery trophies fell, into the weeping brook. Her clothes spread out wide, and for a while they held her up the way a mermaid would, while she sang bits of old tunes, like someone who can't understand her own predicament or like a creature whose natural habitat is water. But it couldn't be long before her clothes, heavy with their drink of water, pulled the poor creature down from her melodious song into a muddy death.

Laertes Alas, then; she is drowned.

Queen Drowned, drowned.

Laertes You've had your share of water, Ophelia, so I won't let myself cry. But it's the way we do things; nature will have its way; no matter how shameful it looks. [*He cries*] When these tears are gone, all that's womanly in me will also be gone. Farewell, my lord. I have a fiery speech in me that wants to blaze forth, but these foolish tears douse it.

[**Laertes** *exits*]

King Let's follow him, Gertrude. I had to work so hard to calm his rage! Now I fear that this will start it going again. So let's follow.

[*The* **King** *and* **Queen** *exit*]

Comprehension **Check What You Know**

1. What does the King discuss with Rosencrantz and Guildenstern in Scene 2?

2. What information does the Captain share with Hamlet?

3. What disturbs Hamlet about his meeting with the Captain? How does he compare it to his own problems?

4. What do the Queen and Ophelia discuss?

5. What news does the Messenger bring about the public's mood? How has Laertes affected events in the kingdom?

6. Why is Ophelia giving flowers and herbs to Laertes and the Queen?

7. What information is in Hamlet's letter to Horatio?

8. Describe people's descriptions of the fencing skills of Laertes and Hamlet.

9. What do you learn about Ophelia at the end of this act?

Activities & Role-Playing **Classes or Informal Groups**

Majority Rules Imagine you are a group of Danish citizens at a "town meeting," arguing about who you would like to be king. Have different members try to persuade the rest to support Hamlet, Laertes, Claudius, or Fortinbras. As you debate each one's merits, consider what the Danish people may have heard or not heard about what's really going on in the royal court.

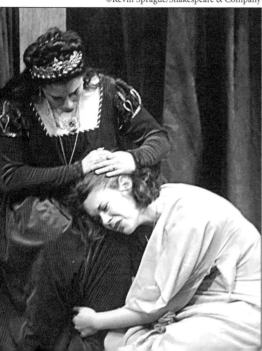

©Kevin Sprague/Shakespeare & Company

Picturing Shakespeare Ophelia has often been depicted in paintings, and her "mad scenes" in Act 4 have been vividly presented on stage. Discuss how you think Ophelia should look when she hands out her flowers and herbs in Scene 5. How would you make her appearance reflect her state of mind? Is her hair up or down? How is she dressed? Is she wearing makeup? If you want, research the Internet or look in the library for reproductions of paintings and photos of stage productions that show Ophelia during this scene. How did your ideas match actual productions?

Order in the Court In Scene 5 of Act 4, troubles are mounting at court. Suppose you wanted to present this scene for an audience. You would use everything possible—the way people dress, how they are grouped together, how they enter and exit the stage, even the music that is playing—to contribute to the overall mood of the scene. Discuss your ideas with others.

Discussion **Classes or Informal Groups**

1. How does the King prepare Laertes for his meeting with Hamlet? Describe the King's motivations. Why do you think he talks so much to Laertes about the way that the French horseman, Lamond, praised Laertes's skills?

2. Compare and contrast the Queen and Ophelia. What qualities do they share? How do they handle events differently?

3. How has Hamlet come to understand the King's plans for him? Who does Hamlet trust? Who does Hamlet distrust?

4. Discuss the relationship between Laertes and Ophelia. How do the events of this act affect Laertes? How would you feel if you were Laertes?

5. Update the chart you created for Ophelia in Act 3. Include any new information from Act 4 that has influenced your view of her behavior or her relationships with other characters in the Danish court.

Suggestions for Writing **Improve Your Skills**

1. Review the conversation between Hamlet and the King in Scene 3 (lines 20–39). List the images Hamlet uses during the exchange. Which images would you say are "high" and noble and which seem "low" or disgusting? Write a paragraph explaining whether you think the combination of images is effective and why or why not.

2. Ophelia has little chance to speak for herself in the play. Imagine you are Ophelia, and write a letter expressing some of her feelings about her experiences with either Hamlet, Laertes, or the Queen.

3. Imagine that you are Horatio and that somehow you have uncovered Laertes and the King's plan. Write a short letter to Hamlet describing the plan and give Hamlet advice on how to foil their scheme.

4. Ophelia gives flowers to Laertes, the Queen, and the King. Each symbolizes such things as remembrance, love, flattery, ingratitude or lack of chastity, corruption, repentance, and lying. List each person who received flowers. After each name write the name of the flower given to that person and the characteristic that the flower symbolizes. Finally, write a paragraph about each character explaining why the flower was appropriate.

All the World's a Stage Introduction

Hamlet has returned home safely. The characters head toward a final conflict. But first, Ophelia must be buried. At this point in the play, a funeral is a rather regular event.

Hamlet was absent for most of Act 4, which gave you some time to think about his character. You may find that you just don't know who he is or what he stands for. Given his cruelty to Ophelia, can Hamlet be considered a hero? Is he mad after all? And should he be punished for his hurtful acts?

What's in a Name? Characters

The situations are rather sad and grim. But that doesn't stop Shakespeare from introducing two amusing new characters: the Clowns. They act as gravediggers in Act 5's first scene. Osric, a courtier (member of the royal court), also makes his first appearance in the play.

The Clowns provide some comic relief. Shakespeare's clowns play up the physical and vulgar comedy that were a specialty of medieval clowns. But they also "comment" on the action in a new way. Because they act like buffoons, they can talk about topics that might be risky to chat about in Shakespeare's day—like interpreting the Bible. They could also share sly "in-jokes" easily with the audience. Some scholars think that when the gravedigger asks his pal to get him a drink, he sends him to a local tavern in London!

COME WHAT MAY Things to Watch For

What did Hamlet gain by being born a prince? Is Claudius a big winner by murdering for the crown? Shakespeare's graveyard imagery suggests an old Christian theme: earthly versus heavenly pursuits. The vanity or unimportance of earthly glories was a constant subject of medieval art and religion. Jesuits encouraged people to think about death as a part of their religious exercises. Gazing at a skull was sometimes a part of such activities.

Hamlet's mind is locked into a death mode. Shakespeare's language of corruption and decay furthers this theme of death. In Act 5, the idea of humankind's return to dust reaches its greatest intensity.

All Our Yesterdays Historical and Social Context

Act 5 combines kings and princes with gravediggers. You may sense the hang-up with rank, "degree," in the Elizabethan world. But in Shakespeare's era, people could move up in social status. It helped to have great ability or talent, but it was even better to own land.

Among the wealthy and titled, funerals marked a show of status. Polonius's hasty burial upsets Laertes. As the gravediggers note, high rank brings special treatment and privileges.

The Play's the Thing Staging

Should Hamlet go hatless? Not in Shakespeare's day. Noblemen of his time wore hats indoors. The Globe stage served for both outdoor and indoor scenes. Richard Burbage, the actor who played Hamlet at the Globe, very likely wore a hat throughout most of the play, for both exterior and interior scenes. Osric, however, is another matter. Most of the audience in Shakespeare's day would have considered him a dandy, and the actors usually portrayed him as flighty and effeminate.

In Act 5, Hamlet has a running exchange with Osric over the wearing of hats. As a sign of respect, gentlemen usually took off their hats to greet one another, but then they placed the hats back on their heads. However, a subject kept his hat off at all times when in the presence of his king. Since Shakespeare's audience paid great attention to costumes on stage and to social rank in the daily world, they would have understood why Hamlet asks Osric to wear his hat. They would also have noted that in keeping his head bare, Osric may be trying to flatter the prince.

In one early version of *Hamlet*, Osric is called "Ostricke," suggesting that Shakespeare's company may have had some fun with this character's costume. Some of the fanciest Elizabethan hats were decorated with an ostrich feather. It might also have helped the audience keep track of the character.

My Words Fly Up Language

The richest and most fashionable members of Shakespeare's audience would have been sharp judges of the sword-fighting scenes. Gentlemen were expected to learn the art of fencing. These men would have known the technical terms that may baffle modern-day audiences. Fighting with both a rapier and a dagger (for parrying) was common.

Hangers are straps used for hanging swords from the fencer's girdle. (Osric calls hangers "carriages," a term that would have been more likely to refer to gun-carriages than swords.) A *pass* was a bout and to *answer* meant to engage in a match. A *hit* was scored by touching an opponent's body with one's sword.

Shakespeare plays with the word *foil.* A foil is a fencing sword with a blunted point. But to *foil* also means to *defeat,* and *to be someone's foil* means to serve in contrast or opposition to someone.

Act V

Scene I

Enter two Clowns – a **Grave-digger** *and* **Another.**

Grave-digger Is she to be buried in Christian burial, when she wilfully seeks her own salvation?

Other I tell thee she is, therefore make her grave straight. The crowner hath sat on her and finds it Christian burial.

5 **Grave-digger** How can that be, unless she drowned herself in her own defence?

Other Why, 'tis found so.

Grave-digger It must be se offendendo, it cannot be else. For here lies the point: if I drown myself wittingly, it argues
10 an act, and an act hath three branches – it is to act, to do, to perform; argal, she drowned herself wittingly.

Other Nay, but hear you, Goodman Delver –

Grave-digger Give me leave. Here lies the water: good. Here stands the man: good. If the man go to this water and drown
15 himself, it is, will he nill he, he goes, mark you that. But if the water come to him and drown him, he drowns not himself. Argal, he that is not guilty of his own death shortens not his own life.

Other But is this law?

Two Clowns—a **Gravedigger** *and the* **Other** *laborer—enter.*

Gravedigger Is she getting a Christian burial, even though she willfully took her own life?

Other I tell you she is, so dig her grave quickly. The coroner conducted an inquest and he says it's to be a Christian burial.

Gravedigger How can that be, unless she drowned herself in self-defense?

Other Why, that's what the coroner found.

Gravedigger [*using mangled Latin legal terminology*] It must be *se offendendo,* it couldn't be anything else. For here's the point: If I drown myself on purpose, that has to be considered an act, and an act has three branches—to act, to do, and to perform. *Argal* [*he means* "Ergo," *Latin for* "therefore"], she drowned herself on purpose.

Other No, but listen, Digger—

Gravedigger Let me finish. Here lies the water: good. Here stands the man: good. If the man goes to this water and drowns himself—whether he wants it or not, willy-nilly—it's a fact that he goes. Note that. But if the water comes to him and drowns him, he doesn't drown himself. *Argal,* the man who isn't guilty of his own death hasn't shortened his own life.

Other But is this the law?

20 **Grave-digger** Ay, marry is't, crowner's quest law.

Other Will you ha' the truth on't? If this had not been a
gentlewoman, she should have been buried out o'Christian
burial.

Grave-digger Why, there thou say'st. And the more pity
25 that great folk should have countenance in this world to
drown or hang themselves more than their even – Christian.
Come, my spade. There is no ancient gentlemen but
gardeners, ditchers, and grave-makers – they hold up
Adam's profession. [*He digs*]

30 **Other** Was he a gentleman?

Grave-digger He was the first that ever bore arms.

Other Why, he had none.

Grave-digger What, art a heathen? How dost thou
understand the Scripture? The Scripture says Adam digged.
35 Could he dig without arms? I'll put another question to thee.
If thou answerest me not to the purpose, confess thyself –

Other Go to.

Grave-digger What is he that builds stronger than either the
mason, the shipwright, or the carpenter?

40 **Other** The gallows-maker, for that frame outlives a thousand
tenants.

Grave-digger I like thy wit well in good faith, the gallows
does well. But how does it well? It does well to those that do
ill. Now, thou dost ill to say the gallows is built stronger
45 than the church; argal, the gallows may do well to thee. To't
again, come.

Other Who builds stronger than a mason, a shipwright, or a
carpenter?

Gravedigger Yes, indeed it is—coroner's inquest law.

Other Do you want the truth? If she hadn't been a gentlewoman, she wouldn't get a Christian burial.

Gravedigger You said it. And the more's the pity that the rich and powerful should have permission in this world to drown or hang themselves more than their fellow Christians can. Give me my spade. In ancient times, there were no gentlemen except gardeners, ditch-diggers, and gravemakers. They maintain Adam's profession. [*He digs*]

Other Was he a gentleman?

Gravedigger He was the first who ever bore arms.

Other [*Thinking his partner means a heraldic coat of arms*] Why, he didn't have any!

Gravedigger What are you, a heathen? Do you understand the Bible? The Bible says, "Adam digged." Could he dig without arms? I'll ask you another question. If you don't give me a straight answer, confess yourself [*he is interrupted before completing the phrase "confess yourself and be hanged"*]—

Other Go on.

Gravedigger Who builds stronger than either the mason, the shipmaker, or the carpenter?

Other The gallows maker, because that structure outlasts a thousand tenants.

Gravedigger That's a good one; the gallows is a good answer. But how is it good? It does a good turn to those who do bad. Now, it's bad of you to say that the gallows is built stronger than the church: *Argal,* the gallows may do *you* some good. Come on, try again.

Other Who builds stronger than a mason, a shipmaker, or a carpenter?

Grave-digger Ay, tell me that and unyoke.

50 **Other** Marry, now I can tell.

Grave-digger To't.

Other Mass, I cannot tell.

Grave-digger Cudgel thy brains no more about it, for your
dull ass will not mend his pace with beating. And when you
55 are asked this question next, say, 'A grave-maker.' The
houses he makes lasts till doomsday. Go, get thee to
Yaughan; fetch me a stoup of liquor.

[*Exit the* **Other Clown.** *The* **Grave-digger** *continues digging*]

[*Sings*] *In youth when I did love, did love,*
Methought it was very sweet:
60 *To contract – O – the time for – a –*
my behove,
O methought there – a – was
nothing – a – meet.

[*While he is singing, enter* **Hamlet** *and* **Horatio**]

Hamlet Has this fellow no feeling of his business that he
65 sings in grave-making?

Horatio Custom hath made it in him a property of easiness.

Hamlet 'Tis e'en so, the hand of little employment hath the
daintier sense.

Grave-digger *But age with his stealing steps*
70 *Hath clawed me in his clutch,*
And hath shipped me intil the land,
As if I had never been such.

[*He throws up a skull*]

Gravedigger Yes, tell me.

Other Aha, now I've got it!

Gravedigger Go on.

Other By the Mass, I don't know.

Gravedigger Don't beat up your brains about it anymore. You can't make a dumb ass go faster by beating it. And the next time someone asks you this riddle, say, "A gravemaker." The houses he makes last until Doomsday! Go; head over to Yaughan's tavern and get me a bottle of booze.

[*The* **Other Clown** *leaves. The* **Gravedigger** *keeps digging. He sings and grunts while he works*]

In youth when I did love, did love,
*   I thought it was very sweet:*
To shorten (oh) the time for (ah) my own good,
Oh I thought there (ah) was nothing so (ah) right!

[**Hamlet** *and* **Horatio** *enter while he sings*]

Hamlet Does this fellow have no feeling for what he's doing, that he sings while he's digging a grave?

Horatio He's so used to it he doesn't think about it.

Hamlet Very true. People who don't work have more delicate feelings.

Gravedigger *But age with his stealthy steps*
*   Has clawed me in his clutch*
*   And sends me back into the land*
*   As if I had never been such.*

[*He tosses up a skull*]

Hamlet That skull had a tongue in it, and could sing once.
How the knave jowls it to the ground, as if 'twere Cain's
75   jawbone, that did the first murder! This might be the pate of
a politician which this ass now o'er-reaches, one that would
circumvent God, might it not?

Horatio It might, my lord.

Hamlet Or of a courtier, which could say, 'Good morrow,
80   sweet lord. How dost thou, sweet lord?' This might be my
Lord Such-a-one, that praised my Lord Such-a-one's horse
when he meant to beg it, might it not?

Horatio Ay, my lord.

Hamlet Why, e'en so, and now my Lady Worm's, chopless,
85   and knocked about the mazard with a sexton's spade. Here's
fine revolution and we had the trick to see't. Did these bones
cost no more the breeding but to play at loggats with 'em?
Mine ache to think on't.

Grave-digger   *A pickaxe and a spade, a spade,*
90   *For and a shrouding-sheet,*
                  O a pit of clay for to be made
                  For such a guest is meet.

[*Throws up another skull*]

Hamlet There's another. Why, may not that be the skull of a
lawyer? Where be his quiddities now, his quillities, his cases,
95   his tenures, and his tricks? Why does he suffer this rude
knave now to knock him about the sconce with a dirty
shovel, and will not tell him of his action of battery? Hum!
This fellow might be in's time a great buyer of land, with his
statutes, his recognizances, his fines, his double vouchers,
100   his recoveries. Is this the fine of his fines and the recovery of

Hamlet That skull had a tongue in it and could sing once. How the villain dashes it to the ground, as if it were the jawbone of Cain, who did the first murder! This might be the head of a shrewd intriguer, whom this ass now gets the better of, the kind who would try to bypass God, might it not?

Horatio It might, my lord.

Hamlet Or it might be some member of a royal court, who could say, "Good morning, sweet lord. How are you, sweet lord?" This one might be my Lord Such-and-Such, who praised my Lord Such-and-Such's horse when he meant to borrow it, might it not?

Horatio Yes, my lord.

Hamlet Yes, just so. And now he's at my Lady Worm's disposal, jawless, and knocked about the head by a sexton's spade. Here's a fine turn of events, were we able to see it. Were these bones made for no better use than to play games with them by tossing them around? My own bones ache to think about it.

Gravedigger [*singing*]
A pickaxe and a spade, a spade,
That and a shrouding sheet,
Oh a pit of clay that's to be made
For such a guest is fit.

[*He tosses up another skull*]

Hamlet There's another. Why, might that not be the skull of a lawyer? Where are his loopholes now, his quibbles, his cases, his title deeds, his tricks? Why does he now let this rube knock him on the head with a dirty shovel and not take him to court for battery? Hmm! In his time, this fellow might have been a great buyer of land, with his bonds and mortgages, his fines, his twice-signed vouchers, his recoveries to transfer possession. Is this the fine end of his fines and the recovery of his recoveries, to have his fine pate full of fine dirt? Will his vouchers vouch him no more of his purchases, and double ones too, than the length and breadth of a pair of indentures? The very conveyances of his lands will hardly lie in this box, and must th'inheritor himself have no more, ha?

Horatio Not a jot more, my lord.

Hamlet Is not parchment made of sheepskins?

Horatio Ay, my lord, and of calves' skins too.

Hamlet There are sheep and calves which seek out assurance in that. I will speak to this fellow. Whose grave's this, sirrah?

Grave-digger Mine, sir.

[*Sings*] *Oh a pit of clay for to be made* –

Hamlet I think it be thine indeed, for thou liest in't.

Grave-digger You lie out on't, sir, and therefore 'tis not yours. For my part, I do not lie in't, and yet it is mine.

Hamlet Thou dost lie in't, to be in't and say 'tis thine. 'Tis for the dead, not for the quick: therefore thou liest.

Grave-digger 'Tis a quick lie, sir, 'twill away again from me to you.

Hamlet What man dost thou dig it for?

Grave-digger For no man, sir.

Hamlet What woman then?

Grave-digger For none neither.

Hamlet Who is to be buried in't?

Grave-digger One that was a woman, sir; but rest her soul, she's dead.

his recoveries, to have his fine head full of fine dirt? Will his voucher—and twice-signed, too—vouch for his purchases only so far as the length and breadth of a two-sided legal document? The parchment titles to his lands will hardly fit in this box of his skull, and must the buyer himself have no more, ha?

Horatio Not one bit more, my lord.

Hamlet Isn't parchment made of sheepskins?

Horatio Yes, my lord, and of calves' skins, too.

Hamlet Then people are just like sheep and dumb calves if they seek safety in parchment documents. I'll speak to this fellow. [*To the* **Gravedigger**] You—whose grave is this?

Gravedigger Mine, sir.

[*Singing*] *Oh a pit of clay that's to be made—*

Hamlet I think it's yours after all, since you're lying in it.

Gravedigger You lie out of it, sir, and therefore it's not yours. For my part, I'm not lying in it, and yet it's mine.

Hamlet *You* lie in it, to be in it and claim it's for you. It's for the dead, not the living. Therefore, you're lying.

Gravedigger It's a lively lie, sir; it goes from me to you.

Hamlet What man are you digging it for?

Gravedigger No man, sir.

Hamlet What woman, then?

Gravedigger No woman either.

Hamlet Who's going to be buried in it?

Gravedigger Someone who was a woman, sir. But, rest her soul, she's dead.

Hamlet How absolute the knave is. We must speak by the
card or equivocation will undo us. By the Lord, Horatio,
130   these three years I have taken note of it, the age is grown so
picked that the toe of the peasant comes so near the heel of
the courtier he galls his kibe. How long hast thou been a
grave-maker?

Grave-digger Of all the days i'th'year I came to't that day
135   that our last King Hamlet o'ercame Fortinbras.

Hamlet How long is that since?

Grave-digger Cannot you tell that? Every fool can tell that.
It was the very day that young Hamlet was born – he that is
mad and sent to England.

140 **Hamlet** Ay, marry. Why was he sent into England?

Grave-digger Why, because he was mad. He shall recover
his wits there. Or if he do not, 'tis no great matter there.

Hamlet Why?

Grave-digger 'Twill not be seen in him there. There the
145   men are as mad as he.

Hamlet How came he mad?

Grave-digger Very strangely, they say.

Hamlet How 'strangely'?

Grave-digger Faith, e'en with losing his wits.

150 **Hamlet** Upon what ground?

Grave-digger Why, here in Denmark. I have been sexton
here, man and boy, thirty years.

Hamlet How long will a man lie i'th'earth ere he rot?

Grave-digger Faith, if he be not rotten before he die – as we
155   have many pocky corses nowadays that will scarce hold the
laying in – he will last you some eight year or nine year. A
tanner will last you nine year.

Hamlet How precise in his meanings the rogue is! We must speak perfectly clearly, or ambiguity will ruin us. By our Lord, Horatio, I've noticed in these last three years that our times have grown awfully refined. A peasant's toe follows so close behind a courtier's heel that he practically rubs off the calluses. [*To the* **Gravedigger**] How long have you been a gravedigger?

Gravedigger Out of all the days of the year, I started on the day that our last King Hamlet defeated Fortinbras.

Hamlet How long ago was that?

Gravedigger Don't you know? Every fool knows that. It was the very day that young Hamlet was born—the one who's mad and been sent to England.

Hamlet Yes, certainly. Why was he sent to England?

Gravedigger Why, because he was mad. He'll get his wits back there. Or, if he doesn't, it won't matter much there.

Hamlet Why?

Gravedigger It won't be noticed there. There all the men are as mad as he is.

Hamlet How did he go mad?

Gravedigger Very strangely, they say.

Hamlet "Strangely" how?

Gravedigger Truly, from losing his wits.

Hamlet Upon what ground?

Gravedigger Why, here in Denmark. I've been the sexton here for thirty years, as a man and a boy.

Hamlet How long will a man lie in the earth before he rots?

Gravedigger Truly, if he isn't rotten before he dies—we have many diseased corpses nowadays that will scarcely hold together long enough to be buried—he'll last you some eight or nine years. A man who worked as a tanner will last you nine years.

Hamlet Why he more than another?

Grave-digger Why, sir, his hide is so tanned with his trade
160   that he will keep out water a great while, and your water is a
sore decayer of your whoreson dead body. Here's a skull now
hath lien you i'th'earth three and twenty years.

Hamlet Whose was it?

Grave-digger A whoreson mad fellow's it was. Whose do
165   you think it was?

Hamlet Nay, I know not.

Grave-digger A pestilence on him for a mad rogue! He
poured a flagon of Rhenish on my head once. This same
skull, sir, was Yorick's skull, the King's jester.

170 **Hamlet** This? [*Takes the skull*]

Grave-digger E'en that.

Hamlet Alas, poor Yorick! I knew him, Horatio: a fellow of
infinite jest, of most excellent fancy. He hath borne me on
his back a thousand times. And now, how abhorred in my
175   imagination it is! My gorge rises at it. Here hung those lips
that I have kissed I know not how oft. Where be your gibes
now, your gambols, your songs, your flashes of merriment,
that were wont to set the table on a roar? Not one now to
mock your own grinning? Quite chop-fallen? Now get you to
180   my lady's chamber and tell her, let her paint an inch thick,
to this favour she must come. Make her laugh at that.
Prithee, Horatio, tell me one thing.

Horatio What's that, my lord?

Hamlet Dost thou think Alexander looked o' this fashion
185   i'th'earth?

Horatio E'en so.

Hamlet And smelt so? Pah! [*Throws down the skull*]

Hamlet Why will he last more than someone else?

Gravedigger Why, sir, his hide is so tanned with his trade that he'll keep out water for a long time. And your water is a nasty decayer of your lousy dead body. Now here's a skull that's been lying in the earth for 23 years.

Hamlet Whose was it?

Gravedigger A mad scoundrel's it was. Whose do you think it was?

Hamlet No, I don't know.

Gravedigger Curse him for being a mad rogue! He poured a pitcher of Rhine wine on my head once. This same skull, sir, was the skull of Yorick, the King's court jester.

Hamlet This? [*Taking the skull*]

Gravedigger The very same.

Hamlet Alas, poor Yorick! I knew him, Horatio. A fellow of infinite jests, full of excellent silliness. He carried me on his back a thousand times. And now, how horrible it is to remember it! It makes me feel sick. Here hung those lips that I kissed I don't know how many times. Where are your witty insults now, your slapstick, your songs, your flashes of merriment that made everyone at the table roar with laughter? Not one of these left to mock at your own grinning? Jaw-dropped for good? Now go to my lady's room. Tell her she can paint her face an inch thick, but she'll still wind up looking like you. Make her laugh at that. Horatio, tell me one thing.

Horatio What's that, my lord?

Hamlet Do you think Alexander the Great looked like this in the earth?

Horatio Exactly so.

Hamlet And did he smell so bad? [*He throws down the skull*]

Horatio E'en so, my lord.

Hamlet To what base uses we may return, Horatio! Why,
190   may not imagination trace the noble dust of Alexander till he
find it stopping a bung-hole?

Horatio 'Twere to consider too curiously to consider so.

Hamlet No, faith, not a jot, but to follow him thither with
modesty enough, and likelihood to lead it. Alexander died,
195   Alexander was buried, Alexander returneth to dust, the dust
is earth, of earth we make loam, and why of that loam
whereto he was converted might they not stop a beer-barrel?

> *Imperial Ceasar, dead and turned to clay,*
> *Might stop a hole to keep the wind away.*
> 200   *O that that earth which kept the world in awe*
> *Should patch a wall t'expel the winter's flaw.*

But soft, but soft awhile. Here comes the King,
The Queen, the courtiers.

[*Enter a* **Priest, King, Queen, Laertes,** *and a coffin, with*
Lords attendant]

                              Who is this they follow?
205   And with such maimed rites? This doth betoken
The corse they follow did with desp'rate hand
Fordo its own life. 'Twas of some estate.

Laertes What ceremony else?

Hamlet That is Laertes, a very noble youth. Mark.

210 **Laertes** What ceremony else?

Priest Her obsequies have been as far enlarged
As we have warranty. Her death was doubtful;
And but that great command o'ersways the order,
She should in ground unsanctified have lodged
215   Till the last trumpet: for charitable prayers,

Horatio   Exactly so, my lord.

Hamlet   How low we'll all end up, Horatio! Why, can't the imagination trace a path for Alexander's noble dust, so that he winds up serving as a barrel stopper?

Horatio   That's looking at it a little *too* closely.

Hamlet   No, surely not, not a bit. See if you can follow this: Alexander died; Alexander was buried; Alexander returns to dust; the dust is made of earth; we make mortar out of earth. So if he was converted into mortar, why wouldn't he be the type of clay they use to stop up beer barrels?

> *Imperial Caesar, dead and turned to clay,*
> *Might stop a hole to keep the wind away.*
> *Oh, that that earth, which kept the world in awe,*
> *Should patch a wall to keep cold gusts at bay.*

But quiet, that's enough for now. Here come the King, the Queen, the courtiers.

[*A* **Priest,** *the* **King,** *the* **Queen,** *and* **Laertes** *enter with Lords, Attendants, and bearers carrying a coffin.* **Hamlet** *and* **Laertes** *hide in order to watch*]

Who's this they're following? And with such minimal rites? This indicates that the body they're following died by its own desperate hand. It was someone of high rank.

Laertes   [*Speaking to the* **Priest**]   What other ceremonies?

Hamlet   [*To* **Horatio**]   That is Laertes, a very noble youth. Listen.

Laertes   What other ceremonies?

Priest   We have observed her funeral rites as fully as we may. The manner of her death was questionable. If higher authorities hadn't commanded that we ignore the usual procedure, she would have been laid in unsanctified ground until the last trumpet of Doomsday. Instead of charitable

Shards, flints, and pebbles should be thrown on her.
Yet here she is allowed her virgin crants,
Her maiden strewments, and the bringing home
Of bell and burial.

220 **Laertes** Must there no more be done?

Priest   No more be done.
We should profane the service of the dead
To sing sage requiem and such rest to her
As to peace-parted souls.

225 **Laertes**   Lay her i'th'earth,
And from her fair and unpolluted flesh
May violets spring. I tell thee, churlish priest,
A minist'ring angel shall my sister be
When thou liest howling.

230 **Hamlet**   What, the fair Ophelia!

Queen [*scatters flowers*] Sweets to the sweet. Farewell.
I hoped thou shouldst have been my Hamlet's wife:
I thought thy bride-bed to have decked, sweet maid,
And not have strewed thy grave.

235 **Laertes**   Oh, treble woe
Fall ten times treble on that cursed head
Whose wicked deed thy most ingenious sense
Deprived thee of. Hold off the earth awhile,
Till I have caught her once more in mine arms.

[*Leaps in the grave*]

240   Now pile your dust upon the quick and dead,
Till of this flat a mountain you have made
To o'ertop old Pelion or the skyish head
Of blue Olympus.

prayers, she would have had shards, flints, and pebbles thrown into her grave. Yet here she is allowed her virgin's garlands, her funeral flowers strewed on maidens' graves, and consecrated burial with the tolling of a bell.

Laertes Can't any more be done?

Priest No more can be done. We would profane the burial rituals if we sang a solemn dirge and laid her to rest like a soul that died in peace.

Laertes Lay her in the earth, and let violets grow from her fair and unpolluted flesh. Begrudging priest, I tell you that my sister will be a ministering angel when you lie howling down in hell.

Hamlet What? The fair Ophelia!

Queen [*scattering flowers*] Sweets to the sweet. Farewell. I hoped that you would be my Hamlet's wife. Sweet girl, I thought I would have decked your bridal bed with flowers, not strewn them on your grave.

Laertes Oh, let triple woe fall ten-times-triple on his cursed head, that man whose wicked deeds deprived you of your reason! Keep the earth off her a while, until I have held her once more in my arms.

[*He leaps into the grave*]

Now pile your dust upon the living and the dead, till you've turned this flat ground into a mountain higher that the top of old Mount Pelion, higher than the sky-high head of blue-peaked Olympus.

Hamlet   What is he whose grief
245   Bears such an emphasis, whose phrase of sorrow
        Conjures the wand'ring stars and makes them stand
        Like wonder-wounded hearers? This is I,
        Hamlet the Dane.

Laertes   [*grappling with him*] The devil take thy soul!

250 **Hamlet**   Thou pray'st not well.
        I prithee take thy fingers from my throat,
        For though I am not splenitive and rash,
        Yet have I in me something dangerous,
        Which let thy wisdom fear. Hold off thy hand.

255 **King** Pluck them asunder.

Queen Hamlet! Hamlet!

All Gentlemen!

Horatio Good my lord, be quiet.

Hamlet Why, I will fight with him upon this theme
260   Until my eyelids will no longer wag.

Queen O my son, what theme?

Hamlet I loved Ophelia. Forty thousand brothers
        Could not with all their quantity of love
        Make up my sum. What wilt thou do for her?

265 **King** O, he is mad, Laertes.

Queen For love of God forbear him.

Hamlet 'Swounds, show me what thou't do.
        Woo't weep, woo't fight, woo't fast, woo't tear thyself,
        Woo't drink up eisel, eat a crocodile?
270   I'll do't. Dost come here to whine,
        To outface me with leaping in her grave?
        Be buried quick with her, and so will I.
        And if thou prate of mountains, let them throw

Hamlet [*Coming out of hiding*] Who is this whose grief carries such emphasis? Whose fine phrases of sorrow hold the wandering planets spellbound, so they stand there like an audience struck with amazement? [*Using a title that usually applies to the King of Denmark*] This is I—Hamlet the Dane!

Laertes [*Wrestling with him*] The devil take your soul!

Hamlet That's an unkind prayer. Kindly take your fingers off my throat—for though I'm not impetuous and rash, I've still got something dangerous inside me, which you'd be wise to fear. Take your hands off me.

King [*To some attendants*] Pull them apart.

Queen Hamlet! Hamlet!

All Gentlemen!

Horatio Good my lord, calm down.

Hamlet Why, I will fight with him over this matter until my eyes are permanently shut.

Queen Oh my son, what matter?

Hamlet I loved Ophelia. Forty-thousand brothers could not equal the sum of my love with all their love combined. What will you do for her?

King Oh, he is mad, Laertes.

Queen For the love of God, ignore him.

Hamlet By God's wounds, show me what you'll do. Will you weep, will you fight, will you fast, will you claw at yourself, will you drink up vinegar, eat a crocodile? I'll do it. Do you come here to whine, to outdo me by leaping in her grave? Be buried alive with her, and so will I. And if you prattle about

275 Millions of acres on us, till our ground,
Singeing his pate against the burning zone,
Make Ossa like a wart! Nay, and thou'lt mouth,
I'll rant as well as thou.

Queen   This is mere madness,
And thus awhile the fit will work on him.
280 Anon, as patient as the female dove
When that her golden couplets are disclosed,
His silence will sit drooping.

Hamlet   Hear you, sir,
What is the reason that you use me thus?
285 I loved you ever. But it is no matter.
Let Hercules himself do what he may,
The cat will mew, and dog will have his day.

[*Exit*]

King   I pray, thee, good Horatio, wait upon him.

[*Exit* **Horatio**]

[*To* **Laertes**] Strengthen your patience in our last night's
290   speech;
We'll put the matter to the present push.
Good Gertrude, set some watch over your son.
This grave shall have a living monument.
An hour of quiet shortly shall we see;
295 Till then in patience our proceeding be.

[*Exeunt*]

mountains, let them throw millions of acres over us, until the ground singes its head against the sun's burning zone. It will make Mount Ossa look like a wart! No, if you're going to be an orator, I'll rant as well as you do.

Queen   This is pure madness. He'll suffer from this fit for a while. But soon he'll sit drooping silently, as calmly as the dove when her yellow chicks are hatched.

Hamlet   Listen to me, sir, why are you treating me this way? I have always liked you. But never mind. The cat will still meow, and every dog will have his day, even if Hercules himself tries to stop them.

[**Hamlet** *exits*]

King   Good Horatio, please look after him.

[**Horatio** *exits*]

[*To* **Laertes**] Strengthen your patience by remembering what we talked about last night. We'll soon put this matter to the test. Good Gertrude, make sure your son is watched. This grave will have an enduring monument. We'll have a quiet hour soon; till then we'll have to be patient.

[*They exit*]

Act V

Scene II

Enter **Hamlet** *and* **Horatio.**

Hamlet So much for this, sir. Now shall you see the other.
You do remember all the circumstance?

Horatio Remember it, my lord!

Hamlet Sir, in my heart there was a kind of fighting
5   That would not let me sleep. Methought I lay
Worse than the mutines in the bilboes. Rashly –
And praised be rashness for it: let us know
Our indiscretion sometimes serves us well
When our deep plots do pall; and that should teach us
10   There's a divinity that shapes our ends,
Rough-hew them how we will.

Horatio   That is most certain.

Hamlet Up from my cabin,
My sea-gown scarfed about me, in the dark
15   Groped I to find out them; had my desire,
Fingered their packet, and in fine withdrew
To mine own room again, making so bold,
My fears forgetting manners, to unseal
Their grand commission; where I found, Horatio –
20   Ah, royal knavery! – an exact command,
Larded with many several sorts of reasons
Importing Denmark's health, and England's too,
With ho! such bugs and goblins in my life,

Hamlet *and* **Horatio** *enter.*

Hamlet So much for this, sir. Now you'll learn the rest. Do you remember all the circumstances I wrote you about?

Horatio Remember it, my lord! [*Meaning he could hardly forget it*]

Hamlet Sir, there was a kind of struggle in my heart that wouldn't let me sleep. I lay there feeling worse than the mutineers in chains. On an impulse— [*he interrupts himself*] And praised be impulsiveness for it; let's acknowledge that our slip-ups sometimes serve us well when our best-laid plans come to nothing. And that should teach us that there's something divine that shapes our lives, no matter how we sketch out our plans.

Horatio That's certainly true.

Hamlet [*resuming his story*] I came up from my cabin, with my sea-clothes wrapped around me, and groped in the dark to find Rosencrantz and Guildenstern. I did find them, stole their packet of documents, and finally withdrew to my own room again. Then I made so bold as to open their royal communiqués, for my fears overrode protocol. There I found, Horatio—ah, royal villainy!—there I found a clear command, embellished with assorted reasons regarding the King of Denmark's welfare and the King of England's too—with ho! predictions of such bugaboos and goblins to be unleashed if

That on the supervise, no leisure bated,
25   No, not to stay the grinding of the axe,
My head should be struck off.

Horatio   Is't possible?

Hamlet Here's the commission, read it at more leisure.
But wilt thou hear now how I did proceed?

30   **Horatio** I beseech you.

Hamlet Being thus benetted round with villainies –
Ere I could make a prologue to my brains,
They had begun the play – I sat me down,
Devised a new commission, wrote it fair –
35   I once did hold it, as our statists do,
A baseness to write fair, and laboured much
How to forget that learning, but, sir, now
It did me yeoman's service. Wilt thou know
Th'effect of what I wrote?

40   **Horatio**   Ay, good my lord.

Hamlet An earnest conjuration from the King,
As England was his faithful tributary,
As love between them like the palm might flourish,
As peace should still her wheaten garland wear
45   And stand a comma 'tween their amities,
And many such-like 'as'es of great charge,
That on the view and knowing of these contents,
Without debatement further more or less,
He should those bearers put to sudden death,
50   Not shriving-time allowed.

Horatio   How was this sealed?

Hamlet Why, even in that was heaven ordinant.
I had my father's signet in my purse,
Which was the model of that Danish seal;
55   Folded the writ up in the form of th'other,

I were left alive. The command stated that once the letter was read, without waiting a moment—no, not even long enough to sharpen the axe—my head should be cut off.

Horatio Can that be possible?

Hamlet Here's the order; read it at your leisure. But would you like to hear what I did then?

Horatio Please.

Hamlet Surrounded this way by a net of villainy (for they had started to act the play before I could understand the plot), I sat down and thought up a new commission. I wrote it out in fine handwriting. I used to think, as our statesmen do, that it showed low rank to write with a fine hand, and I tried hard to unlearn that skill. But now, sir, it did me indispensable service. Would you like to know the gist of what I wrote?

Horatio Yes, my good lord.

Hamlet An earnest appeal from the King of Denmark. It requested that—as the English king was the king of Denmark's faithful subject; as the love between them should flourish like the palm tree; as Peace with her garland of wheat should link them in friendship; and many more such "as"es loaded with significance—that once the letter's contents had been read and understood, the English king should put the letter's bearers immediately to death, without further debate. And he should do this with no time for absolution or confession.

Horatio How did you seal this letter?

Hamlet Why, even in that heaven provided. I had my father's signet ring in my pouch, which was a copy of the King of Denmark's seal. I folded up what I had written just like the other had been folded, signed it, sealed it with the ring, and

Subscribed it, gave't th'impression, placed it safely,
The changeling never known. Now the next day
Was our sea-fight, and what to this was sequent
Thou knowest already.

60 **Horatio** So Guildenstern and Rosencrantz go to't.

Hamlet Why, man, they did make love to this employment.
They are not near my conscience, their defeat
Does by their own insinuation grow.
'Tis dangerous when the baser nature comes
65 Between the pass and fell incensed points
Of mighty opposites.

Horatio   Why, what a king is this!

Hamlet Does it not, think thee, stand me now upon –
He that hath killed my King and whored my mother,
70 Popped in between th'election and my hopes,
Thrown out his angle for my proper life,
And with such cozenage – is't not perfect conscience
To quit him with this arm? And is't not to be damned
To let this canker of our nature come
75 In further evil?

Horatio It must be shortly known to him from England
What is the issue of the business there.

Hamlet It will be short. The interim is mine.
And a man's life's no more than to say 'one'.
80 But I am very sorry, good Horatio,
That to Laertes I forgot myself;
For by the image of my cause I see
The portraiture of his. I'll court his favours.
But sure the bravery of his grief did put me
85 Into a towering passion.

Horatio   Peace, who comes here?

[*Enter* **Osric,** *a Courtier*]

safely replaced it. They never detected the substitution. Now the next day was our fight at sea, and what happened after that you already know.

Horatio   So Rosencrantz and Guildenstern are done for.

Hamlet   Why, man, they begged for this employment. They're not on my conscience. Their downfall was the result of their own interfering. It's dangerous when inferior natures come between the fierce swordpoints and thrusts of mighty enemies.

Horatio   Why, what a king this is!

Hamlet   Don't you think it's incumbent upon me now? Now that he's killed my King and made a whore out of my mother, intruded between the throne and my hopes of succession, thrown out his hook to bait my very life, and with such trickery—isn't it perfect justice to pay him back for this myself? And wouldn't it be damnable to let this ulcer grow and do more evil?

Horatio   He'll hear back from England soon about what took place there.

Hamlet   It *will* be soon. The meantime is mine. A man's whole life is short. It lasts no longer than it takes to count to "one." But I'm very sorry, good Horatio, that I forgot myself with Laertes, since I see the mirror-image of his cause in my own. I'll try to get in his good graces. But, truly, the blustery way he expressed his grief put me in a towering rage.

Horatio   Hush, who's that?

[**Osric,** *a member of the court, enters*]

Osric Your lordship is right welcome back to Denmark.

Hamlet I humbly thank you sir. Dost know this water-fly?

Horatio No, my good lord.

90 **Hamlet** Thy state is the more gracious, for 'tis a vice to know him. He hath much land and fertile. Let a beast be lord of beasts and his crib shall stand at the king's mess. 'Tis a chough, but, as I say, spacious in the possession of dirt.

Osric Sweet lord, if your lordship were at leisure, I should
95 impart a thing to you from his Majesty.

Hamlet I will receive it, sir, with all diligence of spirit. Put your bonnet to his right use: 'tis for the head.

Osric I thank your lordship, it is very hot.

Hamlet No, believe me, 'tis very cold, the wind is northerly.

100 **Osric** It is indifferent cold, my lord, indeed.

Hamlet But yet methinks it is very sultry and hot for my complexion.

Osric Exceedingly, my lord, it is very sultry – as 'twere – I cannot tell how. My lord, his Majesty bade me signify to you
105 that he has laid a great wager on your head. Sir, this is the matter –

Hamlet [*signing to him to put on his hat*] I beseech you remember –

Osric Nay, good my lord, for my ease, in good faith. Sir, here
110 is newly come to court Laertes; believe me an absolute gentleman, full of most excellent differences, of very soft society and great showing. Indeed, to speak feelingly of him, he is the card or calendar of gentry; for you shall find in him the continent of what part a gentleman would see.

Osric Your lordship is very welcome back to Denmark.

Hamlet I humbly thank you, sir. [*To* **Horatio**] Do you know this water fly?

Horatio No, my good lord.

Hamlet That's a state of grace, since it's a vice to know him. He owns much fertile land. Let a beast be the lord of other beasts, and his trough will stand at the king's table. He's a boor, but, as I say, he owns a lot of dirt.

Osric Sweet lord, if your lordship has time for me, I'd like to give you a message from his Majesty.

Hamlet I will receive it, sir, with the utmost attentiveness. Put your hat to its proper use: It's for the head.

Osric I thank your lordship; it is very hot.

Hamlet No, believe me, it's very cold; the wind is from the north.

Osric It is a little cold, my lord, indeed.

Hamlet And yet I think it's very muggy and hot for my taste.

Osric Exceedingly, my lord, it is very muggy—as if it were— I can't exactly say. My lord, his Majesty asked me to let you know that he has made a large bet on your head. Sir, these are the circumstances—

Hamlet [*Making signs to* **Osric** *to put on his hat*] Please, your hat—

Osric No, my good lord, if you'll kindly excuse me. Sir, Laertes has recently returned to court. Believe me, he's an absolute gentleman, full of excellent qualities, with very charming manners and distinguished looks. Indeed, to do him justice, he's the very map or model of good breeding, for you'll discover that he contains everything a gentleman wants to see.

115 **Hamlet** Sir, his definement suffers no perdition in you;
though I know to divide him inventorially would dozy
th'arithmetic of memory, and yet but yaw neither, in respect
of his quick sail. But, in the verity of extolment, I take him
to be a soul of great article and his infusion of such dearth
120 and rareness as, to make true diction of him, his semblable is
his mirror and who else would trace him his umbrage,
nothing more.

Osric Your lordship speaks most infallibly of him.

Hamlet The concernancy, sir? Why do we wrap the
125 gentleman in our more rawer breath?

Osric Sir?

Horatio Is't not possible to understand in another tongue?
You will do't, sir, really.

Hamlet What imports the nomination of this gentleman?

130 **Osric** Of Laertes?

Horatio His purse is empty already, all's golden words are
spent.

Hamlet Of him, sir.

Osric I know you are not ignorant –

135 **Hamlet** I would you did, sir. Yet in faith if you did, it would
not much approve me. Well, sir?

Osric You are not ignorant of what excellence Laertes is –

Hamlet I dare not confess that, lest I should compare with
him in excellence; but to know a man well were to know
140 himself.

Osric I mean, sir, for his weapon; but in the imputation laid
on him, by them in his meed, he's unfellowed.

Hamlet [*Imitating **Osric**'s wordy speech*] Sir, his definition suffers no loss in your description, though I know that making a list of his fine points would dizzy the arithmetic of memory and even then would simply lumber off course, compared to his speedy sailing. But to praise him truthfully, I take him to be a soul with many articles in his inventory, one whose essence is of such rarity that, to speak of him correctly, his only likeness is his mirror. Anyone who'd try to copy him would be his shadow, nothing more.

Osric Your lordship speaks of him infallibly.

Hamlet The pertinence, sir? Why do we wrap the gentleman in our grosser speech?

Osric Sir?

Horatio Can't this be put in another tongue? You'll do it, sir, really.

Hamlet What's the reason for naming this gentleman?

Osric Laertes?

Horatio His pocket's empty already. All his golden words are spent.

Hamlet Him, sir.

Osric I know you are not ignorant—

Hamlet I wish you did, sir. Though certainly, if you did, that wouldn't reflect well on me. Well, sir?

Osric You are not ignorant of Laertes's excellence—

Hamlet I don't dare admit that, in case I'd be implying a similar excellence in myself. Though it's true that to know somebody else well, one must also know oneself.

Osric I mean, sir, excellence in the use of his weapon. According to the reputation he's been given by those of his rank, he's unmatched.

Hamlet What's his weapon?

Osric Rapier and dagger.

145 **Hamlet** That's two of his weapons. But well.

Osric The King, sir, hath wagered with him six Barbary
horses, against the which he has impawned, as I take it, six
French rapiers and poniards, with their assigns, as girdle,
hanger, and so. Three of the carriages, in faith, are very dear
150 to fancy, very responsive to the hilts, most delicate carriages,
and of very liberal conceit.

Hamlet What call you the carriages?

Horatio I knew you must be edified by the margin ere you
had done.

155 **Osric** The carriages, sir, are the hangers.

Hamlet The phrase would be more german to the matter if
we could carry a cannon by our sides. I would it might be
hangers till then. But on. Six Barbary horses against six
French swords, their assigns, and three liberal-conceited
160 carriages; that's the French bet against the Danish. Why is
this – impawned, as you call it?

Osric The King, sir, hath laid, sir, that in a dozen passes
between yourself and him he shall not exceed you three hits;
he hath laid on twelve for nine. And it would come to
165 immediate trial if your lordship would vouchsafe the answer.

Hamlet How if I answer no?

Osric I mean, my lord, the opposition of your person in trial.

Hamlet Sir, I will walk here in the hall. If it please his
Majesty, it is the breathing time of day with me. Let the
170 foils be brought, the gentleman willing, and the King hold
his purpose, I will win for him an I can; if not, I will gain
nothing but my shame and the odd hits.

Hamlet What's his weapon?

Osric Rapier and dagger.

Hamlet That's two of his weapons. However.

Osric The King, sir, has bet Laertes six Barbary horses, against which Laertes has ventured, as I take it, six French rapiers and daggers along with their gear (such as girdles, hangers, and so on). Three of the carriages, truly, are very delightful to imagine, very well-fitted to the swords' hilts—very delicate workmanship, elaborately wrought.

Hamlet What are you calling the "carriages"?

Horatio I knew you'd need marginal notes before you were through.

Osric The carriages, sir, are the hangers.

Hamlet The term would fit better if we had cannons strapped to us, instead of swords. I prefer that we use "hangers" until then. But go on. Six Barbary horses against six French swords, their accessories, and three elaborately wrought carriages: That's the French bet against the Danish. Why is this "ventured," as you called it?

Osric The King, sir, has bet, sir, that in a dozen bouts between you and Laertes, Laertes won't beat you by three bouts. Laertes bet he would win by making nine hits out of twelve. And it will be decided immediately if your lordship would be so kind as to answer.

Hamlet What if I answer "no"?

Osric I mean, my lord, "answer" by accepting the challenge to a match.

Hamlet Sir, I'll walk here in the hall. If his Majesty pleases, this is the time of day I usually exercise. If the foils are brought, the gentleman is willing, and the King is still firm in his intention, I will win for the King if I can. If not, I'll gain nothing except my shame and a few hits.

Osric Shall I deliver you so?

Hamlet To this effect, sir, after what flourish your nature
175   will.

Osric I commend my duty to your lordship.

Hamlet Yours.

[*Exit* **Osric**]

He does well to commend it himself, there are no tongues
else for's turn.

180 **Horatio** This lapwing runs away with the shell on his head.

Hamlet He did comply with his dug before he sucked it.
Thus has he – and many more of the same bevy that I know
the drossy age dotes on – only got the tune of the time and
outward habit of encounter, a kind of yeasty collection,
185   which carries them through and through the most fanned
and winnowed opinions; and do but blow them to their trial,
the bubbles are out.

[*Enter a* **Lord**]

Lord My lord, his Majesty commended him to you by young
Osric, who brings back to him that you attend him in the
190   hall. He sends to know if your pleasure hold to play with
Laertes or that you will take longer time.

Hamlet I am constant to my purposes, they follow the King's
pleasure. If his fitness speaks, mine is ready. Now or
whensoever, provided I be so able as now.

195 **Lord** The King and Queen and all are coming down.

Hamlet In happy time.

Osric Shall I say that's what you said?

Hamlet To that effect, sir, with whatever verbal flourishes you like.

Osric I commend my duty to your lordship.

Hamlet Yours.

[**Osric** *exits*]

He does well to "commend" it himself; no one else would praise it for him.

Horatio [*Referring to* **Osric**'*s hat*] This brave bird runs away with the shell on its head.

Hamlet He begged gracious pardon of his mother's nipple before he sucked it. He's like many more of the same ilk that I know our frivolous age dotes upon. He's only got the tune of the time and the style of speaking, a kind of frothy dictionary of current phrases. It carries them through in the presence of people with more cultivated opinions. If you so much as blow on them to test them, their bubbles will burst.

[*A* **Lord** *enters*]

Lord My lord, his Majesty conveyed a message to you through young Osric, who reported back that you are waiting for him in the hall. He would like to know if you'd still care to compete with Laertes now, or if you would prefer to do it later.

Hamlet My intentions are the same; they'll serve the King's pleasure. If he says he's ready, I am too. Now or whenever, provided I'm as able to fight as I am now.

Lord The King and Queen and the rest are coming down.

Hamlet With good timing.

Lord The Queen desires you to use some gentle entertainment to Laertes before you fall to play.

Hamlet She well instructs me.

[*Exit* **Lord**]

200 **Horatio** You will lose this wager, my lord.

Hamlet I do not think so. Since he went into France, I have been in continual practice. I shall win at the odds. Thou wouldst not think how ill all's here about my heart; but it is no matter.

205 **Horatio** Nay, good my lord.

Hamlet It is but foolery, but it is such a kind of gaingiving as would perhaps trouble a woman.

Horatio If your mind dislike anything, obey it. I will forestall their repair hither and say you are not fit.

210 **Hamlet** Not a whit. We defy augury. There is a special providence in the fall of a sparrow. If it be now, 'tis not to come; if it be not to come, it will be now; if it be not now, yet it will come. The readiness is all. Since no man of aught he leaves, knows aught, what is't to leave betimes? Let be.

[*A table prepared. Trumpets, Drums, and Officers with cushions. Enter* **King, Queen, Laertes, Osric,** *and all the State, and Attendants with foils and daggers.*]

215 **King** Come, Hamlet, come, and take this hand from me.

[*Puts* **Laertes'** *hand into* **Hamlet's**]

Lord The Queen wishes you to greet Laertes courteously before you start the match.

Hamlet She instructs me well.

[*The* **Lord** *exits*]

Horatio You'll lose this bet, my lord.

Hamlet I don't think so. Since he went to France, I've been practicing continually. I'll win at the odds they've made. You can't imagine what a bad feeling I have in my heart, but it doesn't matter.

Horatio No, my good lord.

Hamlet It's just nonsense; it's the kind of misgiving that might perhaps trouble a woman.

Horatio If your mind senses something's wrong, obey it. I'll stop them from coming here and say that you're not well.

Hamlet By no means. We defy superstition. Everything happens for a reason: There's a special providence even in a sparrow's death. If it's going to be now, it won't be still to come. If it's not still to come, it will be now. If it's not now, it will still be to come. What matters is to be ready. Since no man knows what he's leaving behind, what does it matter if he leaves early? Let it be.

[*A table is set up. The sound of trumpets and drums announces the arrival of the court, preceded by Officers with cushions. The* **King, Queen, Laertes, Osric,** *members of the Court, and Attendants carrying foils and daggers enter*]

King Come Hamlet, come, and take this hand from me.

[*He puts* **Laertes***'s hand into* **Hamlet***'s*]

Hamlet Give me your pardon, sir. I have done you wrong;
But pardon't as you are a gentleman.
This presence knows, and you must needs have heard,
How I am punished with a sore distraction.
220 What I have done
That might your nature, honour, and exception
Roughly awake, I here proclaim was madness.
Was't Hamlet wronged Laertes? Never Hamlet.
If Hamlet from himself be ta'en away,
225 And when he's not himself does wrong Laertes,
Then Hamlet does it not, Hamlet denies it.
Who does it then? His madness. If't be so,
Hamlet is of the faction that is wronged;
His madness is poor Hamlet's enemy.
230 Sir, in this audience,
Let my disclaiming from a purposed evil
Free me so far in your most generous thoughts
That I have shot my arrow o'er the house
And hurt my brother.

235 **Laertes**   I am satisfied in nature,
Whose motive in this case should stir me most
To my revenge; but in my terms of honour
I stand aloof, and will no reconcilement
Till by some elder masters of known honour
240 I have a voice and precedent of peace
To keep my name ungored. But till that time
I do receive your offered love like love
And will not wrong it.

Hamlet   I embrace it freely,
245 And will this brother's wager frankly play.
Give us the foils.

Laertes Come, one for me.

Hamlet I'll be your foil, Laertes. In mine ignorance
Your skill shall like a star i'th'darkest night
250 Stick fiery off indeed.

Hamlet Give me your pardon, sir. I have done you wrong. But pardon it, as you are a gentleman. The Court knows, and you must have heard, how I am afflicted with a painful derangement. Whatever I might have done to provoke your feelings, your sense of honor, or your disapproval—I here proclaim it was madness. Was it Hamlet who wronged Laertes? No, never Hamlet. If Hamlet has been severed from himself, and when he's not himself does wrong to Laertes, then Hamlet doesn't do it. Hamlet denies it. Who does it then? His madness. If that's so, Hamlet is one of the wronged parties; his madness is poor Hamlet's enemy. Sir, before this company, let my denial that I meant to do you harm serve to free me—in your generous thoughts—from the charge that I unintentionally injured you, as if I had shot my arrow over the house and hurt my brother.

Laertes I am satisfied regarding my personal feelings, which in this case should most stir me to revenge. Where my honor is concerned, I'll remain aloof. To keep my good name uninjured, I won't reconcile until recognized experts in such matters have authoritatively judged that we should make peace. But until that time, I receive your offered love *as* love, and I will not reject it.

Hamlet I embrace it freely, and I will play out this brotherly wager without ill feeling. Give us the foils.

Laertes Come, one for me.

Hamlet I'll be *your* foil, Laertes. Against the background of my inexperience, your skill will shine out brilliantly, like a star in the darkest night.

Laertes　　　　　　　　You mock me, sir.

Hamlet　No, by this hand.

King　Give them the foils, young Osric. Cousin Hamlet,
　　You know the wager?

255 **Hamlet**　　　　　　　　Very well, my lord.
　　Your Grace has laid the odds o'th'weaker side.

King　I do not fear it. I have seen you both,
　　But since he is bettered, we have therefore odds.

Laertes　This is too heavy. Let me see another.

260 **Hamlet**　This likes me well. These foils have all a length?

Osric　Ay, my good lord.　[*They prepare to play*]

　　[*Enter Servants with flagons of wine*]

King　Set me the stoups of wine upon that table.
　　If Hamlet give the first or second hit,
　　Or quit in answer of the third exchange,
265　Let all the battlements their ordnance fire:
　　The King shall drink to Hamlet's better breath,
　　And in the cup an union shall he throw
　　Richer than that which four successive kings
　　In Denmark's crown have worn. Give me the cups –
270　And let the kettle to the trumpet speak,
　　The trumpet to the cannoneer without,
　　The cannons to the heavens, the heavens to earth,
　　'Now the King drinks to Hamlet.' Come, begin.
　　And you, the judges, bear a wary eye.

275 **Hamlet**　Come on, sir.

Laertes　Come, my lord.　[*They play*]

Hamlet　One.

Laertes You're mocking me, sir.

Hamlet No, upon my word.

King Give them the foils, young Osric. Cousin Hamlet, you know the wager?

Hamlet Very well, my lord. Your Grace is betting on the weaker side.

King I'm not worried. I have seen both of you, but since he's improved, we've adjusted the odds accordingly.

Laertes [*Rejecting a rapier*] This is too heavy. Let me see another.

Hamlet I like this one. Are these foils all the same length?

Osric Yes, my good lord.

[*They prepare to fence. Servants enter with decanters of wine*]

King Set the wine decanters on the table. If Hamlet gives the first or second hit, or if he wins the third bout after Laertes has won the first two, let all the castle battlements fire their cannons. The King shall drink to Hamlet's improved stamina, and he'll throw a pearl into the cup of wine—a pearl more valuable than the one four successive Danish kings wore in their crown. Give me the cups. And let the kettledrum say to the trumpet, the trumpet say to the men outside firing the cannons, the cannons say to the heavens, and the heavens say to the earth: "Now the King is drinking to Hamlet." Come, begin. And you, the referees, watch carefully.

Hamlet Come on, sir.

Laertes Come, my lord. [*They fence.* **Laertes** *holds the poisoned rapier*]

Hamlet One.

Laertes No.

Hamlet Judgment.

280 **Osric** A hit, a very palpable hit.

Laertes Well, again.

King Stay, give me drink. Hamlet this pearl is thine.
Here's to thy health.

[*Drums; trumpets; and shot goes off*]

Give him the cup.

285 **Hamlet** I'll play this bout first. Set it by awhile.
Come   [*They play again*]
Another hit. What say you?

Laertes A touch, a touch I do confess.

King Our son shall win.

290 **Queen**   He's fat and scant of breath.
Here, Hamlet, take my napkin, rub thy brows.
The Queen carouses to thy fortune, Hamlet.

Hamlet Good madam.

King Gertrude, do not drink.

295 **Queen** I will, my lord, I pray you pardon me.

[*She drinks and offers the cup to* **Hamlet**]

King [*aside*] It is the poisoned cup. It is too late.

Hamlet I dare not drink yet, madam; by and by.

Queen Come, let me wipe thy face.

Laertes My lord, I'll hit him now.

300 **King**   I do not think't.

Laertes No.

Hamlet A ruling.

Osric A hit, a clear hit.

Laertes Well, again.

King Wait, give me a drink. Hamlet, this pearl is yours. Here's to your health.

[*Drums, trumpets, and cannon fire sound as the* **King** *drinks*]

Give him the cup.

Hamlet I'll play this bout first. Set it by for a while. Come [*they fence again*], another hit—what do you say?

Laertes A touch, a touch, I must admit.

King Our son will win.

Queen He's out of shape and winded. Here, Hamlet, take my handkerchief and wipe your brow. The Queen toasts your good fortune, Hamlet.

Hamlet Good madam.

King Gertrude, don't drink.

Queen I will, my lord, if you'll pardon me.

[*She drinks and offers the cup to* **Hamlet**]

King [*aside*] It's the poisoned cup. It's too late.

Hamlet I don't dare drink yet, madam; I'll drink by and by.

Queen Come, let me wipe your face.

Laertes My lord, I'll hit him now.

King I don't think so.

Laertes [*aside*] And yet it is almost against my conscience.

Hamlet Come for the third, Laertes. You do but dally.
I pray you pass with your best violence.
I am afeard you make a wanton of me.

305 **Laertes** Say you so? Come on. [*They play*]

Osric Nothing neither way.

Laertes Have at you now.

[**Laertes** *wounds* **Hamlet**; *then, scuffling, they change rapiers*]

King Part them; they are incensed.

Hamlet Nay, come again.

[*He wounds* **Laertes**. *The* **Queen** *falls*]

310 **Osric** Look to the Queen there, ho!

Horatio They bleed on both sides. How is it, my lord?

Osric How is't, Laertes?

Laertes Why, as a woodcock to mine own springe, Osric.
I am justly killed with mine own treachery.

315 **Hamlet** How does the Queen?

King   She swoons to see them
bleed.

Queen No, no, the drink, the drink! O my dear Hamlet!
The drink, the drink! I am poisoned. [*Dies*]

320 **Hamlet** O villainy! Ho! Let the door be locked.
Treachery! Seek it out.

[*Exit* **Osric**]

Laertes [*aside*] And yet, it's almost against my conscience.

Hamlet Come on, Laertes, let's have the third bout. You're just stalling. And why don't you give it your best shot? I'm afraid you're only toying with me.

Laertes You think so? Come on. [*They fence*]

Osric Nothing either way.

Laertes Have at you now.

[**Laertes** *wounds* **Hamlet** *with the poisoned rapier. The men begin to scuffle. When they start to fence again, they change rapiers.* **Hamlet** *now holds the poisoned rapier*]

King Separate them; they are incensed!

Hamlet No; come again!

[**Hamlet** *wounds* **Laertes**. *The Queen falls to the floor*]

Osric Look to the Queen there, ho!

Horatio They're both bleeding. [*To* **Hamlet**] How are you, my lord?

Osric How are you, Laertes?

Laertes Why, I'm like a bird, caught in my own trap, Osric. I've been justly killed by my own treachery.

Hamlet How is the Queen?

King The sight of their blood makes her faint.

Queen No, no, the drink, the drink! Oh, my dear Hamlet! The drink, the drink! I've been poisoned! [*The* **Queen** *dies*]

Hamlet Oh, villainy! Ho! Lock the door! Treachery! Find it.

[**Osric** *exits*]

Laertes It is here, Hamlet. Hamlet thou art slain.
No medicine in the world can do thee good;
In thee there is not half an hour of life.
325 The treacherous instrument is in thy hand,
Unbated and envenomed. The foul practice
Hath turned itself on me. Lo, here I lie,
Never to rise again. Thy mother's poisoned.
I can no more. The King – the King's to blame.

330 **Hamlet** The point envenomed too! Then, venom, to thy
work.

[*Stabs the* **King**]

All Treason! Treason!

King Oh yet defend me, friends. I am but hurt.

Hamlet Here, thou incestuous, murd'rous, damned Dane,
335 Drink off this potion. Is thy union here?
Follow my mother.

[**King** *dies*]

Laertes   He is justly served.
It is a poison tempered by himself.
Exchange forgiveness with me, noble Hamlet.
340 Mine and my father's death come not upon thee,
Nor thine on me. [*Dies*]

Hamlet Heaven make thee free of it. I follow thee.
I am dead, Horatio. Wretched Queen, adieu!
You that look pale and tremble at this chance,
345 That are but mutes or audience to this act,
Had I but time – as this fell sergeant, Death,
Is strict in his arrest – O, I could tell you –
But let it be. Horatio, I am dead,
Thou livest. Report me and my cause aright
350 To the unsatisfied.

Laertes It is here, Hamlet. Hamlet, you've been slain. No medicine in the world can help you; you won't live a half-hour longer. The treacherous means is in your hand, unblunted and poisoned. The foul plot has turned against me. See, here I lie, never to rise again. Your mother's been poisoned. I'm done for. The King—the King's to blame.

Hamlet The point is poisoned, too? Then, venom—do your work.

[*He stabs the* **King**]

All Treason! Treason!

King Oh, defend me, friends. I'm just wounded.

Hamlet [*Forcing the* **King** *to drink from the poisoned cup*] Here, you incestuous, murderous, damned Dane, drink off the rest of this potion! Is your pearl here? Follow my mother.

[*The* **King** *dies*]

Laertes He is justly served. It's a poison he mixed himself. Exchange forgiveness with me, noble Hamlet. You won't be blamed for my death and my father's, and I won't be blamed for yours.

[**Laertes** *dies*]

Hamlet May heaven acquit you of it. I follow you. I am dead, Horatio. Wretched Queen, farewell! You who look pale and who tremble at this bad fortune, who merely look on as silent witnesses, if I had time—for this cruel sergeant, Death, wastes no time in making his arrests. . . . Oh, I could tell you. . . . But let it be. Horatio, I am dead. You live. Tell the truth about me and my cause to those who don't already know.

Horatio   Never believe it.
I am more an antique Roman than a Dane.
Here's yet some liquor left.

Hamlet   As thou'rt a man
355   Give me the cup. Let go, by heaven I'll have't.
O God, Horatio, what a wounded name,
Things standing thus unknown, shall I leave behind me.
If thou didst ever hold me in thy heart,
Absent thee from felicity awhile,
360   And in this harsh world draw thy breath in pain
To tell my story.

[*A march afar off and shot within*]

What warlike noise is this?

[*Enter* **Osric**]

Osric   Young Fortinbras, with conquest come from Poland,
To the ambassadors of England gives
365   This warlike volley.

Hamlet   O, I die, Horatio.
The potent poison quite o'ercrows my spirit.
I cannot live to hear the news from England,
But I do prophesy th'election lights
370   On Fortinbras. He has my dying voice.
So tell him, with th'occurrents more and less
Which have solicited – the rest is silence. [*Dies*]

Horatio   Now cracks a noble heart. Good night, sweet prince,
And flights of angels sing thee to thy rest!

[*March within*]

375   Why does the drum come hither?

Horatio Never believe it. The Romans chose to kill themselves rather than live in dishonor. I'm more of an ancient Roman than a Dane. There's still some of the drink left. [*He takes up the poisoned cup*]

Hamlet By your manhood, give me the cup! Let go, by heaven, I'll have it. [**Hamlet** *gets the cup*] Oh God, Horatio, what a wounded reputation I'll leave behind if the truth is left untold! If you ever held feeling for me in your heart, stay out of heaven for a while, and draw your breath in pain in this harsh world to tell my story.

[*The sound of marching and cannon fire can be heard from far off*]

What's that warlike noise?

[**Osric** *enters*]

Osric Young Fortinbras has come from his conquest in Poland. He's firing this warlike volley in honor of the English ambassadors.

Hamlet Oh, I die, Horatio. The potent poison crows over me in triumph. I can't live long enough to hear the King of England's news, but I predict that Fortinbras will be made the Danish king. He has my dying vote. Tell him that, along with the general events that have urged me—the rest is silence.

[**Hamlet** *dies*]

Horatio A noble heart has cracked. Good night, sweet prince, and may flights of angels sing you to your rest!

[*The sound of marching is heard*]

Why are they marching this way?

[*Enter* **Fortinbras,** *and the* **English Ambassadors,** *and Soldiers with drum and colours.*]

Fortinbras Where is this sight?

Horatio   What is it you would see?
    If aught of woe or wonder, cease your search.

Fortinbras This quarry cries on havoc. O proud Death,
380   What feast is toward in thine eternal cell,
    That thou so many princes at a shot
    So bloodily hast struck?

1st Ambass.   The sight is dismal;
    And our affairs from England come too late.
385   The ears are senseless that should give us hearing
    To tell him his commandment is fulfilled,
    That Rosencrantz and Guildenstern are dead.
    Where should we have our thanks?

Horatio   Not from his mouth,
390   Had it th'ability of life to thank you.
    He never gave commandment for their death.
    But since, so jump upon this bloody question,
    You from the Polack wars, and you from England,
    Are here arrived, give order that these bodies
395   High on a stage be placed to the view,
    And let me speak to the yet unknowing world
    How these things came about. So shall you hear
    Of carnal, bloody, and unnatural acts,
    Of accidental judgments, casual slaughters,
400   Of deaths put on by cunning and forced cause,
    And, in this upshot, purposes mistook
    Fallen on th'inventors' heads. All this can I
    Truly deliver.

Fortinbras   Let us haste to hear it,
405   And call the noblest to the audience.
    For me, with sorrow I embrace my fortune.
    I have some rights of memory in this kingdom,
    Which now to claim my vantage doth invite me.

[**Fortinbras** *and the* **English Ambassadors** *enter, along with Soldiers bearing drums and colors*]

Fortinbras Where is this sight?

Horatio What do you want to see? If you want to see something full of woe or wonder, stop searching.

Fortinbras This pile of dead announces a slaughter. Oh, proud Death, what feast are you preparing in your eternal cell, causing you to kill so many nobles with one bloody blow?

1st Ambass. It's a terrible sight, and our news from England comes too late. [*Referring to the* **King**] The ears that should have heard us are senseless. They can't hear that his command has been fulfilled, that Rosencrantz and Guildenstern are dead. Where will we find thanks for this?

Horatio Not from his mouth, even if it was alive to thank you. He never ordered their deaths. [*To* **Fortinbras**] But since you've come here from the Polish wars—[*to the* **Ambassadors**] and since you've arrived here from England— just at this bloody turn of events, order these bodies to be placed high on a platform to be viewed. And let me tell the still-uninformed world how these things came about. In that way you'll hear of carnal, bloody, and unnatural acts; of accidental retributions, accidental slaughters; of deaths caused by cunning and plotting; and of botched plans that backfired on their own inventors, in this last result. All this I can truly relate.

Fortinbras Let's hear it quickly, and call the noblest members of the court to listen. As for me, with sorrow I embrace my good fortune. I have some traditional rights to this kingdom, which I now have the opportunity to claim.

Horatio Of that I shall have also cause to speak,
410   And from his mouth whose voice will draw on more.
        But let this same be presently performed
        Even while men's minds are wild, lest more mischance
        On plots and errors happen.

Fortinbras   Let four captains
415   Bear Hamlet like a soldier to the stage,
        For he was likely, had he been put on,
        To have proved most royal; and for his passage,
        The soldier's music and the rite of war
        Speak loudly for him.
420   Take up the bodies. Such a sight as this
        Becomes the field, but here shows much amiss.
        Go, bid the soldiers shoot.

[*A dead march. Exeunt, bearing off the bodies, after which a
                            peal of ordnance is shot off*]

Horatio I will also have reasons to speak about that, acting as a voice for someone whose vote will influence others. But let's do this immediately while everyone's still unsettled, to prevent worse things from happening on top of these recent plots and errors.

Fortinbras Let four captains bear Hamlet like a soldier to the platform. He was likely to have proved a most royal king, had he been given the chance. To commemorate his passing, let martial music and military salutes speak loudly for him. Take up the bodies. Such a sight as this should be seen on the battlefield. Here, it shows much amiss. Go tell the soldiers to shoot.

[*Soldiers bear away the bodies. All exit, marching slowly and solemnly. The sound of cannons firing salutes is heard*]

Comprehension **Check What You Know**

1. Who are the gravediggers talking about at the beginning of Scene 1?

2. What hint does the gravedigger give about Hamlet's age?

3. Compare the two types of burials that the priest describes in Scene 1. What is the difference between the two? Why are they different?

4. What happens when Hamlet comes out of hiding during Ophelia's funeral?

5. What did Hamlet do to save himself on the ship that set sail for England? Whose orders did he reverse, and what were these orders?

6. By the end of Act 5, what has happened to Rosencrantz and Guildenstern?

7. Describe Laertes's fencing skills and his preparations with the foils.

8. Describe the duel. How does the mood of the fighters and spectators change as the fencing continues?

9. How does the Queen become part of the action during the duel? What happens to her?

10. How does the play conclude? What happens to the characters?

11. What characters enter near the end of Act 5? Why have they come to Denmark and how do they react to what they find?

Activities & Role-Playing **Classes or Informal Groups**

Electing a King During the period in which *Hamlet* is set, Denmark's kings had to be elected by a council of senior court members. Before Hamlet dies, he tells Horatio that Fortinbras has his "voice," or vote, as the best choice for the

©Kevin Sprague/Shakespeare & Company

next king. What do you think of Hamlet's choice? Role-play a debate among the councilors to choose a new monarch after King Claudius's and Prince Hamlet's deaths. Discuss the merits and drawbacks of Fortinbras as king. Base your arguments upon what you have heard and seen about Fortinbras in the play.

Staging a Funeral Research The Globe's stage in reference books, on the Internet, or in other sources recommended in the list at the back of this book. How would you describe the action in lines 202–287 of Scene 1?

Discussion **Classes or Informal Groups**

1. Discuss Ophelia's funeral. How did people in Shakespeare's day view suicide? How is that viewpoint different or similar to the way suicide is thought of today?

2. Discuss Rosencrantz and Guildenstern's role in the play. Do you agree with Hamlet's opinion that Rosencrantz and Guildenstern deserved their fates? Why or why not?

3. What is your conclusion about the character of Hamlet? Was he an honorable person, less than honorable, or something in between? Describe his good qualities and his flaws. What makes him a tragic character?

Suggestions for Writing **Improve Your Skills**

1. At the end of Act 5, Fortinbras states that Hamlet would have made a good king (Scene 2, 416–417). Do you agree with Fortinbras? Write two paragraphs explaining why you agree or disagree that Hamlet would have been a good king. Give examples of passages from the play that support your opinion.

2. Review Act 5's Scene 1. Write two or three sentences explaining how the graveyard setting contributes to the mood of the scene and foreshadows the end of the play. List any images that express the corrupt and tragic Danish court.

3. Imagine you are one of the English ambassadors arriving at the end of Act 5. Write a two-paragraph letter to the English king, reporting on what you saw in Elsinore and what may happen there now that the King is dead.

4. Horatio is left alive to explain events at the end of the play. Write a paragraph explaining what you think are his most important character traits and explaining why. Is Horatio an important character? Will he report Hamlet's story accurately?

Hamlet
Additional Resources

Books

Title: *The Riverside Shakespeare*
Author: J. J. M. Tobin, et al. (editors)
Publisher: Houghton Mifflin
Year: 1997
Summary: This volume features all of Shakespeare's plays, along with 40 pages of color and black-and-white plates. Each play is introduced by scholarly commentary from one of the volume's editors. The book also contains general background material on the Shakespearean stage and Elizabethan history.

Title: *The Complete Works of Shakespeare*
Author: David Bevington (editor)
Publisher: Addison-Wesley Publishing Company
Year: 1997
Summary: This book offers the complete, unabridged works of Shakespeare as edited by the current president of the Shakespeare Association of America. Editor David Bevington also provides an introductory essay for each play and a general introduction to Shakespeare's life, times, and stage.

Title: *Shakespeare: A Life*
Author: Park Honan
Publisher: Oxford University Press
Year: 1999
Summary: Using the little available data that exists, Honan pieces together this biographical account of Shakespeare's life.

Title: *Shakespeare A to Z: The Essential Reference to His Plays, His Poems, His Life and Times, and More*
Author: Charles Boyce
Publisher: Facts on File
Year: 1990
Summary: This book features over 3,000 encyclopedic entries arranged alphabetically. It covers several areas of Shakespeare, including historical background, play synopses, entries for individual characters, and critical commentary.

Title: *The Shakespearean Stage: 1574–1642*
Author: Andrew Gurr
Publisher: Cambridge University Press
Year: 1992 (3rd ed.)
Summary: An overview of Shakespearean staging by Andrew Gurr, one of the foremost experts in this area. The book highlights the many different theater companies of the day and how they performed.

Title: *A Shakespeare Glossary*
Author: C. T. Onions (editor)
Publisher: Oxford University Press
Year: 1986
Summary: This classic reference book defines all of the now-obscure words used by Shakespeare in his plays and shows how the meaning of words that are still common may have changed. The book provides examples and gives play locations for the words.

Title: *Shakespeare's Book of Insults, Insights & Infinite Jests*
Author: John W. Seder (editor)
Publisher: Templegate
Year: 1984
Summary: This entertaining book covers several categories of jabs and mockeries taken straight from the text of Shakespeare's plays.

Title: *What Happens in Hamlet*
Author: John Dover Wilson
Publisher: Cambridge Unversity Press
Year: 1951
Summary: Wilson's in-depth analysis of the play includes scene summaries, background on Danish and Elizabethan history, and a discussion of ghosts in drama.

Title: *Everybody's Shakespeare: Reflections Chiefly on the Tragedies*
Author: Maynard Mack
Publisher: University of Nebraska Press
Year: 1994
Summary: Mack offers essays on *Romeo and Juliet, Julius Caesar, Hamlet, Othello, King Lear, Macbeth,* and *Antony and Cleopatra,* plus four chapters covering general topics. The essays are written specifically for the general reader by the author, a noted scholar.

Title: *The Meaning of Shakespeare* (2 vols.)
Author: Harold Goddard
Publisher: University of Chicago Press
Year: 1960
Summary: Originally published in 1951, this classic, hefty work of Shakespearean criticism includes essays on all of Shakespeare's plays. (Note: Because Goddard's work is in two volumes, readers who seek information on particular plays should make sure they obtain the volume containing commentary on that play.)

Videos

Title: *Hamlet*
Director: Michael Almereyda
Year: 2000
Summary: The hero is portrayed as a filmmaker in this version of *Hamlet* set in modern-day New York City.

Title: *Hamlet*
Director: Kenneth Branagh
Year: 1996
Summary: This is a four-hour, full-text production. It is set in the second half of the nineteenth century.

Title: *Hamlet*
Director: Franco Zeffirelli
Year: 1991
Summary: Mel Gibson stars in this two-hour version of the Shakespeare play.

Title: *Hamlet*
Director: John Gielgud
Year: 1964
Summary: Gielgud's three-hour production was originally devised for the stage.

Title: *Hamlet*
Director: Laurence Olivier
Year: 1948
Summary: Lasting two and one-half hours, this black-and-white version cuts liberally from the Shakespeare text.

Audiotapes

Title: *King Lear, Othello,* and *Hamlet*
Producer: DH Audio
Year: 2000
Summary: n/a

Title: *Hamlet: From Shakespeare Stories by Leon Garfield*
Producer: Chivers Audio Books
Year: 1999
Summary: This is a BBC radio presentation.

Title: *A Study Guide to William Shakespeare's* Hamlet
Producer: Time Warner Audio Books
Year: 1998
Summary: This cassette includes historical background, plot overviews, and a companion booklet.

Title: *Hamlet*
Producer: Modern Library
Year: 1996
Summary: This is a BBC radio presentation.

Title: *All the World's a Stage: An Anthology of Shakespearean Speeches Performed by the World's Leading Actors*
Producer: BBC Radio
Year: 1995
Summary: A collection of some of the finest performances of Shakespeare's famous passages. Laurence Olivier, Richard Burton, and Vanessa Redgrave are featured, along with several other notable actors.

Web Sites

URL: *www.rdg.ac.uk/globe/research/research_index.htm*
Summary: Associated with The Globe Theatre's web site, this collection of research links offers information on the building and rebuilding of The Globe, Shakespeare's relationship to the theater, and miscellaneous articles on theatrical traditions and practices during Shakespeare's time.

URL: *www.tech-two.mit.edu/Shakespeare/hamlet/index.html*
Summary: This web site from the Massachusetts Institute of Technology (MIT) features the full text of many of Shakespeare's plays in a searchable format.

URL: *http://shea.mit.edu/ramparts2000/intro.htm*
Summary: This co-product from the Folger Shakespeare library and MIT offers instructional aids (texts, images, and film) for portions of *Hamlet.*

URL:
http://www.english.wayne.edu/~aune/2200W00Contents.html
Summary: This site offers introductory information for students studying Shakespeare. Offerings include tips for reading and writing about Shakespeare as well as information on individual works.

URL: *http://daphne.palomar.edu/Shakespeare/*
Summary: "Mr. William Shakespeare and the Internet" offers a wide variety of links to other Shakespeare sites. "Criticism," "Educational," and "Life & Times" are just a few of the categories offered.

URL: *www.hamlet.org*
Summary: Operated by the Society for the Study of *Hamlet,* this site is devoted to researching and archiving commentary and discussion of *Hamlet.*

Software

Title: *Literature Survival Series:* Hamlet
Developer: Lawrence Productions
Grades: 9–12
Platform: Mac
Summary: This software aids students who are writing about *Hamlet*. It includes advice on finding a topic, stating a thesis, using quotes (with more than 100 quotes from the play), planning, and revising. It also includes information about the characters in the play.

Title: *Hamlet*
Developer: Bookworm Student Library
Grades: 7–12
Platform: Mac
Summary: The play is presented using film, sound, graphics, unabridged original texts, and relevant criticism.

Title: *Shakespeare Trivia*
Developer: Cascoly Software
Grades: All
Platform: Windows
Summary: A trivia game for any ability or knowledge level. The program includes 37 plays, more than 1,200 characters, more than 400 scenes, and 500 individual quotes. Players may choose the difficulty and type of question as they test their knowledge of Shakespeare.

Title: *Shakespeare's Language*
Developer: Randal Robinson and Peter Holben Wehr
Grades: 9–12, College
Platform: Mac
Summary: This program is created to help readers identify and respond to various types of difficulty in Shakespeare's language. Problems addressed include syntactical difficulties, unfamiliar words, figurative language, unexpected and multiple meanings of words, and special connotations of words.

Notes

Notes

Notes

The plays take on new meanings with . . .

Simply *Shakespeare*

This brand-new illustrated series presents six of Shakespeare's most frequently taught plays. The original Elizabethan text appears complete, side-by-side and line-by-line with a modern "translation" on facing pages. Preceding each act of every play, an explanatory spread describes what is about to take place with—

- An Introduction explaining the play's background
- Character descriptions
- Things to watch for as the story unfolds
- The play's historical and social context
- Staging at Shakespeare's original Globe Theatre
- Language, puns, and poetic images

Identifying icons preceding each of the above noted "Study Points" appear in a second color, then are located again as cross-references in the original text. Extra teachers' aids include test questions and themes for class discussion.

Each book: Paperback, approx. 288 pp., 6" x 9"
$8.95   Canada $12.50

Hamlet—ISBN 0-7641-2084-0
Julius Caesar—ISBN 0-7641-2089-1
Macbeth—ISBN 0-7641-2086-7
Romeo and Juliet— ISBN 0-7641-2085-9
The Tempest—ISBN 0-7641-2087-5
Twelfth Night—ISBN 0-7641-2088-3

BARRON'S

Barron's Educational Series, Inc.
250 Wireless Blvd.
Hauppauge, NY 11788
Order toll-free in the U.S.
1-800-645-3476
In Canada phone
1-800-247-7160
www.barronseduc.com

(#113) R 12/01